PSYCHOLOGIST'S GUIDE TO ADOLESCENTS AND SOCIAL MEDIA

PSYCHOLOGIST'S GUIDE TO ADOLESCENTS AND SOCIAL MEDIA

PIERRE COURT

Educational Psychologist, Government of Jersey, Jersey, Channel Islands
Chartered Member, British Psychological Society, Leicester, United Kingdom
Practitioner Psychologist, Health Care Professions Council, London, United Kingdom
Member, Association of Educational Psychologists, Durham, United Kingdom

ELSEVIER

ACADEMIC PRESS
An imprint of Elsevier

Academic Press is an imprint of Elsevier
125 London Wall, London EC2Y 5AS, United Kingdom
525 B Street, Suite 1650, San Diego, CA 92101, United States
50 Hampshire Street, 5th Floor, Cambridge, MA 02139, United States
The Boulevard, Langford Lane, Kidlington, Oxford OX5 1GB, United Kingdom

Library of Congress Cataloging-in-Publication Data
A catalog record for this book is available from the Library of Congress

British Library Cataloguing-in-Publication Data
A catalogue record for this book is available from the British Library

ISBN: 978-0-323-91898-5

For information on all Academic Press publications
visit our website at https://www.elsevier.com/books-and-journals

Publisher: Nikki Levy
Acquisitions Editor: Joslyn Chaiprasert-Paguio
Editorial Project Manager: Barbara Makinster
Production Project Manager: Punithavathy Govindaradjane
Cover Designer: Matthew Limbert

Typeset by STRAIVE, India

Contents

About the author ix
Acknowledgments xi
Introduction xiii

I

The positives and purposes of using social media

1. Identity and construction of the self

The Ship of Theseus 4
Ecological systems theory 5
How much do we know ourselves? 8
Social identity theory 11
Congruence and true self 14
Lesbian, gay, bisexual, transgender, questioning, intersex, asexual, plus (L.G.B.T.Q.I.A.+) 18

2. Social connectedness

Social conformity 27
The Houseparty saga 28
The displacement hypothesis 31

3. Emotional regulation

Uses and gratifications theory 37

II

The unintended consequences of using social media

4. Cyberbullying

Finding a definition of cyberbullying 44
Methods of cyberbullying 45
Harassment 45
Photo and video shaming 46

Impersonating someone 47
Subtweeting or vaguebooking 48
Cyberstalking 48
Trolling 49

5. Unfulfilled expectations

Signaling theory 54
Reassurance seeking 56
The thought behind an upload 59

6. Internet addiction

Defining addiction 66
Internet addiction 66
The problem owner 68
Who is vulnerable? 70
Measuring internet addiction 72
Behavioral addictions "on" the Internet 76
The design of technology and the battle for your attention 76

7. The educational impact of social media usage

A brief psychology of procrastination 86

III

Researching the impact of social media on UK secondary school students

8. Delving in deeper

Research questions 94
How to find out? 94
Time to get to work: Designing the questionnaire 96
Results 98
Analysis 98
To what extent does social networking occupy the minds of secondary aged young people? Can they be considered behaviorally addicted? 106

9. "Tell me more about that"

Semi-structured interviews 116
Interview design 116
Interview schedule 117
Qualitative analysis 118
The process of interpretative phenomenological analysis (IPA) 120
Results 120

10. Connection to others: Social connection, relationship maintenance, the monitoring of others

Social connection 122
Relationship maintenance 125
The monitoring of others 128

11. Identity and construction of the self: Change over time; A part of you; The role of parent

Change over time 134
A part of you 137
The role of parent 141

12. Cyberbullying: Group judgment & reaction; A venue and channel for negativity; The use of "blocking" as protection

Group judgment and reaction 146
A venue & channel for negativity 150
The use of "blocking" as protection 152

13. From online to in-school: Interference of work; Threats, intimidation or violence

Interference of work 158
Threats, intimidation or violence 160

14. "A cup of tea and a notebook"

IV

What can be done to help those who need support with their social media use?

15. "You can lead a horse to water..."

What is society's responsibility? 174
Self-governance 175
What can parents do? 177
They're in, so now what? 180
How long is too long? 181
Help parents to practice what they preach 182
Three minute take-away 183
The minefield of apps 184
HOLLA: Live random video chat 185
Yolo: Q&A 185
IMVU: 3D Avatar creator and chat 185
Likee—let you shine 186

Calculator% 186
Burnbook 186
Wishbone 187
Chatroulette 187
Parents using technology to their advantage 187

16. "... But you can't make it drink, or can you?"

Schools 192
Working 1:1 196
Stages of change model 196

17. Getting a measure of the situation

Understanding the individual's social media usage 200
Understanding the individual's social media usage: Results analysis with the child 203
Understanding the individual's social media usage: Results analysis with the parent 208
Planning and implementing an intervention 211
Reviewing progress of the intervention 215

18. Drawing everything to a close

Epilogue 223
Glossary of terms 227
Appendix 229
Sources and References 231
Index 241

About the author

Dr. Pierre Court is an Educational and Child Psychologist currently living and working in Jersey. He has a Doctorate in Educational, Child and Community Psychology and Qualifications in Counseling, Psychotherapy, and Hypnotherapy.

Working in education and psychology for over 10 years, Dr. Court is a Chartered Member of the British Psychological Society, registered with the Health Care Professions Council as a practitioner psychologist and a member of the Association of Educational Psychologists.

In professional practice, Dr. Court provides strategic support to a range of schools, alternative education settings and families—including psychological assessment, stress management for school staff, collaborative problem solving for the most challenging of cases and clinical supervision for practicing school-based counselors, supporting professional development, refining reflective practice, and bridging the gap between therapeutic support, mental health, and educational contexts.

Born in Bristol (United Kingdom), Pierre moved to Jersey in 2019. He is married with one daughter.

Acknowledgments

This book would not have been possible without the countless young people who were, and still are, willing to share their thoughts with me. Their openness and honesty are a refreshing reminder of the importance of listening.

I dedicate this book to my wonderful wife Faye and daughter Alba. Without you, this book would not have been written. Without you, I would not have been able to pursue my dreams and for that, I am eternally grateful.

Introduction

The Internet plays an ever-growing role in our lives. While this is true of the adult world, it is happening on an even greater level in the lives of the younger generation. Children grow up immersed in technology to a level that keeps surprising earlier generations, but to young people is simply an inherent element of their habitat.

People growing up in this "immersion of technology" are variously known as the Net Generation, Digital Natives, Millennials, and Generation Y. But these titles don't matter, and they certainly don't convey much information. The commonalities between the above groups are an ability to access the internet rapidly using a variety of media devices. Adults and children are frequent users of computers, games consoles, mobile phones, and music players, the majority of which have the functionality to connect to the internet. Never before has the world been so connected... and yet, somehow, disconnected.

The internet has become a principal venue for social interaction. There is an expanding evidence base exploring the internet use in facilitating communication, developing virtual communities, instigating new friendships, in the formation of romantic connections and in the maintenance and furtherance of already established relationships. Sounds great right? But while the Internet expands horizons, facilitates connection, builds on learning, and provides entertainment, heavy use can cause psychological and social problems—such as social isolation, depression, loneliness, and failure in school and work. Not so great.

But before we dive further into it, I should tell you who I am and how this book came to be.

My name is Pierre Court and I am a psychologist. I studied educational, child and community psychology at a doctoral level. Years before that, I studied psychology and counselling as an undergraduate. And along the way I gained qualifications in psychotherapy and hypnotherapy. I have a keen interest in the analysis of interpersonal communication, the impact of technology on psychological wellbeing and the resilience people can show when recovering from adversity. I work as an Educational Psychologist for the Government of Jersey, in the Channel Islands. I am a husband, a father, a son, a brother, a friend to many and a close friend to a few. I am a gamer and a user of social media—although these distinctions are blurring. I'm also a terrible cook—paradoxically, as my dad is a chef. My dad is French, my mum is from the North of England and I grew up in the South West…am i oversharing? perhaps I am, but more on that later.

This book started as a sigh. Multiple sighs, over multiple years. While working in a secondary school as a head of year I had pastoral responsibility for 350 students. Students who, if they were having any difficulties, would come to me for the "solution." Or to vent, but more often than not, they would want me to "fix" what was wrong, to get justice for them in some way. When I look back, I often picture the head of year role as an internal school police force for my assigned year group.

During this time, I was regularly presented with young people experiencing difficulties in school, because of something that had either started over social media, or been exacerbated using social media. It was therefore my job to try and mediate these difficulties, and help pupils come to a resolution regarding the situations they have found themselves in on-line, and subsequently in-school, or vice versa.

I found myself in awe at the value young people placed on their access and use of social networking. In addition, the scale of the numbers of young people who were members of social networks, connected to one another, was seemingly massive. I was out of my depth. Wading into situations that spanned the internet, the school, people's news feeds, offline friendships, online friendships, and families. Situations involving bullying, racism, threats, assault, humiliation, bribery, extortion, exploitation, indecent images, identity, sexuality… all of which had a presence online, all of which was happening in the lives of children between 11 and 18 years old.

You can see why this book started with a sigh… and with me needing to know more. So, when I was given the opportunity to conduct research as part of my doctorate, I knew exactly what subject I wanted to focus my efforts. This book is my attempt to share what I learned along the way and continue to learn through my work with young people to this day.

If technology is evolving and changing rapidly, then social media is changing at light speed. It has never been more important to stay up to date with these evolving media platforms. Gaining an understanding of how young people are using technology is important in deepening an understanding of the tools they are using to socialize.

There is another aspect here however, and that is one of understanding the cultural worlds inhabited by young people. There is a risk of professionals and parents losing touch with the cultural worlds inhabited by children and young adults. The disjuncture between social worlds across (and increasingly, within) generations leads to real problems for those working or living with young people.

Understand the technology, understand the psychology—and you will understand why people feel drawn to social media, and why it seems they can't stop. It is vitally important to understand the "places" that young people inhabit, both online and offline, in order to support them effectively throughout childhood and into adulthood.

A note on style

This book is written in a relaxed style. I have spent years reading textbooks, psychological papers, research articles, and theses. They are difficult to digest. I find them overly complex and littered with references, which can interrupt the flow of reading. I wanted to write a book that was more like a narrative, a discussion, infused by psychology and easy to understand. If you would like to know the sources and information I have used to inform this book, you will find this in a section at the back titled: Sources and References.

This book will not capture every nuanced psychological aspect of social media use for teenagers. That is not possible, it would be like writing a book on every aspect of life… and although that is a tempting thing to create, I am not up to the challenge, my family would never forgive me and I'm not smart enough to do it. What this book will do is guide you through some key psychological foundations of social media use, the underlying mechanisms of what you will see online and what young people will experience. Part 1 of this book opens up by introducing you to the psychology of identity and why social media platforms act as a stage to present one's self. It will then meander into the psychology of social connection and how we are biologically driven to connect to one another before diving into the psychology of emotional regulation and how social media use can facilitate and foster positive mood. In short, Part 1 of this book will shine a light on the purposes and positives of using social media. Then, In Part 2, we take a nose-dive into the unintended consequences of using social media… the dark side, if you will allow me to use a Star Wars metaphor to satisfy my inner (outer?) geek. This part of the book will explore cyberbullying and what form it can take through the internet, it will also expose the unfulfilled expectations of social media users and how this can exacerbate feelings of isolation and dis-connection, before taking a longing gaze at the controversial topic of "internet addiction"—if this is something that can exist as an addiction and how ingenious programming is designed to hold your attention to your preferred technology. Part 2 will end by exploring the impact social media use can have on a young person's education.

By this point in the book you will find yourself at a crossing point, you will have heard the positives and the negatives of social media, you will have been introduced to research, theory and real-life examples and may already have your own views on what you think about social media. But it doesn't end there. Part 3 will uncover what I found out conducting research with teenagers in the UK, bringing the reality of the teenage experience of social media to your eyes through the medium of psychological research methods, which can be cumbersome techniques to write about, but, produce a rich tapestry to highlight young people's experiences.

When you get to the end of Part 3 you will be thinking something along the lines of "blimey, I know a lot now, but what the heck can I do about it?" Well, take a deep breath because, believe or not, that's what Part 4 is all about... and... (looks over shoulder to make sure no other authors in this field are listening) is what is massively lacking in the field of social media research. Part 4 will guide you through a broad and systematic view of what is being done to police social media, what can be done to educate those who don't know and importantly, what can be done to assess, intervene and support a young person to overcome any difficulties they are experiencing. You will finish this book with everything you need, informed and resourced to the max.

So whether you bought this book because you have concerns about adolescent's use of social media, you work with children and feel like you're in the dark about it all, or you just want to know more... this book will give you a rounded understanding about the underlying psychology involved—the good, the bad, the in-between, and what you can do about it. Before we really get started though, let's tackle some definition of what social media is.

What counts as social media?

This isn't as easy to define as you might think. What are social media? And is there a difference between social media and social networks? There are several difficulties when it comes to trying to define the concept of social media. One of which is certainly the speed at which technology is advancing and the cross compatibility of services via multiple devices—be it computers, laptops, tablets, mobile phones, smart watches, smart TVs' and games consoles. The other difficulty is the similarities between what social media can offer vs technology that is already in operation... are e-mails considered social media? The telephone? Both of which facilitate connection utilizing technology.

Boyd and Ellison, researcher's writing in the *Journal of Computer-Mediated Communication*, define social networking sites as web-based services that allow individuals to:

1. Construct a public or semi-public profile within a bounded system.
2. Articulate a list of other users with whom they share a connection.
3. View and traverse their list of connections and those made by others within the system.

In an article titled: *Social Media Definition and the Governance Challenge*, Obar and Wildman compared multiple definitions of social media and synthesized the commonalities between them to produce what they deem a working definition of social media:

1. Social media services are (currently) Web 2.0 internet-based applications.
2. User-generated content is the lifeblood of social media.
3. Individuals and groups create user-specific profiles for a site or app, designed and maintained by a social media service.
4. Social media services facilitate the development of social networks online, by connecting a profile with other individuals and/or groups.

I like both of these definitions; they help boundary what we're talking about. Create an online profile, see other people's profiles, connect with them (or not) and upload "content" to the social media services. And to answer a question I posed earlier—there is no agreed consensus as to if there is a difference between "social networking sites" and "social media." Both terms will be used interchangeably in this book, and both will mean I'm talking about the above definitions in combination.

But let's get specific. What are the most popular social networking sites across the world, right now, at the time of writing (because this landscape shifts quickly)? To answer this, I'm relying on earnings data. Earnings data are the best source to determine the most popular social platforms, gathered direct from company statements and earning announcements. Let me explain... The more "active" users a social network has, the more that company can charge to advertisers to use it to reach our eyes. So, social media companies track their number of active users carefully, because that number is directly linked to the profitability of their app/site.

For the figures, I'm relying on Simon Kemp—and his company Kepios. Kepios are teamed up with the networks "We Are Social" and "Hootsuite" and gather a huge collection of data and trends relating to digital, social media, mobile, and e-commerce use around the world. If you like data, there is a lot you can learn from the information they gave garnered and it can be found at https://kepios.com. But for now, let's get back to social networks, or "social platforms" as they refer to them… you can see how the language used can muddy the waters.

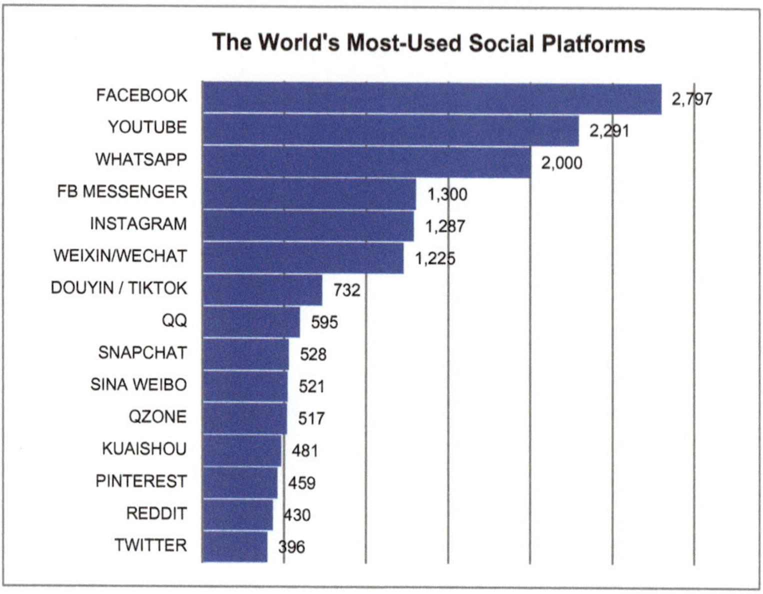

The information above is based on monthly active users, active user accounts, advertising agencies or unique monthly visitors (in millions). Market leader Facebook was the first social network to surpass 1 billion registered accounts and currently sits at over 2.7 billion monthly active users. Facebook is closely followed by YouTube, WhatsApp, Facebook Messenger, Instagram, WeChat and TikTok. If you are finding yourself lost already about what each of these networks are, then head to the "glossary of terms" at the back of the book where you'll find a brief description of each.

Social media companies have grown to be technology powerhouses, providing a multitude of services for their users. Those who use social media can traverse from uploading personal information on Facebook, to shopping, to watching a video on how to cook on YouTube, to real-time chat conversations on WhatsApp, to building levels and playing with/against people from all over the world through games. All of this can be done through a variety of online games and platforms. For example, through the Xbox and PlayStation consoles and smartphone/tablet game applications. All those features are not solely limited to one or another technological platform, many of those aforementioned social media applications are available on multiple devices, and often with a capability to sync and connect with one another. Quite clearly, people have multiple opportunities, through multiple means, to "check-in" with their chosen networks.

Social networks are changing the way hundreds of millions of people relate to one another and share information. To sustain the success of a social media site, it is important that members continuously and constantly access and use the site to maintain its vitality... to remain active users... and so companies are invested in keeping you "using" their site. Later on, in this book you will find out how social media companies use psychological tactics to their advantage—keeping people glued to their networks. There is nothing stopping you from skipping to that section now. However, this book has been designed to be read in the order it is written. By reading it in its designed order you will take more away at the end than if you dip in and out of various chapters. You will then be in the best place to utilize the resources and face the challenge of discussing social media with young people... I can't stop you though, I'm not watching you read... or am I? (no, no I'm not) ... anyway, I digress, where was I?

A rapidly growing body of research has accompanied the meteoric rise of Facebook, as social scientists attempt to assess the impact of Facebook on social life. But the truth is, social media is advancing and becoming available faster than the impact of using it over time can be researched. Research into social media is in its infancy, there is a lot to learn, and much to iron out.

I'll give an example of the difficulties in researching social media. One particular mammoth challenge is that there is a massive amount of "data" that exists—times of day that apps are used, how long they're used, what is being clicked on etc... which could be analyzed and researched and compared. However, this information is owned by social media companies, who are often not willing to share such information. Imagine the scandal, if research were to highlight that children were self-harming and certain apps were used moments before the harm took place... it could destroy the business. This information is guarded fiercely. Therefore, researchers must rely on other methods of assessment to explore the impact of social media... such as self-report measures, which can be biased, all the while knowing that a goldmine of information is denied to them.

Social media is a tough landscape to navigate, and an even tougher one to research. But what became clear to me, in dealing with first-hand accounts of the impact of social networking, in reading countless articles and designing and conducting research, is that despite the numerous apps that exist, the underlying psychology doesn't fundamentally shift. The apps may change, but the psychology remains. So as this book continues, specific sites may be mentioned, but rest assured the psychology is often transferable to multiple platforms and applications... or as a friend of mine once put it, "the recipe might have been tweaked, but it's still a curry."

I was recently talking with a colleague about writing this book and he asked me a question that stumped me. He asked, "why do I need to know this?" It stumped me not because I didn't know what to say, but because I was shocked into forgetting everything I knew for about 7 s. He had a habit of asking questions that did that, or perhaps I have a habit of forgetting everything. Either way, I responded with a challenge—"go somewhere where teenagers gather and watch them for 10 min, come back and tell me what you saw." I met that same colleague later in the afternoon and he said "OK, I don't know why... I don't know why phones have become so integral to teenage interaction, and I want to know why."

So, put your phones on silent, there are no planned fire alarm tests, if the fire alarm goes off we'll gather by the tree at the edge of the carpark, feel free to use the toilets if you get the urge, you don't have to ask. Let's get started.

PART I

The positives and purposes of using social media

CHAPTER

1

Identity and construction of the self

https://doi.org/10.1016/B978-0-323-91898-5.00008-4

Identity presentation on most social networks centers around the user profile, which serves as a platform on which people can make public or semi-public presentations of themselves. Despite the name "social networks," much user activity is self-focused. On Facebook, for example, people can post pictures of themselves, complete a personal profile listing their personal information and preferences, join common interest groups, and post status updates for other users to see and comment on. It is important that you understand some key aspects of the psychology of "identity" because this will play an important role in many teenagers' social media behaviors.

Psychologists have long agreed that the concept of the self is multifaceted. There are countless textbooks written on the subject. It would be impossible to do the subject justice in its entirety in a chapter. Moreover, the multifaceted nature of the self means that researchers have taken different directions with regard to studying how it relates to a social media society. What this chapter will do is introduce you to some relevant research and psychological theory which are pertinent to understanding identity, self, and social media.

The Ship of Theseus

The ship of Theseus is a thought experiment that raises the question of whether an object that has had all its parts replaced remains fundamentally the same object. This concept is one of the oldest in philosophy, having been discussed by the likes of Heraclitus and Plato circa 500–400 BCE. There are a few different iterations of the story of Theseus' ship, but generally, they adhere to the following form:

> Theseus was a hero in ancient Greek mythology, on his missions he sailed a famous ship, traveling the high seas battling monsters and gods… these battles resulted in wear and tear on the ship, as a result Theseus replaced parts of his ship that had worn out. After many years Theseus had replaced every single part of his ship piece by piece…

So, the question is if every single piece had been replaced, is it still the same ship?

But wait, there's more:

> What if, unbeknown to Theseus, each part of his Ship that was discarded, was collected and carefully repaired by an expert shipwright… Whom put them all back together and rebuilt the famous ship. So now, we have two ships.

The question now becomes—which is the "real" Theseus' ship?

Let's give our brains a break from that conundrum for a moment and consider what we know about biology. Our bodies are in a continual process of duplicating and replicating cells and discarding/recycling the unused. So, are we the same people we were 5 months ago? 5 years ago? 10 years ago? The idea here in biology is that identity is continuous, each person alters over time, piece by piece and so eventually, you are a completely different person than who you started as. But some things don't change, right? The "Theseus" of us, what makes us who we are apart from or outward appearance? Our values? Our qualities? Our personality? I know many people whose values, qualities, and personalities have changed over time. Time changes all, mortality beckons revelation. So, which is the "real" Theseus' ship? You'll need to decide for yourself. And when thinking about your own identity over time, one thing is for certain, you need to understand that multiple influences shape you as an individual. To do this, I'm relying on the work of Urie Bronfenbrenner, who formulated the ecological systems theory.

Ecological systems theory

Urie Bronfenbrenner (April 29, 1917—September 25, 2005) was a Russian-born American psychologist. He was best known for developing the ecological systems theory in 1979. This is a theory in which individuals are seen as developing not in isolation, but within the context of multiple relationships, such as those involving families, friends, schools, neighborhoods, and society. Bronfenbrenner organized the ecological system (in which human growth occurs) into five subsystems: the microsystem, mesosystem, exosystem, macrosystem, and chronosystem. It's hard to explain on paper, but much easier to understand when seen visually, see below:

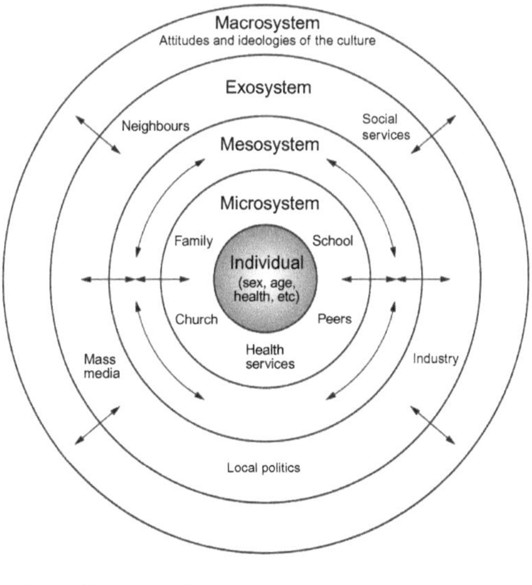

Bronfenbrenner's ecological systems theory.

Place yourself in the center of the circle above, this is you and everything within you—your sex, age, health, natural hair color, your genetics, etc. From that point, Bronfenbrenner suggests that we develop as part of the interactions and context of multiple variables.

Microsystem—The most proximal level of interaction. This includes the settings in which individuals directly interact and the people who inhabit them. For example, our families, our friends, the neighborhood we live in, local schools, after-school clubs, religious groups, health services, and local parks. These are the direct connections you have with your surroundings.

Mesosystem—The mesosystem covers the interaction of the different microsystems that people find themselves in. It is, broadly speaking, a series of microsystems showing the links possible between them—between home and school, between peer group and family and between family and community. For example, certain peers might meet up in a neighborhood play area, certain religious groups might be a part of a school curriculum delivery. If parents get on well with a child's peers—then this can lead to positive experiences, if they do not, then disharmony can occur between the interacting systems. All of these connections start to shape the environment one is developing within.

Exosystem—The exosystem refers to the connections that may exist between two or more settings. One of these may not contain the developing individual but affect them indirectly. For example, social welfare services and the school may have issues with the family and their care practices which impacts the individual in the center. Police, mass media, and neighbors may highlight an issue with a local play area, resulting in its closure—which will interfere with the "spaces" the individual gets to occupy—in potentially good and bad ways depending on your outlook. Another example of how the exosystem can impact a developing child would be related to a parent's experience. If a parent is going to work, repeatedly passed for promotion is underappreciated and mistreated—they may come home and take their frustration out on their family (in psychodynamic theory this is known as displacement and is a defense mechanism).

Macrosystem—The macrosystem is the most distant collection of people and places to the individual. However, there is still a significant impact on how this influences development. The macrosystem is composed of the individual's cultural patterns and values, specifically their dominant beliefs and ideas, as well as political and economic systems of the country that they are growing up in. At this level, the existence of the internet would appear here and the available politics of a country and that country's economic planning. For example, children in war-torn areas will experience a different kind of development than children in peaceful environments.

Chronosystem—The chronosystem adds the invaluable dimension of time. This shows the impact of both change and constancy in the surrounding environment and relationships. Over time, this could include a change in family structure, housing, employment status, and immense societal changes such as economic cycles, wars, or the recent coronavirus pandemic.

If we imagine that our current identity sits mapped out on the top of this log, using Bronfenbrenner's Ecological Systems theory. If we were to take a slice out of this log and look down upon it, we would likely see a completely different set of relationships and links, depending on what "year of growth" we cut into. This is the chronosystem. Identity and development, through relationships with multiple systems, over time.

This concept of change over time is important. It is particularly important when considering social media use. You may have seen in the media multiple high-profile people getting into trouble for things that they have posted online when they were much younger. Politician's losing their jobs due to outfits worn at parties 10 years earlier, or statements that they have made on social media that are now considered offensive to different groups. This doesn't simply remain on social media either. Recently the film Ace Ventura was put under the spotlight for its choice of supposed humor toward the LGBTQ community. But is this simply a reflection of the time in which they were made or posted online? A reflection of how our thinking has evolved that allows us to re-think what has come before us? I used to find the show Little Britain hilarious but upon re-watching, it did not find it humorous at all. What is written online leaves a trace, much like the Chronosystem in Bronfenbrenner's Ecological Systems Theory. You will find much "trimming" happening online with people seeking to adapt and adjust the "imprint" of their selves which has been left behind, and perhaps, represents someone they used to be. After all, it is not uncommon for employers to search through social media to vet prospective candidates for jobs to ensure they are getting what is written "on the tin."

Bronfenbrenner's Ecological Systems Theory highlights the diversity of the connected influences on our development and identity. It also allows us to reflect on our current situations. If you desire to change for yourself, consider what would need to change in the context and relationships that you are living with.

I. The positives and purposes of using social media

So now that we have an understanding of the multiple interacting influences on our development and identity, we can begin to explore other aspects of identity, such as whether or not we can truly know ourselves.

How much do we know ourselves?

This feels like it could be a title of a magazine column. Where you would have to tick lots of boxes, do some careful addition and then you would get an answer about the type of person you are—ending with some sort of parentheses that reads: *"You're a Lion personality—A strong a silent type, reliable to your friends, trustworthy, but you're no pushover… you don't take any prisoners."* Although undeniably fun while it's being completed, they are often anti-climactic. You might get identified as a Codfish instead of a Lion…and then have to change your answers so that you get the result you desired, not that that has happened to me… moving swiftly on, I can assure you that approach has no place here, but interestingly, does in diagnostics… more on that later.

It's important to explore this question because time and time again you will see teenagers behaving a certain way online, seemingly in a haze of naivety, believing they are presenting themselves in one way, but appearing to us and others in a completely different way—the psychology of this is fascinating. To answer the question of *how much do we know ourselves*? I'm relying on some psychology that has stood the test of time. A technique that was created by psychologists Joseph Luft

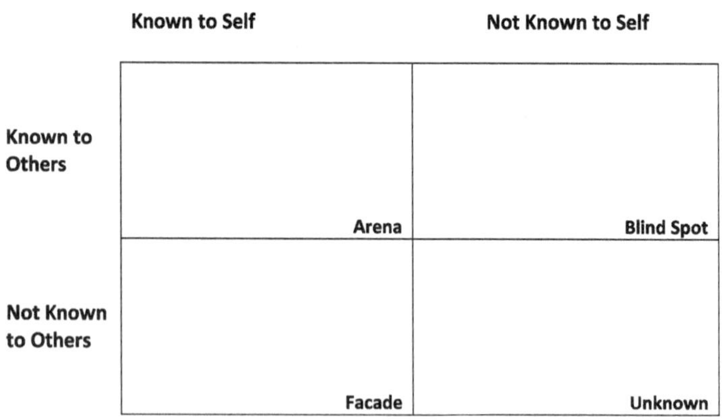

The Johari Window.

(1916–2014) and Harrington Ingham (1916–1995) in 1955: The Johari Window.

The Johari window is a technique that helps people better understand their relationship with themselves and others. There are four quadrants to it:

The Arena—Things that are known to self and known to others. This could include personal characteristics and traits that you openly accept and that your friends know you for. Factual information can be here as well as feelings and desires that you openly express.

The Façade—Things that are known to self but not known to others. This could include personal characteristics that we hide from others—jealousy, nervousness, or perhaps parts of ourselves we have not wanted to share—growing up in care? Having been divorced multiple times? Hidden sexual desires? Being in an abusive relationship?

The Blind Spot—Things that are not known to self but known to others. These might include habits people have noticed of you, certain ways of speaking, certain repetitive phrases or facial expressions too often used. Perhaps a level of meanness, or a funny-sounding laugh we don't recognize of ourselves, a funny way of walking or perhaps narcissistic tendencies. Often when we see ourselves on film, we can become aware of how we may be seen by others—I never realized how hunched I sit at a table until I was filmed delivering a psychological consultation.

The Unknown—Things not known to self and not known to others. These characteristics tend to appear in certain unexpected circumstances, and are unknown until the circumstance triggers it. For example—standing up to a bully, showing leadership skills during an emergency, handling significant pain in a calm and measured way. Once the characteristic appears, it moves from the unknown box into the *blind spot* or *arena.*

I encourage you to sketch a copy of the Johari window and try to complete some of it. I've included a blank one at the back of the book for you to write on/tear out if you so desire. It is a powerful exercise of self-reflection. It is also very personal, so when completing yours consider how honest you want to be with yourself and others if they are going to see what you have written. Also, speaking from experience, if you're the type of person who lends a book to someone else once you've finished reading it, tearing out the page or sketching it may be the best option. To demonstrate, I'll go first...

	Known to Self	Not Known to Self
Known to Others	Father/ Husband/ Psychologist Relaxed approach to life & work Organised Humorous Sarcastic Honest – sometimes unsocially so **Arena**	Makes 'a face' when looking in the mirror* Changes posture and baritone of voice when meeting new people* Holds chest when laughing hard* Lights up when talking about Alba* Snores louder than a vacuum cleaner* Very easily distracted* **Blind Spot**
Not Known to Others	Gets extremely nervous when having to speak in front of a crowd. Experiences impostor syndrome. Unhappy with how I physically look. Regularly wonders if I would have been happier in different career – perhaps archaeology or astronomy **Facade**	? **Unknown**

*Throwing caution to the wind, I asked my wife to complete this section for me... we are still married

The Johari Window: Completed example.

If you're feeling brave, you can use the Johari window as an activity with others. By cutting out descriptors on paper, such as:

Able	Extroverted	Modest	Sensible
Bold	Helpful	Nervous	Sentimental
Calm	Idealistic	Observant	Spontaneous
Complex	Ingenious	Patient	Tense
Confident	Intelligent	Quiet	Trustworthy
Dependable	Introverted	Reflective	Warm
Empathetic	Loving	Relaxed	Witty
Energetic	Mature	Searching	Woeful

You can then arrange them yourself in the Arena/Façade area... then ask the other/others to arrange the remaining in the Blind Spot, leaving any remaining items in the Unknown, yet to be discovered.

So how much can we know ourselves? We can know what we know, and we can know what we hide, but there will always be a blind spot of what others know and we know nothing about. And there will always be "the unknowns," waiting for the right conditions to become evident.

So far, we have looked at multiple interacting influences on our development and identity and seen the self as multifaceted. But there is more to discuss when understanding identity, and it is important to understand these concepts before we throw social media into the mix once more... because a lot will suddenly make sense, stay with me. If psychology is the sky, and theories are clouds, I'm pulling from multiple clouds to bring together a climate for us to bask in. And right now, I'm going to pull something from Henri Tajfel's cloud. Henri Tajfel (22 June 1919–3 May 1982) studied psychology in London, becoming a lecturer, first at the University of Durham and then at Oxford University. He was a social psychologist of profound renown, most famous for social identity theory.

Social identity theory

Social identity is an individual's perception of who they are based on their group memberships. Social identity theory espouses that the groups that we belong to, or are drawn to—family; clubs; teams; social class; music genre; are all an important source of pride and self-esteem. The groups that we identify with and belong to give us a sense of social identity: a sense of belonging to the wider social world.

Human beings are profoundly social, we are drawn toward connection with others. To realize the importance of human connection you only have to glance at Bruce Perry's book—*The boy who was raised as a dog*. His book is full of phenomenal accounts of the importance of connecting to others in meaningful ways, but for now, back to Tajfel.

Henri Tajfel proposed that stereotyping is based on a normal cognitive process—the tendency to group things together. In doing this, we have a habit of also engaging in the exaggeration of the differences between groups and the similarities within "our group". Essentially, creating an "us" and "them."

This is known as in-group (us) and out-group (them) bias. The fundamental premise of social identity theory is that group members of an in-group will seek to find negative aspects of an out-group, thus enhancing their self-image. On a small scale, this creates people who love rock music disliking pop music fans... On a country-sized scale, prejudice can turn into racism (think back to WWII—Nazis and the Jews).

It is proposed that there are three stages to group identification that happen cognitively when "assessing the other person"—to work out if they are in-group or out-group if they are "us" or "them". These stages are Social Categorization, Social Identification, and Social Comparison. Let's look at them further:

(1) Social Categorization

We naturally categorize things in order to understand them, to make sense of them and for convenience. We categorize most things in life—plants that you can eat, plants that you can't, animals which you can eat, animals which you can't. Picture for a moment how you organize your kitchen, fresh food, tinned food, condiments, tea/coffee/sugar (close to the kettle of course), pots and pans. We as a species tend to lean toward organization and categorization.

In a very similar way, we categorize people (including ourselves) in order to understand the social environment around us. We even create social categories like White; Black; English; French; Buddhist; Christian; Muslim; Student; Rich; Middle Class; Poor; Gay; Straight; Vegetarian; Vegan; Tourist, Laborer, Academic and Train Driver. We do this because categories are useful. These categories are useful because they tell us something about the individual. And if categories didn't exist, then day-to-day functioning would be difficult. Take the train driver example, if you are on a train, without the category of driver, how do you refer to this man? If I am cooking for you and you tell me you're a vegetarian...well, hang on, I would first panic because 90% of the meals I normally cook would no longer be appropriate, and secondly, I would panic because I'm a terrible cook. My cooking was already likely to ruin our friendship and now I have to consider vegetables. Who am I kidding...? I wouldn't be cooking for you, I'd be ordering takeaway for you because I like you and you don't deserve to be put through my cooking. But the point stands, categories help us understand situations and people better.

In a similar vein, we find out things about ourselves by understanding what groups we belong to. Understanding where we belong better helps us to understand what the expectations are for us—how should we be? But you can only do this if you are able to "find your tribe"... and people can belong to many different groups.

My wife once threw a surprise birthday party for me, it was such a wonderful gesture of love—she had invited everyone I am friends with: people I studied with, colleagues from work, people I grew up with, my close family, my extended family. On the one hand, a grand gesture of love and an amazing evening, but for me, on the other hand—a clashing of tribes. Here under one roof were all my groups... how many different people would I need to be over an evening? A calm sense of dread washed over me as I note the group of friends I grew up with who have seen me at my worst—teenage years of drinking, embarrassment, and hangovers, stood talking with my new colleagues I've known for only a few months... where can I hide?

(2) Social Identification

In the second stage, social identification, we begin to assume the identity of the group that we have categorized our self as belonging to. When I got my first job in a secondary school, I had to wear a suit and tie every day. I amassed 32 different ties and multiple tie shirt combinations to go with my 5 subtlety different suits... I looked at the part, which was important to me at the time. When I moved into training to be a psychologist no one wore suits, and no one was wearing ties. I saw Chino-shirt combos, suit trouser-shirt combos... oh, a jumper shirt mix (is that allowed?). Time for a wardrobe upgrade... or was it downgrade? Was I now so qualified that ties were somehow beneath me? I quickly found someone I trusted to talk me through the "male educational psychologist wardrobe expectation." The advice went like this: "dress smart enough, but not too smart that it makes the rest of us look scruffy... apart from if you to go to court as an expert witness, then wear a suit and tie". This brief bit of advice helped me fit in and assume the identity of the group I'd just joined.

The same applies if you become a student, a civil servant, or a lawyer, you start to assume the role and identity of the group. There is a high level of emotional significance to your identification with a group, and your self-esteem will become symbiotic with that group membership.

(3) Social Comparison

The third stage is social comparison. To maintain our self-esteem and maintain the value of "our group," we begin to compare our group to other groups. There is an interesting aspect of social comparison, that of "rivalry." If we find ourselves belonging to a group, we can find rivalry with those unlike "us", but also those like us. The league tables that rank schools are a prime example of this—all educators and supporting staff, yet in competition to have the best results. The success of "your" school (or identified group) feeds into your self-worth and self-esteem.

The groups that we identify with are an important aspect of our identity, unlike my multiple tie-shirt combos, they can't be easily taken on and off, they become an integral aspect of our *self* and *identity*. If you want to know more about certain aspects of social comparison you should look up Leon Festinger's Social Comparison Theory and read more on Henri Tajfel.

Let's re-cap—we have multiple interacting factors that influence our development, the self is multi-faceted, we are biologically drawn to connecting with others, and identity is largely driven by the various groups that we belong to, which give us a sense of social identity. This is quite the tapestry we've created and there is a thread that weaves its way through this tapestry and every now and pulls at us, and we notice it, and that is the concept of congruence and true self.

Congruence and true self

Another word for congruence is harmony. If our identity doesn't fit with who we feel we are then we become incongruous. You might meet people like this at work, at restaurants or anywhere interaction takes place. If you ever get the sense that someone is playing a role and not being genuine then this person may have found themselves in an incongruent or disharmonious identity.

The true self is referred to as many different things. In other books and articles, it will be referred to as ideal self, real self, idealized self, and authentic self amongst others. It is a concept originally introduced into psychoanalysis in 1960 by Donald Winnicott who called it—the spontaneous authentic experience and feeling of being alive. It is a sense of being content with oneself, connected to one's surroundings and present with the experience. One's true self also consists of qualities that an individual currently possesses, but perhaps, does not normally express to others in everyday life.

Carl Rogers (January 8, 1902—February 4, 1987) was a distinguished American psychologist who is widely regarded as the founding father of person-centered/humanistic psychotherapy. Rogers' methods and unique approach to psychology are applied to multiple fields of work—including student-centered learning in education and countless counseling practices. In his book: *On Becoming a Person,* Rogers explores his experiences of helping people discover their path to personal growth. Using client examples from therapy to highlight a shift in his client's experiencing life and perception—moving toward becoming their true selves. Rogers guides the reader through this process, a process where you find yourself moving away from façades, away from "oughts," away from meeting expectations, away from pleasing others, toward self-direction, toward "being," toward openness to experience, toward acceptance of others, toward trusting one's self. You will find that teenagers particularly go through a phase of wanting to be seen as "real" or "authentic" from their unique perspective of the world. As social media can often act as an imprint of someone's identity at any given time, this will be notable in how a young person expresses themselves online.

That's enough theory for now. To build on the metaphor I stated earlier, we now have a climate of understanding about identity and construction of the self. This climate is what young people take with them wherever they go, it is what adults take with them wherever they go. So, what happens when a platform is created where we get to create a virtual representation of ourselves for others to see? This is exactly what social media has provided for billions across the world. People's representations of their selves online for all (or nearly all) to see.

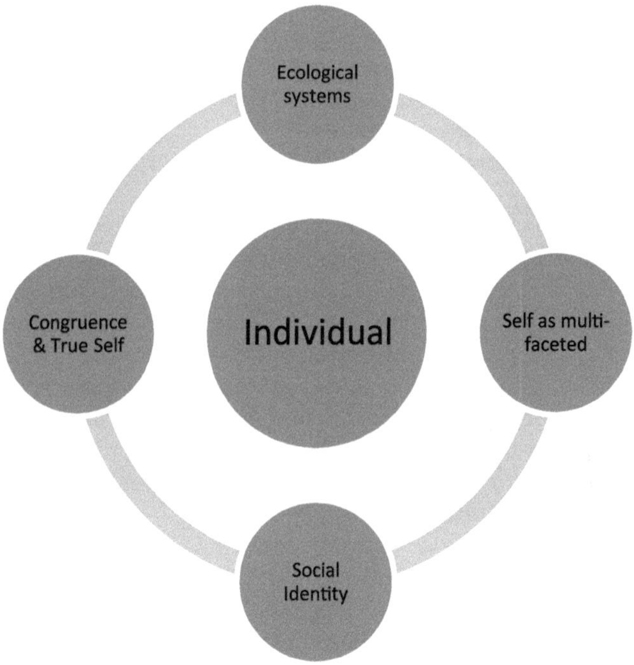

Carl Rogers once described the goal of life as the journey to be the self which one truly is, but is this possible? are people expressing their true selves online? Recent research has focused on the use of social media in the achievement of this goal. One such researcher was Gwendolyn Seidman, writing for the captivating Journal *"Computers in Human Behavior."* In 2014, Seidman gathered up 184 undergraduate university students and then asked them to complete an online survey that assessed "True Self" expression to their friends online (Study 1a). Answering the question of whether or not this is present through social media use.

While this was happening 41 different undergraduate students also completed the same survey and had screenshots of their Facebook profiles saved and coded to detect levels of personal disclosure on their profiles and others' walls (Study 1b).

The results of Study 1a found that true self-expression was indeed evident online. The results also suggested that those who express their "true self" online tend to post for more self-oriented reasons, such as getting attention and feeling included, rather than other reasons—like expressing care for others.

The results of Study 1b confirmed that those who express their true self online are more likely to post on others' walls and are more likely to disclose intimate information on Facebook. Seidman also noted that despite the increase in self-disclosure of their participants, this did not elicit a reciprocal response from their online friends. This highlights some differing underlying reasons for using social media, it seems that not everyone is solely channeling their "true self"... Self-disclosure will be discussed a little later when we consider some of the unintended consequences of social media use and, in particular, the use of reassurance seeking.

A couple of years ago, prior to Seidman's study, Leman Pinar Tosun created a study looking into motives for Facebook use and expressing "true self" on the internet. Surveying 143 students, Tosun uncovered four main motives for Facebook use. These were—to maintain long-distance friendships, for entertainment purposes, for photo-related activities, and for organizing social activities. Individuals' tendency for expressing one's true self online had an influence on their Facebook use motives: The participants with a high tendency to express their "true self" on the Internet reported using Facebook for establishing new friendships and for initiating/terminating romantic relationships more than the individuals' with low and medium levels of the same tendency did.

This seems to highlight a level of online confidence, to be putting oneself "out there" to meet others, to start relationships and to end them. This is also an indicator that those who utilize social media in part to represent their "true selves" show a large amount of trust in the information they are posting online about themselves and are gathering online from others. There are elements of a reciprocal nature here, to put yourself "out there" in the belief you will be meeting like-minded people who are doing the same.

Tosun suggests that people may find it difficult to express some aspects of their "true self" during their face-to-face communication; especially if those aspects conflict with social norms and expectations, and that those individuals may also find it difficult to gather information from others during face-to-face communication. So, what social media is allowing, is a dedicated space for people to create a digital version of their identity. It is allowing people the option to connect. And if in day-to-day life, they struggle to connect with others, or struggle to read social situations, it is giving them time to construct their responses exactly as they would like them to be. It is allowing people to channel their true selves. Let me give an example:

Let's say that that you are massively into "furries." If you don't know what a "furry" is, it is a fandom of enjoying to dress as animals that have anthropomorphic features—simply put, people dressed as animals. The likelihood is that in your local community, be it a school or a workplace, you're not likely to find many other people with that interest. It is quite a niche. To use Johari's window, your love of this is probably known by you, but not known by others (for fear of prejudice). How do you then find your tribe? You can see the "footballers" have all found one another, the "cake makers" have all found one another, the "fashion conscious" have found one another... but what about you? One quick search of "furries" through social media and suddenly...

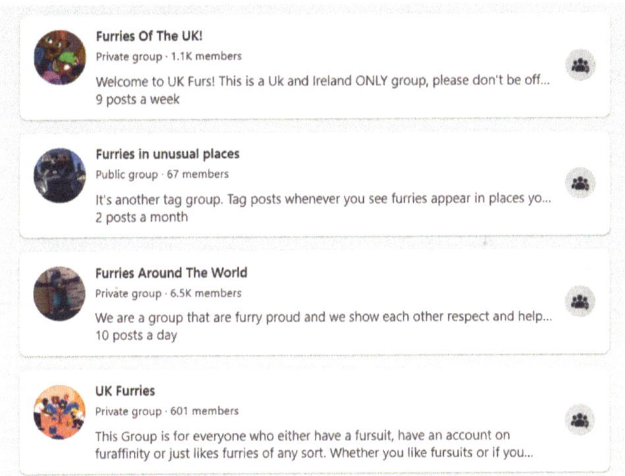

Hundreds of groups appear, you're not alone. Social identity theory kicks into action, you have found people, like you... you become more congruent and closer to being your true self. You found your tribe. How powerful is that?

This is one reason that it will always be difficult to stop using social media. Or why a teenager will roll their eyes at a parent saying, "just delete it, get rid of it." Our identities are knitted into the fabric of our being, social media is allowing a venue to express our true selves. To "get rid of it" for some, would be akin to asking them to sever their right hand. Now, let's look at another group with whom identity and finding like-minded people has always been important.

Lesbian, gay, bisexual, transgender, questioning, intersex, asexual, plus (L.G.B.T.Q.I.A.+)

For young people who identify as L.G.B.T.Q.I.A.+, the internet is often turned to as a place to find out more. In the early days of realizing there may be a "difference," the internet is often utilized by young people to explore what that difference may be and to then find others who may be the same. There is an internal drive to find one's identity and then socially connect with others to share it, explore it and develop it... all of which can take place before the young person has "come out" to those around them.

For the young people who identify as L.G.B.T.Q.I.A.+ social media is often used for them to feel 'normal'. They need to see videos, read stories, and hear the voices of others who may look like them, identify under the same labels and either be on or have been on a similar journey as they are. This is particularly evident for young people who are not yet 'out' in their local communities, but also for those who are. There is comfort and unity in finding others that are like them. This is particularly true for groups for whom there is still 'marginalization' and targeted attacks for existing.

Identity and connection aside, social media is allowing marginalized voices to be heard, and the more voices that can be heard then the better the situation will eventually become. This is the basis of Parasocial Contact Hypothesis theory—when a person or a group of people learn to better understand the object of their prejudice, discrimination, of their hate, through the use of technology, TV, Movies, and/or social media, then their acceptance levels of that group go up and their pre-held biases go down.

For those young people who identify as L.G.B.T.Q.I.A.+, social media is providing that space for them to be themselves, they may even only be 'out' online. Social media is then transformed into a powerful protective factor for that individual.

What we will be seeing, for many, is the use of social media to represent their ideal selves. The best pictures uploaded, the best moments described filtered photos, adapted and adjusted to represent 'the ideal'. While some may view this as a dishonest representation of that person's 'life', I would view it as a goal state—an ideal self. Difficulties in this area would only arise for an individual if the discrepancy, or distance, between their current 'self' and their 'ideal self' is too large to eventually traverse. At all other times, this "social media self" serves as a pinboard to boost one's self-esteem and represent their chosen real or ideal identity.

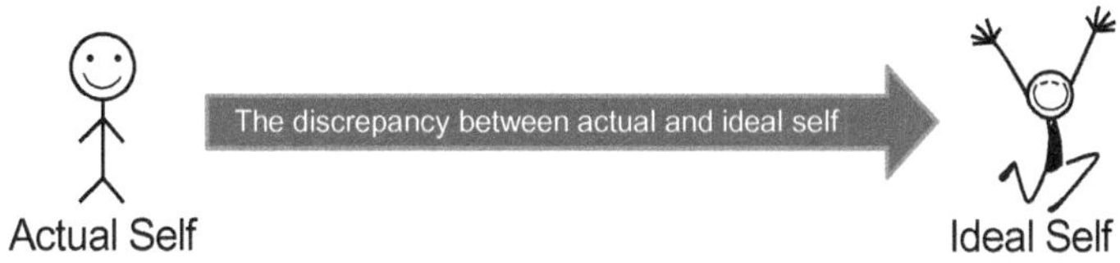

Self-disclosure is viewed as a major factor in the development, maintenance, and deterioration of a relationship. Online and offline worlds are psychologically connected. A person's identity doesn't solely rest on how one presents or expresses themselves, but on multiple factors, including the connections one develops with others and the groups to which they belong. Chapter 2 will explore this further, in considering social connectedness and social media.

CHAPTER

2

Social connectedness

Psychologist's Guide to Adolescents and Social Media
https://doi.org/10.1016/B978-0-323-91898-5.00005-9

At an individual level, social connectedness involves the quality and number of connections one has with other people in a social circle of family, friends, and acquaintances. Social connectedness can be described as a measure of how people come together and interact. On a larger scale, social connectedness is related to social cohesion across populations and wider society.

Adolescence, unlike other life stages, is characterized by establishing many social ties and constantly attempting to strengthen or refine them. With the internet becoming a principal venue for social interaction, young people often feel pressure to join and use social media. The landscape of social media has become the venue to establish or maintain contact with people with whom they share interests or connections.

It seems like the most commonsense statement to make—that social media use allows for social connectedness to take place. Yet, some would argue that using social media is causing the opposite, that people are becoming more disconnected from one another the more they use social networks. So, what is it? Are people becoming more socially connected or less? Let's turn to some research to find out.

7 years ago, a study was designed to explore whether increased social media engagement related to higher levels of social connectedness… it also explored whether social networking usage improved cognitive abilities, but that particular aspect of their study will be discussed later in this book. The study was conducted by Dr. Tracy Alloway and colleagues (et al.) with the results published in the Journal *Computers in Education.* Dr. Alloway recruited 104 students from a UK secondary school to complete a questionnaire on their social networking use. The recruited students were aged between 15 and 18 years old. Incorporated into their questionnaire was Lee and Robbins "Social Connectedness Scale"—developed in 1995 to assess how connected people felt with their family, friends, peers, and society.

The results painted an interesting picture between two social networks. Their study showed that participants who used Facebook for over a year scored highly on social connectedness. However, time spent using YouTube showed no significant levels of social connectedness. What's happening here? Let's consider the style of social network for a moment… the results make sense and have a level of predictability; Facebook's primary design is to connect people and develop social networks, whereas YouTube's primary function is to share videos with a secondary function to comment and join networks. In the discussion of their results, it's highlighted that for secondary school students, most of their day is spent with their peers in school, thus they already feel connected in a social sense to their peers. Therefore, this research also provides evidence that social media is being used as a tool to enhance already established friendships.

In my years of working in secondary schools, I can honestly say there's not been a single day where I haven't either seen a group of children gathered around a phone looking at something on YouTube, or overheard them talking about something they have seen on YouTube. Although YouTube's design does not lend itself, in comparison to Facebook, as a site for social connectedness in and of itself—It certainly is being used as a tool for social connectedness. An "online" platform connecting "offline" relationships through entertainment.

5 years previous—researchers from California State University wanted to explore the connection between online and offline social worlds. Kaveri Subrahmanyam, Stephanie Reich, Natalia Waechter, and Guadalupe Espinoza conducted a study to explore this, which was published in the *Journal of Applied Developmental Psychology*. In their study, they gathered 55 male and 55 female undergraduate students and asked them to complete questionnaires based on their social media usage and social connectedness.

Their results concluded that social media was being used to connect with people from their offline lives and that there was an overlap between online and offline networks. The authors of this research concluded that social media was being utilized to selectively strengthen different social connections, connections which were not as strong in their "offline" networks.

You may be wondering why I'm telling you all of this, but stick with me, it will become clear.

Back in 2011, social network MySpace was at the height of popularity. I loved it… I could choose music to play when someone clicked on my profile, what better way to represent who I am! Researcher's Mazur and Richards conducted a study to see whether or not MySpace was being used to expand connections to people from different ages, localities, and ethnicities, or to connect with people similar to themselves (also known as homophily). Mazur and Richards gathered information randomly from 129 recently updated public profiles of 16–19-year olds using Myspace. The researchers recorded information such as; age, gender, marital status, city, sexual orientation, number of friends, and schools attended. The researchers then counted the number of comments made by individual friends during the last 24h, examining their profiles and comparing the age, gender, ethnicity, and location of the individual.

The results showed that like offline friendship interactions, the majority of online interactions of adolescents and emerging adults are cross-gender with peers of the same age, ethnicity, and locality. These results suggest that rather than a global social connectedness, there is rather a local-social connectedness evident with social media uses. I would counter that point, however, with a hypothesis—that if an individual does not have local connections, then they would be likely to look wider and further afield to find those connections. These would be the people who are finding global connectedness to fulfill their human need for connection. The human need for connection cannot be underestimated. I once worked with a young girl in England who had started living by an American time-zone so that she could wake, connect, play games online, and sleep at the same time as what she saw as her closest friends. The downside of this is that she would sleep when she should have been at school, such was her need to be connected to those she valued.

Social connectedness within families is evolving with technology. I've lost count of the number of parents I meet who send digital messages to their children when they are in the same house. Some studies have begun to explore this dynamic and the social media connectedness between parents and their children.

In 2014 a study by Doty and Dworkin recruited 649 parents to take part in an online survey exploring how they connect with and monitor their children online. Results showed that parents were using social media to communicate with their children, their children's friends, and the parents of their children's friends. However, this presence of parents online is often met with skepticism by some children, weary of being monitored online. It is widely regarded that too much "monitoring" of online activity is damaging to the child–parent relationship. Those parents who have a baseline trusting relationship with their children are more likely to have an insight into their online activities because of the child's self-disclosure. Self-disclosure was already an inherent aspect of the of the parent-child relationship 'offline' which was transferred 'online'. Trust and a strong parent-child relationship being a huge safety net when children venture into new online (and offline) spaces.

From experience, the monitoring of children's social networking is always a touchy subject with teenagers. It is not uncommon for children to have multiple accounts, one of which they "accept" their parents' friendship online, so they can be monitored. However, at the same time creating other accounts which they use, often under a pseudonym, where they can be free to roam unencumbered.

My point in highlighting the above studies is to show that there is clear evidence for the support of social media use in the maintenance and strengthening of already established social networks. It seems that social connectedness is palpable across social media, it is providing what it advertises… and indeed it can be used to target certain relationships to selectively strengthen. I once worked with a young girl who espoused this phenomenon, I have taken an extract from my case notes of our work together to provide as an example—names have been changed to protect identity:

Dr C: *"Last time we met you mentioned that you had been finding it hard to make new friendships, that you felt stuck in your current ones."*
Sarah: *"Yeah."*
Dr C: *"Has anything changed since we last met?"*

Sarah: *"Well, not really, not yet."*
Dr C: *"You mentioned that you knew who you wanted to be friends with, but that they had been friends for a long time and were a kind of 'closed group', already established, difficult to break into."*
Sarah: *"Yeah that's right."*
Dr C: *"Are they not approachable?"*
Sarah: *"I can't just go up to them."*
Dr C: *"What do you plan on doing? What's your way in?"*
Sarah: *"Umm, well there's Chloe, who's like the leader, well not the leader, but she's very bossy so I can't go up to her, but Jen is quite chill and you know, she's smiled at me a few times and spoken to me before so I think that she's my 'in'."*
Dr C: *"So she could bring you into the wider friendship group… But what are you going to do to?"*
Sarah: *"I can't just go up to them, even Jen, and say "oh I want to be your friends and hang out with you"… and I don't want help with this, you can't help with this, or my parents, or any of the teachers—that will ruin everything, you're not going to do anything about this are you?"*
Dr C: *"If you don't want me to do anything then I won't do anything, honestly, I'm really just trying to explore with you if you have a plan, if you have thought about the 'how'… if you don't want to talk about it then we don't have to, I just know that it's important to you and been on your mind a lot, and you probably haven't spoken to anyone about it…"*
Sarah: *"Ok, sorry, umm, so you want to talk about how I'm going to do what? To get in with them?"*
Dr C: *"Only if you're comfortable talking about it?"*
Sarah: *"It's just a bit embarrassing… you know… to say it out loud, but I'm sure that loads of people do it, but, it's just the way… I'm already friends on Facebook, but everyone's friends with everyone in our year, but I'm going to follow them on Instagram… you know, see what they like and that, and I'm going to start liking the stuff that they like…"*
Dr C: *"And that way it shows them that you have things in common?"*
Sarah: *"Yeah, but it sort of puts me on their radar… then I might make some comments or post similar things to see if they like the things I've posted… then we can see how it goes from there."*
Dr C: *"So it would be a sort of 'testing the water' to see if you could be friends, to see if you are liked by them as well?"*
Sarah: *"Yeah, I guess so."*
Dr C: *"So after that has happened, and let's say that you've liked their stuff online, and they've liked yours, and you're more on their radar… what happens next?"*
Sarah: *"I dunno…"*
Dr C: *"But I bet you would know a lot more about them, you'd have common ground, you'd know things that they like, you'd know what they like of yours… whatever it is that you're sharing, you'd have something to build on, maybe with Jen if she's the most approachable?"*

Sarah: *"Yeah, I could talk with Jen about some of that stuff."*
Dr C: *"That sounds like it would be a good start, I mean, she sounds like the most approachable, you've spoken to her the most out of all of them and she's smiled at you before, these are good signs to build a friendship on, plus, you'd be on the radar of the others because of Facebook and Instagram and so in theory you'd be in more likely to be welcomed into the group, is that right?"*
Sarah: *"I guess so, kinda."*
Dr C: *"That's all we can do really… guess… but it's good to hear that you've thought about a plan. Thank you for telling me about it, you shouldn't feel embarrassed, it's actually quite a well thought out graded approach. And I'm not going to 'do anything' or get involved in some way, I'll leave it to you, but the next time we meet I'd love to hear how things are going if you still want to talk about it. Let's leave friendships parked for the rest of the session and talk a little bit about how things are going in your Science lessons, I understand there's been a few issues recently?"*

My work with Sarah went on for a long time and the discussions about friendships were a large part of our sessions together. Throughout our time together I had to hold back the urge to say "just go up to them, be brave, put yourself out there… " not only would that have been bad psychology, but also bad advice for her… it wouldn't have been congruous with her way of being. She had chosen a strategy that she felt would work for her and was implementing it her way, my job was to be a sounding board to explore her approach with her. Besides, she was right. In the end, Jen was her best way in, and although there were ups and downs along this social networking journey into reshaping friendships, it eventually worked. Sarah joined a new social circle.

If we think back to social identity theory explored in Chapter 1—Sarah used *social categorization* to identify a group she wished to be like, she used *social identification* via Instagram and Facebook to gather the evidence of her group and assume the same interests, become more like them… and then once part of the group engaged in *social comparison*, in a school sense, that group's enemies became her enemies. Sarah's self-esteem rose, she became more confident and some of the group's work ethic rubbed off on her—lesson disruption became much less of an issue for her. Social media allowed Sarah the foundations to connect and further develop her friendships.

Sarah knew which social media apps to use in order to get the results she needed. But did she have a "choice" in using those apps? Or did the wider community of users mean that she "followed the flock"? I believe it remains important to consider what social networking sites are being used by people, to gain an understanding of the social connections they keep and why. The "why" certain apps get used and others do not is important to contemplate, because it can give you an idea of what is socially driving young people's social media desires.

Social conformity

Solomon Asch (September 14, 1907—February 20, 1996) was a pioneering social psychologist, most famous for his experiments in conformity. Asch was born in Poland but moved to the United States with his family at the age of 13, settling in New York City. Asch is said to have credited the works of Charles Dickens for teaching him English, and after his education he worked as a professor at Brooklyn College, Swarthmore College and Rutgers University.

It was during the 1950s where Asch's name became famous among psychologists. Asch conducted a series of experiments, later to be known as the Asch Conformity Experiments, where he was looking to explore how far people would go to conform to others in a group—exploring social pressure.

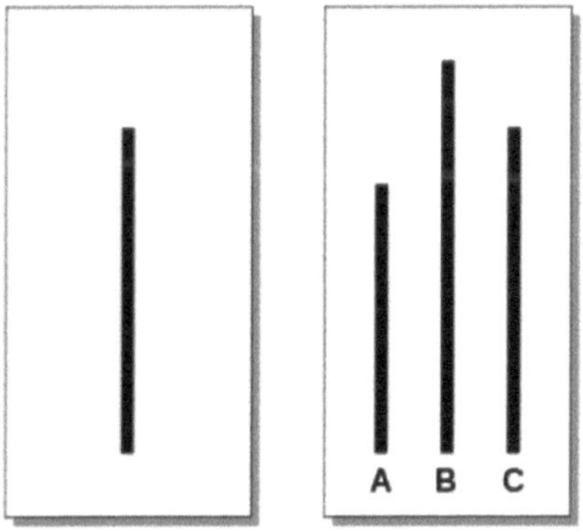

The experiments would roughly go like this—eight participants would be gathered as a group. Seven of these would be actors and one would be the "real participant." The actors knew the true aim of the experiment but were introduced to the "real participant" as other participants. Let's say you (the reader) are the participant. So, you've just been introduced to a group of people to take part in a perceptual activity. You would be given a card that has a line on it, and then another card that has 3 lines on it, labeled A, B, and C. Your job would be to each, in turn, say the line that is a match to the one on the left-hand side card. I mean its obvious right? Your card is most like line C, a simple activity. Everyone else in the group would go first, you would say your answer last.

On some occasions, everyone in the group chooses the correct line, but occasionally, the other participants unanimously declare that a different line is actually the correct match... so what do you do now? Do you go with the group? Or do you go with what you think is right?

The results were fascinating. All in all, a total of 50 students took part in this study... and nearly 75% of the participants went along with the rest of the group at least one time.

At the end of the experiments, the real participants were asked why they had gone along with the rest of the group. Their answers highlight an interesting trend in conformity. They stated that while they knew the rest of the group was wrong, they did not want to risk being made fun of, they didn't want to be 'different'. In addition to this a few of the participants suggested that they genuinely believed the other members of the group must have been correct in their answers, and they must have misjudged the line.

So, conformity in these experiments was influenced both by a need to fit in with the group, and a confidence that other group members are smarter or better informed.

Let's track back to social media for a moment. How do we choose which social networks to download and use? Often because other people are using them… we are influenced by a need to fit in with our wider social groups, and if the people we know, or want to know are using certain apps then we are likely to assume that those who are using them are smarter than us (in the sense of knowing the app) and so we also start using it.

This is how trends in media usage start and can sweep through a population. And as we already know, there is big money to be made by the owners of these apps if people are actively using their software. The Corona Virus lockdown, which has resulted with so many of us socially distancing and sheltering in our homes, has led to new apps and controversy on the social media scene. One such example is with the app *Houseparty*.

The Houseparty saga

Houseparty is an app that lets people video chat on desktop and mobile. This app became very popular in a short space of time during the Corona Virus pandemic as people searched for new and fun ways to connect digitally. *Vogue* even called it "the quarantine app you need to download immediately." I downloaded this app based on a friend's recommendation and had a few group chats using it… it was a decent experience, particularly for quiz lovers.

Then, out of nowhere a number of Houseparty users started to claim that their data had been hacked. A number of tweets ended up suggesting that having Houseparty had compromised their Spotify, PayPal, and Netflix accounts. If this was an Asch experiment, I would be in a long line of people, seeing lots of people deleting the app, then it's my turn, what do I do? These tweets got shared… and the news spread fast, resulting in thousands of people deleting the app, including myself. I didn't want to take the risk, I valued those other apps working, and my data privacy, more than my access to the Houseparty app. But, there's more to this story.

The Houseparty app is owned by Epic Games, the company behind Fortnite, and if you know of Fortnite, then you'll be aware how popular that game is and therefore, how skilled and experienced they are as game makers. Houseparty released a short statement on Monday 30th March 2020 via Twitter, which stated:

"All houseparty accounts are safe – the service is secure, has never been compromised, and doesn't collect passwords for other sites"

Houseparty - March 30th 2020

Interesting… But do we trust them? After such a mass exodus from the app? Has our confidence in the App been compromised by a huge amount of group social media response… is the peer pressure and social conformity shaping my view? And what would it take for me to believe 'Houseparty' is safe again?

The plot thickens a day later:

"We are investigating indications that the recent hacking rumors were spread by a paid commercial smear campaign to harm Houseparty. We are offering a $1,000,000 bounty for the first individual to provide proof of such a campaign to bounty@houseparty.com"

March 31st 2020

The company believes a paid smear campaign took place to harm the apps reputation and are offering $1,000,000 for evidence that can prove it. That certainly is a twist in the tale… and if you consider the massive amount of money that a popular app can be worth, then competitors would have a lot to lose if their clients chose to use a different social media platform.

The spotlight was on and investigations began. Forbes, which is a global media company that focusses on business, investing, technology, and entrepreneurship (among other things) hired cybersecurity and privacy researcher Lukas Stefanko to look at the app. His job was to see if there were any potential security issues as suggested in the social media storm. Here's what he had to say:

> I analyzed the app's permissions usage and since the app provides video chats with your friends it is logical that requested permissions are necessary. I haven't found any shady misusing of them by the app…The app doesn't provide a lot of in-app options and settings, which creates less scenarios for exploiting security issues

If you want to know more about his report then I'd recommend an article by Thomas Brewster: *Houseparty: Is the Hit Coronavirus Lockdown App Safe?* Written for Forbes, a quick Google search will bring up a link to it quickly. There were no apparent issues. Perhaps then, a paid smear campaign was the likely answer to this social media drama.

With Houseparty offering up such a high reward, alongside independent assessments by researchers such as Lukas Stefanko, the stage may be set to bring people back to the app. Trust could be restored to Houseparty, but has the damage already been done? Perhaps our social connectedness and conformity to a wider movement made the decision for us already? It turns out you don't need to think long about it, news dropped in September 2021 that Epic Games Inc will be shutting down the Houseparty app for good... By October 2021 it will be no more, leaving those that use it needing to switch their group chatting to an alternative app.

Decision making regarding what we use to connect with one another may be slightly out of our hands. There will certainly be an influence on what we choose to use depending on what wider society is "consuming" as their social media at the time. But whatever the chosen app, or the "app of the moment" it would seem that evidence lends itself strongly that genuine social connectedness can be made through social media. But wait a moment, what about those naysayers, there is always one in a room, who will lean around the corner with a comment such as:

> Life was better before any of this tappy tap tap technology, people used to talk to each other, people used to listen. Now they're just looking at the phones and the world is passing them by.

It's a compelling argument, and one which I'll admit to thinking from time to time. I often think back to my time as a teenager in secondary school and am grateful that social media was not a massive part of it. The internet, in our house, was dial-up, there was one desktop computer in the house, in the corner of my parents' bedroom. And it was slow, painfully slow. To use it would "engage" the phoneline and so I would need to disconnect often so the phone could be used… and then it would take

10 min to reconnect, hell, the computer would take 30 min to turn on. And the most popular communication software at the time? MSN Messenger, I would spend ages on it messaging my friends. I didn't have a mobile phone, no one I knew did. I would call the home phones of my friends and ask to speak to them... I still remember their numbers, despite the fact they've long since moved. That's how we arranged to meet up outside of school. I can't put my finger on it, but I look back and it seems more wholesome, honest, connected. But is it? Or is it what now would be considered an old-fashioned view, easily dismissed and swept aside as non-sense by the youth of today? When I find myself dancing around the topic of becoming out of touch with technology, I like to turn to Douglas Adams—author of *The Hitchhikers Guide to the Galaxy*. Specifically, I'm turning towards Douglas Adam's rules that describe our reaction to technology:

1. Anything that is in the world when you're born is just a natural part of the way the world works.
2. Anything that's invented between when you're 15 and 35 is new and exciting and revolutionary.
3. ... and anything invented after you're 35 is against the natural order of things.

Increasingly, we need to spend time trying to put ourselves in the young person's shoes... and navigate alongside them or we will end up in the "that's against the natural order of things category"—the "put it away, switch it off category of thinking" which just serves to alienate ourselves from the young people we're talking about. I will talk more on this later in the book. For now, I'm going to lean on psychological theory again, because there is a theory that's related to the 'life was better before all of this' way of thinking. It's called: The Displacement Hypothesis.

The displacement hypothesis

The displacement hypothesis is the theory that there is only so much time in the day, so that if you replace one way of doing something with another... it has been displaced. Here's an example: Video streaming sites such as Netflix, Amazon Prime and Disney+ have revolutionized the choices for people considering watching digital entertainment. This means that for many, these sites have become the media of choice—and Television in its traditional aerial bound form is becoming displaced. Here's another example—my time playing on computer games was significantly displaced the day my daughter was born and has remained so for the last 7 years.

There is a common argument which is built upon the displacement hypothesis, and although it will be delivered in different ways, it often has the same format, and it goes like this:

> If only they would spend less time on their phones, or playing games, and instead spend that time doing something worthwhile, like learning an instrument or revising then they would really be better off.

The idea here is that the use of social media (and games) has replaced another, more analogue way of being… the learning of an instrument, the face to face socialization and the board games. Unfortunately, although it may 'seem right', there really is limited evidence to say that social media is displacing other things. In fact, the evidence seems to point in the other direction, in that it helps to facilitate social connectedness, as opposed to displacing it.

Perhaps the issue here is that social connectedness has evolved and more often than not, we as adults, are putting a blueprint of what we think is "the right way" to be onto teenagers' lives which doesn't fit them and their cultural landscapes.

This fear of the influence of social media on connectedness to others, or in displacing something else, is not a new fear. In fact, when you consider the history of technological advances the same fears seem to be repeating themselves time and time again:

- **Socrates (c. 470–399 BCE)**—Socrates warned against the advent of writing because it would create forgetfulness in the learners' souls because they will not use their memories.
- **Conrad Gessner (1516–1565)**—Swiss scientist who spoke out against the invention of the printing press as too much information is confusing and harmful to the mind, ordinary people cannot handle it.
- **Guillaume-Chrétien de Lamoignon de Malesherbes (1721–1794)**—(What a name!) French statesman who protested the new fashion for news being distributed from the printed page, as it socially isolated readers and detracted from the spiritually uplifting practice of getting news from the pulpit.
- **Gramophone Magazine (1936)**—a magazine article that described how the radio programs were unbalancing children's minds, distracting children from their reading and impacting school success negatively.

I could go on, suffice to say that the same fears came about when television was invented… it would destroy radio, education, families and life as we know it. Personal computers were next in the firing line and the internet is no different. Worries about the impact of new technologies are as old as technology itself. The cycle of fear repeats, just with a different title, and often limited evidence to back up the fears.

Let's take a moment to recap. There is currently ample evidence to suggest that social media sites and apps are facilitating social connection (four studies were selected and explored in this chapter). As well as connecting people, social media sites seem to be used to target and further build upon those connections—whether in building purely online relationships, or in enhancing offline relationships. Specific apps will come and go. The popularity of certain apps and what peers are using, and not using, will influence what media is widely popular—conformity is a difficult weight to resist, particularly when related to connecting within friendships. There will always be fears about new technologies and it seems that a spotlight is on social media at this moment in time.

There is a spotlight of fear aimed at social media sites and apps this moment in society. Often news articles will exacerbate such fears, without paying much attention to the counterargument, the positives that are on offer in using social media, thus the arguments end up imbalanced. One particular area of the benefits of social media builds upon the concepts of identity and social connectedness. This area will be explored in the next chapter and is related to how social media can be used as part of an individual's wider emotional regulation.

CHAPTER

3

Emotional regulation

Psychologist's Guide to Adolescents and Social Media
https://doi.org/10.1016/B978-0-323-91898-5.00004-7

Emotional regulation generally refers to the ability of an individual to effectively manage and respond to an emotional experience. It's often about control, controlling one's reaction to the emotional world they live in and experience.

There are different levels of emotional regulation. The most commonly used form of emotional regulation is something called "down-regulation." This is where we actively try to reduce an emotion we're feeling—deep breathing to reduce anxiety, clenching a fist, and going for a walk when angry. The flip side to this is "up-regulation." This is when we actively try to get in the zone for an activity that might benefit from infusing some excitement into it. Or in trying to shake off whatever may be on your mind to celebrate another's achievements and give them the emotional time and attention they deserve.

The first two chapters of this book took a broad-brush exploration of identity and social connectedness. Those two concepts in and of themselves feed into emotional regulation. Being able to know oneself, and now having online platforms to express oneself, while socially connecting to others feeds into our fundamental human needs. The lack of knowing your identity and a lack of connection to others is also likely to reverberate emotionally within individuals. Whichever way you look at it, this is a powerfully emotional substance we're dealing with, and research has begun to explore the emotional side of social media usage.

It is well known that there are psychological benefits of engaging in expressive writing. Writing is a powerful medium in which to explore one's feelings and engage them in a process. The therapeutic value of writing lies in allowing a person to vent any emotional difficulties, providing them a space for self-reflection and self-understanding. In addition, writing provides a less frightening modality to cope with any interpersonal conflicts being experienced at that time.

Michal Dolev-Cohen is a senior lecturer and researcher at the Oranim Academic College of Education. Together with researcher Azy Barak they began to explore the therapeutic value of writing using social media and instant messaging. If writing can be a powerful medium in which to regulate emotions, surely this would be evident online with the connectedness and available audience of a social network?

Dolev-Cohen and Barak tested 2643 adolescents (aged 14–18 years) by getting them to complete an online questionnaire. This questionnaire had incorporated measures of personality assessment to highlight introversion and extroversion. Once gathered, of the initial 2643 participants, 150 were selected to provide written transcripts of their Instant Messaging conversations to be analyzed by four experts. These experts were tasked with evaluating the participants' emotional state at the beginning of the conversation and at the end.

The results showed that Instant Messaging between friends, as reflected in self-report conversation texts and chat content, produced significant positive changes in emotional state. Dolev-Cohen and Barak's study is evidence that communicating through instant messaging supplies adolescents with an intimate and "private" space where they may share worries and other expressions of bad mood without being judged by others. Teenagers have found a space to be listened to "privately" by friends, and that space is on social media. There was another interesting level to the results of this study, and that was that the participants' level of introversion–extroversion moderated the degree of their perceived emotional relief. In simple terms, the introverted participants profited from instant messaging more than the extroverts did. This adds more evidence to the hypothesis that those who may struggle with the "in-person" and social element of communication benefit greatly from the controlled and structured communication available to them via social media.

Instant messaging, be it through social media or other technological means, has clear positive therapeutic benefits for the users. That's not to say there aren't potential downsides, seemingly "private messages" could be screenshot and sent anywhere. Then again, there's always a chance that what is written on paper could be seen by someone else, copied and shared. When someone takes a step to communicate their emotions, they are putting themselves in a vulnerable position. Some of the unintended consequences of using social media will be discussed further in the next chapters. Writing is a powerful medium for emotional regulation, but so is finding enjoyable things to do with your time.

If you were to ask a teenager today to list 10 things that they do for enjoyment, I guarantee that on that list social media would be present. It would probably be up there for many adults. Let me give an example. The whole reason I have an Instagram account is to follow pages that show me videos and pictures that would make me laugh, or that would show me something that fascinates me. I use Facebook for connecting with friends and seeing what people are selling locally. I use Twitter for news and following a community of social scientists. I use WhatsApp for messaging friends, colleagues, and workgroups. I use Reddit for following fan theories and sci-fi show discussions, and I use YouTube for watching music videos and live performances. Using all the above is enjoyable for me - it provides me entertainment, expands my mind, connects me with others and sometimes I find a bargain being sold locally. To understand why people use certain sites and apps we can turn to psychological theory, in particular—Uses and Gratifications Theory.

Uses and gratifications theory

Uses and Gratifications Theory is an approach that is audience-centered—focusing on what people do with media, as opposed to what media does to people. Several media theories out there view media users as passive, essentially being "done to" by the media. Uses and Gratifications Theory sees users as active agents who have control over their media consumption.

Uses and gratification theory has a long history—evolved from a broader history of communication theories and research. Jay Blumler and Denis McQuail are considered the originators of the theory. They built the foundations in 1969 with their categorization of audience motivations for watching political programs during the time of the 1964 election in the United Kingdom. I'm not going to spend a lot of time delving into the history of Uses and Gratifications Theory, if you are interested then look up - *David L, Uses and Gratification Theory, in Learning Theories, January 26, 2016,* which summarizes it well.

What you need to know about Uses and Gratifications Theory, in a nutshell, is that people are choosing to consume social media for several different reasons. My personal reasons were explored earlier. I could go deeper though. Let's pick on my Facebook use, for connecting with others. I could mention that during 2005 I worked in America for a year teaching rock climbing, caving, kayaking, and mountain hiking. I have maintained my online "friendships" with a number of the people I worked with who are residents in America whom I met that year. It is true that we bonded over that year, and I valued that time in my life, but they are not "active" friends in my life currently. However, I maintain their friendship because if I do go back to America, traveling or whatever fantasy I cook up for suddenly being abroad, I may have someone to call upon, somewhere to stay. Is their friendship then being used as "free accommodation" by me? Is the truth of maintaining the online friendship of 15 years ago a selfish money-saving scheme? Or is it a memory totem of times gone by? People change in 15 years; how much could I milk "that time we worked together in 2005"? My point is that people will have multiple reasons for their social media use and what they choose to do on their social media sites, sometimes not obvious on the surface.

In the literature surrounding social media sites and Uses and Gratifications Theory, there is a consensus that some of the principal gratifications that accompany the use of social media are:

1. Socializing.
2. Finding out information.
3. Entertainment.

Researchers Vanessa Apaolaza, Patrick Hartmann and Jiaxun conducted a study to determine if the gratifications gained from using social media led to a positive mood for those users. They decided to focus on the site Qzone… the most popular social networking site in China. Which, if you have a good memory for statistics, you may remember has approximately 517 million users and is currently the 11th most used social media platform in the world.

The study was conducted with 220 Chinese teenagers between the ages of 14 and 19 years old (91 Male, 129 Female). The participants that took part had to complete a survey designed to test a hypothesis that using Qzone for socializing, information seeking, and entertainment would lead to positive mood for those users. And they were right. The results confirmed that information seeking, socializing, and entertainment derived from using Qzone use led to improved mood. The results highlight the importance of online social networks for Chinese teenagers, assisting them to improve their mood through the emotional gratifications they receive from users. The authors of this study conclude that social media use functions as an important regulator of mood states of adolescents and, likely, adults as well.

Nir Eyal is an internationally best-selling author and is considered a behavioral designer. In his book, *Indistractable* Nir gives an interesting account of the emotional motivation surrounding technology use, exploring the story of Dr. Zoe Chance. Dr. Chance lectured on many things at Yale University, including "mastering influence and persuasion." Looking to research technology and the motivational tools cleverly programmed into them. Dr. Chance found some tech to try out—a Striiv Smart Pedometer. Now, in this pedometer you get points for walking, you can compete with others and be ranked against them and exchange the points you make on a sister app called MyLand, where you can create a small world.

Dr. Chance was hooked and became obsessed with this game. This took a toll on her personal life; she spent more time building up the steps and spending the virtual points than in being in the moment with her family and friends. This is a relatable story, the pull of technology to the expense of the moment. Nir Eyal points out an interesting analysis of this situation, and multiple situations like it:

> We tend to blame things like television, junk food, social media, cigarettes and video games—but these are all proximate causes of our distraction. Solely blaming a smartphone for causing distraction is just as flawed as blaming a pedometer for making someone climb too many steps… Unless we deal with the root causes of our distraction, we'll continue to find ways to distract ourselves.

Nir Eyal, through his discussions with Dr. Chance, explored the underlying reasons surrounding Dr. Chance's obsession with the Striiv Pedometer and MyLand app. It turns out Dr. Chance was in the middle of some of the most stressful events of her life at that time. Dr. Chance was in the middle of job hunting in an extremely competitive field, the same field as her husband who was also job hunting for, in a marriage that was at breaking point. Dr. Chance turned to this technology as an escape, an escape from reality. As Nir Eyal puts it, "most people don't want to acknowledge the uncomfortable truth that distraction is always an unhealthy escape from reality."

Escapism for Dr. Chance was found through the Striiv Pedometer and MyLand app. For other people, that can be found through social media, through digital gaming, through throwing oneself into their work, through reading books, through films and television, through alcohol, and through drugs. Escapism is a powerful motivator and social media is a desirable gateway into a digital world that can be the respite needed from the stressors of daily life.

Let's recap for a moment. Engaging in writing has positive effects on emotional regulation, building on this it's clear that individuals select different social media to meet certain needs in their life, that can lead to a positive mood and enjoyment. Motivations for using social media can be for escapism and previous chapters highlight the importance social media is playing in channeling one's identity and connecting to others... which is in itself highly linked to the emotional landscape of being human.

The evidence suggests that the purposes, and the positives, of social media use are in expressing one's identity and constructing the self, social connectedness and emotional regulation. There is a well-known saying that "too much of a good thing is bad for you," I believe that this is the case for social media use, and there is some research that will be touched upon in the next section which will explore this position.

I take the position that if social media is used to complement an already self-confident/self-assured individual, with a strong offline social network in good psychological health then the user will have a relatively positive experience and social media use will have a positive impact upon them. However, I would also suggest that if there are any deficits in an individual's self-concept, offline social network, and psychological health then social media use may have a negative impact on them, for example with too much time being spent developing online social networks instead of developing offline social networks. It is my position that there is a careful balance that must be consciously maintained so that the use of social media does not cause deficits in one's overall psychological well-being. There will be an ebb and flow of what we, as people, turn to during our emotional times of need. If you notice a change in your normal way of being with technology, it may be time to reflect on the reasons why.

There are consequences of using social media, often unintended or not expected. Part 2 will now explain some of these, including cyberbullying, unfulfilled expectations, and the overuse of the internet.

PART II

The unintended consequences of using social media

The Invention of the ship was also the invention of the shipwreck

Paul Virilio

CHAPTER 4

Cyberbullying

Psychologist's Guide to Adolescents and Social Media
https://doi.org/10.1016/B978-0-323-91898-5.00006-0

This section opened with a quote by Paul Virilio, French Philosopher—the full version goes something like this:

> When you invent the ship, you also invent the shipwreck; when you invent the plane you also invent the plane crash; and when you invent electricity, you invent electrocution... Every technology carries its own negativity, which is invented at the same time as technical progress

I love this quote. It captures the dark side of the technological advances and also the innocence with which it comes into being—"a technical process," not a malicious intent. Where technology advances to connect millions of people across the world, there will be those who use it to communicate ill will.

There is a substantial amount of research that focuses on the rapidly developing mechanisms of Cyberbullying. Yet, there is no agreed definition of cyberbullying. This leaves those that research this field with two options, either construct a definition or select one from multiple options previously constructed. I've decided to select one. However, in doing so I want to take you, the reader, on a journey of the changing nature of 'definition' as more variables are thrown into the mix. So, that eventually, you will come to a new definition yourself, as I did when writing this chapter.

Finding a definition of cyberbullying

Cyberbullying has been defined as:

> An aggressive act or behaviour that is carried out using electronic means, by a group or an individual, repeatedly and over time, against a victim who cannot easily defend him or herself ***(Smith, Mahdavi, Carvalho, Fisher, Russell & Tippett, 2008, p. 376).***

Cyberbullying is a very relevant problem for adolescents using the internet due to the ability to connect with so many people. Robert Slonje, Peter Smith and Ann Frisén, writing for the Journal: *Computers in Human Behavior* conducted a detailed literature review of the nature of Cyberbullying. In this review, it is highlighted that adolescence is a peak period for involvement in Cyberbullying, and in most cases the bullying starts with a face-to-face argument that is then continued online. With regard to the impact that Cyberbullying has on its recipients, Slonje et al. state the following:

> The impact of Cyberbullying is clearly negative, including feelings of anger, fright, depression and embarrassment. However, some victims report being "not bothered"

> about it, in part because it is not "real" or physical. Overall, Cyberbullying and traditional bullying appear to have broadly similar negative impacts; but some features of Cyberbullying, especially anonymity, lack of a safe haven, and embarrassment due to the potentially large breadth of audience, can make the impact of Cyberbullying especially strong, for some young people and in some circumstances (p. 30)

This is an interesting statement that highlights the similarities of the negative experience of traditional bullying and cyberbullying. This statement also brings to the forefront that anonymity, the lack of a break, and the embarrassment due to potentially large audiences mean that Cyberbullying has a nuanced flavor to the impact on the receiver. There is something that is important to consider in discussing bullying and, in particular, the "cyber" aspect, and that is the nature of "intent." Bullying, in general, is about the intention and not the act itself, it is about the intention of the person who bullies to cause harm. When we are dealing with "cyber" it is particularly difficult to analyze the intention of the message. For example, sarcasm could be read as "the words of a bully" when read on a screen—the phrase "aren't you a clever little git" could easily be seen either way, sarcastic or bullying… it would all depend on the intention of the sender. This is important to keep in mind because getting to the "intention" behind an online message, or an online behavior, is half the battle. To build self-awareness of cyberbullying, it's vital to understand the methods of those who cyberbully. In doing so, you will find yourself much more alert to the risks of the social media landscape.

Methods of cyberbullying

Social media, smartphones, text messages, online apps, online gaming forums and websites are all used as tools and weapons for the Cyberbully. But each of those things is not the "problem." Often the problem is the choice that a person makes when choosing to instigate, participate in or observe cyberbullying. Below is a list of six methods of cyberbullying that individuals are likely to come across either themselves or through seeing it happen online in one form or another. This list is by no means exhaustive. I often find myself surprised by the lengths and ingenuity that people can go to in order to cause another person distress.

Harassment

Using messaging services to harass, threaten or embarrass someone. This could take the form of posting rumors, threats or embarrassing information on social media sites. During my time as a head of year in a secondary school, I witnessed a carefully orchestrated harassment of a pupil. This took the form of a planned and targeted stream of abusive text messages from multiple people, started during school hours and continuing into late evening, hundreds of negative messages were received, most sent from free web services and "unknown" numbers. This was devastating for the receiver… it took a long time to unpick and find out who was responsible. And what prompted such an attack?—"she kept looking at me in class."

Another version of harassment that has begun to become evident online is through "false reporting." False reporting is where the harasser "reports" the targets social media account/s to the service provider to try and get their account blocked or removed. There are often in-built "report inappropriate content" functions on various apps that are being misused in order to harass others.

Photo and video shaming

This can take the form of taking pictures/videos of an individual without their consent, or sometimes with their consent, but then using the pictures/videos to threaten the individual. These pictures may be uploaded to photo sharing sites for anyone on the Internet to view—engaging in shaming the individual. Often bullying incidents will be filmed on smartphones and then shared within peer groups or online. These could include acts of physical violence where an individual is punched, kicked and hit multiple times while being filmed.

I once had to confiscate a clump of hair a girl was holding onto after being filmed "ragdolling" (dragging a person by their hair and pulling aggressively on it) a girl on the school field which ripped a large chunk of her hair out. The clump of hair lay in a box in my desk while the police came to collect it—the parent wished to press assault charges and it became "evidence"… along with the phone footage. Filming of fights and incidents of violence seems to be becoming commonplace, I often wonder if people are reaching for their phones to call for help or to film the violence, sadly I feel like the latter has become more prevalent in recent years.

In 2011, I worked with a girl who experienced video shaming from her peers. Jayne was 11 years old when she had a sleepover with some of her friends, and her friends had a plan. During the sleepover, they were playing a game of truth or dare. Jayne was dared to take off her clothes and dance, she decided to do it, in her mind, she was in good company, the atmosphere was jovial, and she was comfortable enough to do it privately for a few seconds. She left the room, stripped her clothes off, came back into the room naked and in dancing to their favorite song, before leaving and putting her clothes back on. It was for less than 5 s. They all laughed together about it and Jayne thought no more of it that night. Except, that one of her friends had filmed it, as they had covertly planned to before the sleepover. The next day at school the video started to get shared between students. Jayne was devastated, the safeguarding officer for the school got involved due to the content of the video and parents were called in immediately. We spent the day rounding up students who had seen the video or had received the video to try and trace all possible copies so that they could be deleted. We did our best, but the truth is we do not know the full extent to which that footage got shared.

Another form of bullying involving video shaming is known as cyberbaiting. This is where an individual will create the conditions for someone to become very upset/distressed while filming the situation. Teachers are often a common target for cyberbaiting.

Impersonating someone

This often involves using, guessing or stealing an individual's password to their social media accounts and posting often harmful messages and material "as them." This is sometimes referred to a "fraping." Once in the account, the impersonator could change pictures, upload new ones, message people, and delete/change information.

Impersonating can also come in the form of creating a social media account using an almost identical screen name as the target individual. Then sending out messages pretending to be them. This can also take place as creating an entirely fake profile if the individual doesn't have an account. I once had a 14-year-old girl called Zara arrive at my office in tears because someone she was "friends" with on Facebook had downloaded all her pictures and created a new account impersonating her. This person had then systematically added Zara's friends to this new account and messaged all of her female friends stating the following—

> Hi, listen, I've never really liked you, in fact, I think you're sly, ugly and a bitch, I'm done fake liking you, don't bother messaging me back, I don't want to talk to talk to you, it would bore me. Let's just put an end to this friendship now.

Brutal right? I can remember panic rising in me in how I could support Zara to socially recover from this. I also remember worrying about how on earth I could find out who did this to her. As it turns out, it was easy. The message that was sent was so incongruous with Zara's personality that a tsunami of pupils came flooding down to my office outraged that someone had created a fake Zara account and was sending out fake messages. They also came down with a list of suspects, and as it turns out, one name stood out repeatedly, Ryan, who was in Zara's form group. Ryan had been bragging to his friends that he had done it... his friends clearly weren't that impressed. It didn't take long for Ryan to confess to what he had done, to send out an apology to everyone he had messaged and delete the account. It also didn't take long for his parents to come into school to meet with me so that Ryan could explain to them why he was in trouble at school that day. And the reason for Ryan doing this? Well, as it turns out he quite fancied Zara, but Zara did not feel the same. It seems Ryan took his emotions about being rebuffed by Zara and engaged in some social media revenge.

Other forms of impersonation can take the shape of "catfishing." This is where an individual will pretend to be someone online in order to lure their chosen "victim" into a fake online relationship. At a secondary school level, I've known this to be done to get the target to share personal information and or pictures which will then be used to humiliate.

Although I have not known this to happen to anyone that I've worked with... It is also possible for a cyberbully to post their target's personal information and contact details on chat rooms/sites known to be frequented by child molesters so that they start receiving messages from strangers wanting to meet... it's the digital version of writing "call this number for sex" on a public restroom wall.

Subtweeting or vaguebooking

These phrases have been created to explain the phenomenon of posting messages on Twitter or Facebook about another person but not using their name in any way. But, the readers in the social circle will "know" who is being spoken about. The issue is that this often-subtle approach goes under the radar of teachers and parents because "it could be about anyone". Here's an example... if there is a post online that reads "I don't understand why people think they can wear fake Superdry clothes on non-school uniform day, we all know, it's obvious, you're not fooling anyone" ... The target of this message will know it's about them. Just like if a post said "if I get looked at like that again I'm going to start cracking skulls"—people involved in reading this would know if they are the target of this message because of the school social circles that they are living in.

Cyberstalking

This a systematic following of an individual's online life. This can include monitoring, false accusations, threats, and is often accompanied by offline stalking. This is why it's particularly important to understand

and utilize the security processes of social media to protect one's account from those you do not wish to have access to your information.

Trolling

Trolling is when a cyberbully will actively make inflammatory comments online with the purpose of upsetting an individual and the audience of a post. There are some people who would argue that Trolling is not a form of cyberbullying, because there may not be repetition and the "bully" tends to not be connected at a personal level with their chosen victim. There is a level of "detachment." It remains up for debate as to if Trolling belongs as a "method" of cyberbullying. I land in the camp that trolling is cyberbullying—because of the "intent to cause harm" of the poster.

But does cyberbullying always start in a negative "something" that happens face-to-face for adolescents? Or can it start/remain purely online? To answer this, I'm turning to the research community once more.

In 2013 researchers Grace Kwon and Marko Skoric conducted a study examining Cyberbullying on Facebook and how it relates to school-based bullying. Kwan and Skoric surveyed 1676 secondary school students (aged 13–17 years) from two different schools exploring their experience of bullying. The results showed that Facebook bullying was relatively common, with 59.4% ($n = 1493$) of Facebook users experiencing at least one form of Bullying in the past year and 56.9% ($n = 1491$) engaging in at least one form of Facebook bullying.

The above study also teased apart the types of bullying incident in which the students took part. The most common bullying incident involved;

- Sending nasty messages.
- Being insulted repeatedly.
- Being made a laughingstock by other users.
- Being excluded from certain groups.
- Being tricked into revealing secrets.

The least common type of bullying incident was:

- Masquerading as someone else.
- Threatening others.
- Hacking into another's account.

An interesting exploration in Kwan and Skoric's study was the correlation between in school bullying and online bullying. The analysis showed that there was a positive correlation between being involved in school bullying to being involved in Facebook bullying. Furthermore, being victimized in school means it's much more likely that an individual would be victimized on their social media.

To me, this is evidence that the power dynamics that are in effect in offline social networks, transfer to online social networks. I believe this is true for the positive maintenance of friendships and also for any negatives that one could experience in school.

One particular difficulty for those who experience regular bullying in school and on social media, is that there is little respite or escape from the negative effects. If we were having this as a conversation in a crowded room, this would often be the point where someone would chime in with the suggestion to "avoid all social media use, cut it out". But the reality is that in doing so that person also stops the positive use of social media (explored in Part 1 of this book). Kwan and Skoric suggest that to tackle the issue of cyberbullying for young adolescents, the focus needs to be on the root of the issue which "very frequently manifests itself in everyday school bullying."

One of the gifts in researching different topics is that often you find the contrary evidence to your opinions and research. As soon as you think you've got an answer, another study can pop up with completely contrasting results. So, in the spirit of a balanced argument, it's important to consider a 2015 study by Kubiszewski, Fontaine, Potard, & Auzoult. They set up their research to explore whether student victims and perpetrators are involved in school bullying only, cyberbullying only, or both, and if there were overlaps/similarities and/or differences between the two forms of bullying. Their study, in which individual interviews were conducted with 1422 junior high and high school students, showed that there was very little overlap between cyberbullying and in-school bullying and that majority of cyber-bullies were not involved in in-school bullying. I wonder if the difficulty here is that there is a lack of a definitional criteria of what constitutes cyberbullying.

A 2015 BBC Learning Poll of 2000 11–16 year olds stated that 57% of those questioned have done something "risky" or anti-social online, that almost two-thirds (62%) told the BBC Learning poll they felt under pressure from others to act in this way and some 20% said they had put pressure on someone else to act negatively online, perhaps a more detailed look at the concepts of negativity online would help bring a deeper understanding of the specifics of the umbrella term cyberbullying.

When I start to think conceptually, I am not sure of the usefulness of teasing apart "cyberbullying" and "in-school bullying." Cyberbullying literature has consistently applied the definition of traditional bullying to the realms of electronic media. However, there is variability in the definitions used across research, this lack of clarity has been described as "the most pervasive methodological drawback in cyberbullying research" (Tokunaga, 2010, p. 283).

So, what has been done to try and right this methodological wrong? A group of researchers led by Dr. Rebecca Dredge (Australian Catholic University) explored the lack of definitional clarity of cyberbullying. They did this by engaging in semi-structured interviews with 25 adolescents who had previously experienced negative social media usage. The results highlighted that from an adolescent victim perspective, the basic criteria for the definition of cyberbullying was either not referenced by participants or was far more complex than initially anticipated. The most referenced criterion was the extent to which the experience has an impact on the victim, which is currently not considered within any definitions. The authors of this study proposed:

> a revised understanding of the definitional criteria for cyberbullying. In particular, it is suggested that focus is given to the social networking behaviours that have a negative impact on victims rather than focusing on the issues of repetition and power imbalance. This will affect the estimation of the prevalence of cyberbullying victimisation and, in turn, it will affect intervention approaches (p. 18)

A unique characteristic of the Rebecca Dredge et al. paper is that it takes a person-centered approach to research. They seek that the views and experiences of the social media users should be considered in revising and complementing definitional criteria of cyberbullying.

Let's consider the definition I selected at the start of this chapter:

> An aggressive act or behaviour that is carried out using electronic means, by a group or an individual, repeatedly and over time, against a victim who cannot easily defend him or herself.

I'm not sure that this definition is fit for purpose. Does a person have to not be able to easily defend themselves to experience cyberbullying? What are the criteria of repetition? If I took a picture of you, without your consent, thought of a humiliating comment and posted it online… I did one thing. But that picture could be seen by millions, re-shared, saved on people's phones, it can be further manipulated, turned into a meme, printed, sent out again. If I am the source, am I then responsible for the re-sharing of that picture? In my view I should be held accountable for it, I would be the source. I see the above incident as something that is experienced repeatedly by the victim because of the number of potential viewers. But I'm not sure, in a school, if I could have been punished as a "bully" because of the traditional model of what is understood as bullying.

What Rebecca Dredge and her team have done is to shift thinking about what is important within a cyberbullying definition. The authors are proposing complementing cyberbullying definitions with person-centered experiences. Dredge et al. believe that "future research should consider the views and experiences of users of technology to further expand the knowledge of an ever expanding and complex area of research"- so do I, without fully understanding young people's experiences, definitions end up as an academic exercise—not a useful framework.

Let's evolve our original definition… This is what I feel fits as a definition of cyberbullying when considering the person-centered experience and the methods utilized by those who choose to bully:

> A purposeful act, targeted towards an individual, or a group, utilising internet-based technology with the intention to humiliate, harass, manipulate, intimidate or threaten—leading to psychological harm.

There is no doubt that cyberbullying is a real issue for those who engage with social media. There will be different levels of it, people may engage in cyberbullying by being the bully, through observing it and doing nothing and through being on the receiving end. The impact of cyberbullying on a "target" will vary depending on the individual make-up of that person. Some people will be able to "shake it off" and others will be devastated by it. There will be times where cyberbullying starts in school as traditional bullying and is transferred online, and times where it will start online and transfer in school. There will also be times where it stays solely online happening within connections that have no direct "real world" link.

Parents and young people need to know about the potential for cyberbullying when engaging in social media use. It is important to understand the methods which can be employed so that one can, where possible, protect oneself from becoming a victim or recognize when cyberbullying is happening and is not for example, "just banter." Young people also need to be able to recognize when they are becoming the bully. There is a fantastic book titled *The Bully in the Greenhouse: exploring why children bully others and what schools can do about it* by Dr. Graham Ramsden. This book highlights that it remains important to support victims of bullying to recover and develop resilience. But also, and most importantly, it delivers a message that it is the person who engages in bullying behaviors who needs support. Those individuals who engage in bullying behaviors need to be supported to make positive change in their interactions with others and how they view themselves.

One potential characteristic of a victim and perpetrator of bullying is that they may have low self-esteem. Some authors argue that using social media can have a positive effect on self-esteem and well-being, I would put myself in that camp. However, just like being on the receiving end of cyberbullying, there are also several negative impacts of using social media. Some recent research has called the benefits into question for certain users, suggesting that individuals with interpersonal problems may use social media in a way that sabotages the potential good it has to offer. The next chapter will now look at some of the ways social media is used and the impact of unfulfilled expectations.

CHAPTER

5

Unfulfilled expectations

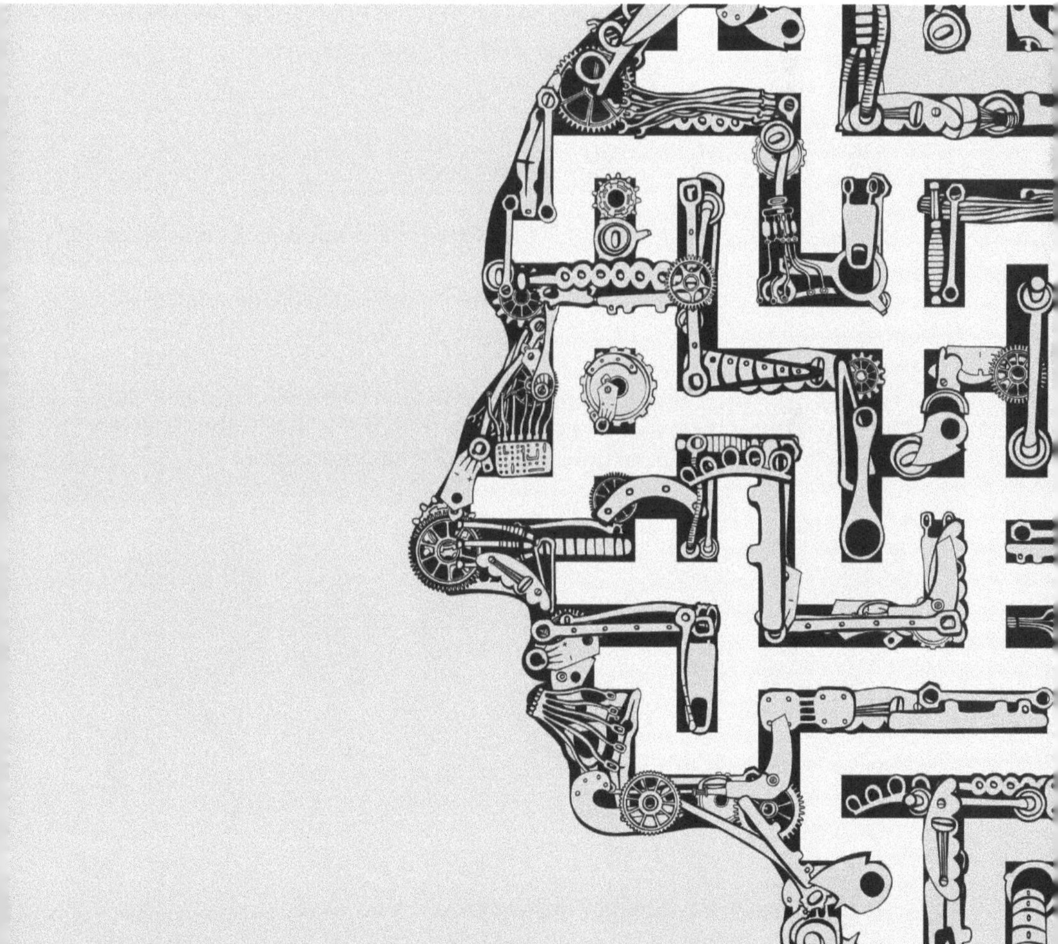

https://doi.org/10.1016/B978-0-323-91898-5.00019-9

Unfulfilled expectations, the internet is full of them. What you hope for and expect to happen when engaging with social media isn't necessarily what you will end up experiencing. I used to have a lecturer during my undergraduate degree who almost always used the phrase "whistle stop tour" during their lectures... it irked me when I heard it. A few fellow students and I would give a sideways glance at one another when the phrase would get used and keep a mental tally of it... If we were using the Johari Window, this phrase would be in the lecturer's unknown to self, known to others box. I have actively avoided using the phrase in my career, especially during any lectures I've been giving. Alas, I find myself now trying to find the words to describe this chapter and it keeps coming back to me. So, I'm going to give in. In homage to my undergraduate lecturer, this chapter is a *whistle stop tour* of various phenomena that teenagers and adults experience online that are a part of the unfulfilled expectations that social media will bring into their lives. It goes without saying that I'm going to throw some psychology theory into the mix as well, for good measure.

Signaling theory

Michael Spence, winner of a Nobel Prize in Economics, is credited for his conceptualization of "signaling theory" in 1973. Signaling Theory, originally developed in biology and economics, describes the relationship between a signal, a received message, and the underlying quality it represents overall.

Typically, within signaling theory, one person (the sender) must decide if and how they are going to communicate something. The "other" person (the receiver) must choose how to interpret the information.

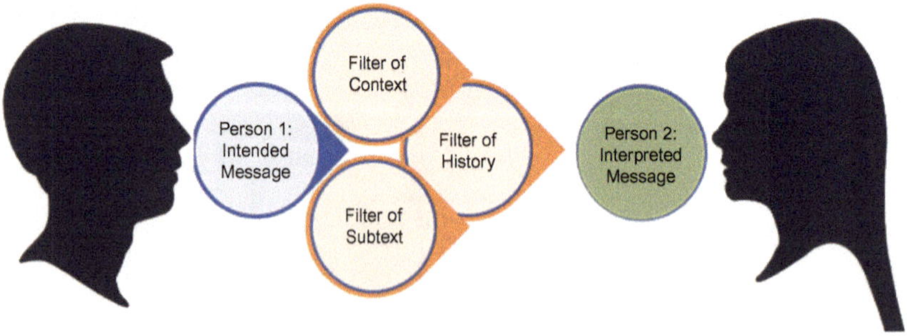

Signaling theory.

You will know of signaling theory even if you haven't heard of the it before. This is because as a society, certain words and phrases have developed a meaning of their own that carry a lot of information. Take for example the phrase "we need to talk"—in a romantic relationship this spells disaster and alarm bells will be ringing. Likewise, if a boss says this to you, a similar dread will be washing over you. However, a close friend whispering this to you, with a cheeky expression, might convey some insanely juicy gossip is about to come your way. There are lots of examples of this in day to day life, I don't know when it happened but the word "fine" has not meant "fine" for a long time... if someone says something is "fine" then it is the opposite. This was captured well in a 2013 episode of the TV series *"2 Broke Girls"* with a conversation between Max Black and Caroline Channing:

Caroline Channing: *"I have to get ready for work, it's fine."*
Max Black: *"Stop saying that, please, stop saying it's fine! Fine doesn't mean fine. The scale goes: great, good, OK, not OK, I hate you, fine. If fine meant fine, that'd be great, but it doesn't, OK?"*

In recent years, signaling theory has been used as a framework to understand social media relationships. Essentially, what "messages" are people sending out based on their social media use. Signaling Theory is explored in a paper by June Ahn, researcher from Maryland University published in 2011. June give's an example of a when a social media user displays a contact as a "friend," they are in an in-direct way vetting that that person is who they claim to be. Therefore, if social media users indiscriminately add any and all friend requests, including of people they do not know and fake profiles, their effort to seem popular may instead damage their credibility and trustworthiness of others.

When I've spoken to teenagers in my work about the "number of friends" they and/or other people have on their social media accounts, they have often cited the phrase "social media whore" when talking about those people in their social circles who have hundreds/thousands of "friends" on their networks. It's like there exists a magic number that nobody really knows, a fine balance, as if you could be quizzed on your "friendships" and if you can't explain who a person is and how you're connected to them, then you get a bad social media reputation. Here's how it looks:

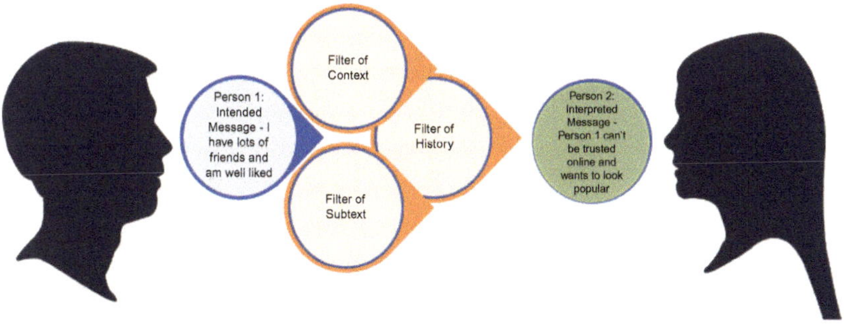

Signaling theory example.

Here's another example of signaling theory in action: Your best friend always posts pictures online of himself and his girlfriend, happy, in love, in lust, loving each other's company. But, behind closed doors you know that he hates his girlfriend, despises their relationship, that they're always arguing, and that the relationship is coming to an end soon. This is a big discrepancy. The signal communicated on social media is one of a happy relationship, the interpreted message, to people who have more information to add to it… context & historical knowledge… is one of a relationships that is struggling. Thus, the posts on social media for this couple are disregarded (by those "in the know") and are considered dishonest. If this continues for a while it may end up in a conversation with your best friend about the nature of their posts online vs face to face conversation.

This above situation can take many forms when analyzing another's social media posts. If someone uploads too much of a "perfect" image without counterbalancing it with some of the messy reality of life, then a "tipping point" will be reached where that person and their representation of "self" suddenly becomes questioned by others… is this person real? A perception of "dishonesty" starts to creep in. It would seem, that balance is key and conscious thought needs to be utilized in managing one's social media portrayal. There is another aspect here, related to signaling theory, and social media is rife with it, and that is a behavioral pattern of "reassurance seeking" posts online.

Reassurance seeking

This is one of my favorite things to witness online, because the psychology is rampant, and the posts really open a plethora of social responses (or lack thereof) from "friends." Reassurance seeking on social media sites can often take different forms. But usually, they are focused on a user posting a message in which they are attempting to invoke a response of reassurance from their friends…Here's an example of one of my favorites:

Jill:	**"Thanks to the amazing staff at accident and emergency last night, you were fantastic."**
Kate:	*"Oh my god Jill what happened, are you alright?"*
Phil:	*"Hope you're ok, if you need anything let me know"*
Simon:	*"OMG What happened? Are you ok now?"*
Alicia:	*"I've just sent you a private message, hope you're ok hun."*

Oh Jill, Jill, Jill, Jill Jill Jill Jill. A provocative post, just enough information to let everyone know that you had some sort of accident (or someone close to you did), but not enough to finish the story. Therefore, people must reach out to you to find out. So, what is Jill getting out of this? She's getting a measure of who cares about her, she's getting attention from people, she gets to appear gracious by thanking the A&E staff in a public forum... and, importantly she gets to hold court in the comments section. Jill will be center stage until she decides to let the cat out of the bag and let us all know what happened. It's fascinating and it's frustrating. I can't tell you how many times I've been hooked by this... not commenting but looking through all the comments to see if Jill has told anyone what actually happened! Come on Jill! I want to know, but I haven't seen you in months so I can't just ask you outright now! 20 comments later and you still haven't let us know... she's clearly loving this. And why shouldn't she? Somethings happened, to break the mundane day to day existence, and Jill wants to tell her story... in a long and drawn out kind of way.

But I need to know now (but do I really?). Maybe I'll message Jill's brother and ask him instead? That's what I did, and I got a reply within minutes—"she broke her toe, kicked a door frame, she's milking it." Let's take a moment and list what's happened to Jill since she broke her toe and had it looked at by her local A&E department. Through social media, Jill's had 20 friends express concern for her by commenting, she's had more post "sad face emojis" in response, she feels heard, listened to, cared about, valued by others. The face-to-face example would be Jill limping into work the next day, colleagues noticing the limp and asking her if she was alright and receiving the attention she's looking for. All in all, this has worked out quite well for Jill when it comes to perceived social support.

But what if it didn't? Jill must have been expecting a certain reply and attention from her friends when she posted such a provocative message. But what if Jill's expectations weren't met? Let's try the scenario again.

Jill:	**"Thanks to the amazing staff at accident and emergency last night, you were fantastic."**
Kate:	...
Phil:	...
Simon:	...
Alicia:	...

Nothing. Not a single comment. Not even from her closest friends. Jill checks to see that the message actually posted to her news feed... it did, and she can see that people have seen it, but nobody has commented. Jill checks her private messages; nobody has messaged her. Jill checks her text messages, her other social networks, her voicemail… nothing.

So, what has Jill experienced now? How is Jill feeling? Lonely, unheard, unloved, uncared for. Her friends don't seem to care that she's been to the hospital. Jill's probably having thoughts like: "if my friends can't rally around me now, when would they? What if something serious had happened? They don't really care about me, does anyone? Are my friends good enough? Screw them all! Am I good enough? Am I disliked by that many people? 479 so-called 'friends' in my list and not one comment, I can see 37 friends currently 'active' online—where are they?!"

All of these feelings could have been avoided if Jill hadn't uploaded that post to her social media accounts. But do you know what else would have been avoided? All the potential positives included in the first example. It certainly is a gamble when posting something online and "expecting" something in return. It is probably why unfulfilled expectations are such a fascinating area of social media usage to me, the gamble of it all and subsequent interpretations of what it all means.

There are many other examples of reassurance seeking through social media. Be it through offering out an opinion on a subject, a political standpoint, a picture of a potential purchase or even house decoration. Anything that is done in an open forum such as social media often has a tinge of seeking some form of social approval. There is a "famous," or perhaps "infamous" version of this, which started to appear on Instagram. Particularly on multiple teen's Instagram accounts. For those who don't know, Instagram is primarily a photo sharing social media site, with messaging as a secondary function. What was this particularly famous phrase that would accompany a selfie?

"Felt cute, might delete later." There is a lot that is communicated with this kind of post. This is reassurance seeking to the max! Let's start taking it apart. "felt cute"—this is my feeling, it is not a fact, I'm not saying it's true, so therefore I am not being big headed, it is just how I felt… "might delete later"—I'm not sure this picture of me is worthy of keeping, perhaps it's not cute, perhaps it's ugly…

The game is on, the comments, the likes, the opinions come flooding in—"this is a great picture, definitely don't delete it," "you look great hun," "Amazing picture," "looking hot," "Definitely a keeper." This type of a post is a recipe for a self-esteem boost, is that the underlying need of the person who posted it? To get a boost in self-esteem? Most likely, and also experience social approval from their peers. This type of social media post isn't solely related to females, this happens across genders but may take slightly different forms. But just like before, what if this post isn't responded to positively by friends? How would they be feeling? Likely unattractive, rejected and now anxious about future uploads, to post a picture is a social gamble if you are expecting something in return.

There has been a host of memes of the "felt cute, might delete later" posts that for a while littered teenager's social media pages. A quick google image search of that phrase and you'll see what I mean.

The thought behind an upload

I have had multiple conversations with teenagers about the pictures they upload to social media and each time I find myself slightly taken aback by the layers of thought that go into a picture upload. Here's an excerpt from a 15-year-old talking to me about their social media use. For context, I asked her to explain to me the step by step process she goes through before uploading a picture, we had a fairly good relationship, so she was refreshingly honest and open with me about it:

Tamika: *"Well firstly, I think about the quality of the picture, is it blurry, is it the best of the bunch I've taken. Then I think about if it needs to be adapted, I always adapt them, so I don't have to think about that for long (Tamika described a secondary App she uses to adjust her pictures). I adjust my nose size, eye brightness, teeth whiteness and remove any spots or blemishes and things like that. Then when I'm done making it look the best it can, it's time to choose a filter for the photo (a filter will change the whole color palate). Then I wait."*

Dr C: *"What are you waiting for?"*

Tamika: *"You can't just upload a picture straight away; you have to wait for the right time of day. Upload it too soon and no-one will see it, it will get lost in the news feed. By timing it right you increase the amount of people who will be*

online to see the picture, and you'll get more likes and comments and reactions."
Dr C: *"When is the best time for you?"*
Tamika: *"I think between 6pm and 9pm, people usually have their phones when they're eating or waiting for food, or they're bored and lots of people are online then."*

I should point out that this will not be everyone experience of uploading a picture. But it certainly will be some people. For Tamika, she had a ritual to go through with her pictures in order to get an optimum response from the audience of her posts. So perhaps she's looking to get an optimum boost to her self-esteem and self-worth. I've known teenagers (and adults) who will upload a picture and if it hasn't been liked within the first 3 min of being online, they will delete it.

Marie, a good friend of mine, once showed me a picture on her phone and asked me if I liked it? I responded with "yes that's a really nice picture." And it was, it was well taken, and she looked good, as did her dog. To which she said "well, will you like it like it then!?" She then held up my phone and waved it about in my face until I took it off her, opened Facebook and "liked" the picture. It seems that simply liking something might not be enough anymore, a public display of liking something in front of an audience was what Marie needed from me. She must have had an optimum number of likes in her head as having a valued meaning to her. As if 50 likes mean it's good—any less and it is a failure, who knows, or perhaps with me publicly "liking" the picture added to the value of the picture because of how Marie valued our friendship? I didn't ask at the time; I just rolled my eyes and did it. There are times and places for wearing a psychologist's hat, and that wasn't one of them.

It's interesting the level of emotional value people place on their pictures. This is true for me when I reflect on my use of social media. To me, my daughter is the most wonderful person; she amazes me, she's funny, kind, intelligent, creative, and beautiful. Everything is enriched when she is around. Therefore, if I take a picture of her and upload it for my friends and family to see, in a way I'm transferring that emotion with the picture. I have emotionalized the picture. Consider now, how that emotion moves with the picture now I've placed it in a public forum. I know people will not feel the same emotions towards that picture as I feel, because they don't feel the same emotions towards my daughter as I do. Yet I can't avoid having the thoughts that she is worth "more" if the picture doesn't garner many "likes." There's an intrusive nature of those thoughts, despite being able to rationally think about social media and knowing about the underlying psychology. It's like putting my greatest achievement on display for the world to see and getting "shrugged shoulders" instead of rousing applause. It is an unfulfilled expectation.

But how harmful to our wellbeing are these unfulfilled expectations? Fortunately, there has been some research looking into this.

Elise Clerkin is a clinical psychologist and associate professor in the Department of Psychology at Miami University. In 2013, alongside her research colleagues April Smith and Jennifer Hames, they looked to explore the interpersonal effects of Facebook reassurance seeking. They wanted to unpick the dilemma of understanding that social networking sites like Facebook can represent a potentially valuable means for individuals with low self-esteem or interpersonal difficulties to connect with others; But, that individuals who are most in need of social benefits from Facebook may be ineffective in their communication strategies, and thereby sabotage their potential to benefit interpersonally from social media.

Elise Clerkin's study tested whether reassurance seeking via Facebook negatively influenced self-esteem, and whether this change in self-esteem made the participants further use "reassurance seeking" and thus get stuck in a cycle of sabotaging the social benefits of social media and positive wellbeing.

To explore this, Elise and her research team designed questionnaires to be completed at two different intervals (24 days apart). They gathered and analyzed 319 completed questionnaires. The results highlighted that those individuals who are looking for certain feedback, but then failed to get it, or alternatively got negative feedback in response to their "reassurance seeking posts" experienced a significant detrimental impact on their self-esteem. In short, Facebook reassurance seeking predicted lower levels of self-esteem, which in turn predicted increased feelings that one does not belong and that one is a burden.

This is important to know because there is a growing body of evidence that the way in which people use social media can elicit psychologically significant information. There is more to social media than the passive use of websites or applications. People are deeply impacted by and emotionally connected to their chosen networks. You need to remember this when talking to people about their social media usage.

Writing for the Journal *"Depression and Anxiety,"* Megan Moreno and her colleagues looked to explore the significance of personal disclosures through social media. The purpose of this study was to evaluate college students' Facebook disclosures that met DSM criteria for a depression symptom or a major depressive episode (MDE). The DSM is a Diagnostic and Statistical Manual that essentially lists all the possible diagnosable psychological conditions. So, armed with the criteria for a diagnosis of depression, Megan Moreno (et al.) took to Facebook and found public (meaning available for all to see) profiles of teenagers and evaluated their "status updates" over a year long period.

In total, 200 profiles were evaluated, and 25% of profiles displayed depressive symptoms and 2.5% met the criteria for Major Depressive Episode. What is particularly interesting about this study is that profile owners were more likely to reference depression, if they averaged at least one online response from their friends to a status update disclosing depressive symptoms, or if they used Facebook more frequently. Megan Moreno and her colleagues conclude that teenagers commonly display symptoms consistent with depression on Facebook. Their findings suggest that those who receive online reinforcement from their friends are more likely to discuss their depressive symptoms publicly on Facebook. They also suggest that:

> Given the frequency of depression symptom displays on public profiles, social networking sites could be an innovative avenue for combating stigma surrounding mental health conditions or for identifying students at risk for depression.

As highlighted earlier, I would add that if you do not get the responses that you are looking for from any given situation then it may exacerbate the negative emotion you are feeling. Facebook has the potential for very negative and far reaching influences on one's interpersonal functioning as well as positives for individuals finding support and a space to connect to others.

With the use of social media for those with interpersonal problems, the benefits and the negatives may be equally prevalent, this position was summed up well in an article by Indian and Grieve (2014) when they stated:

> Facebook interaction may readily facilitate improved well-being in socially anxious individuals, thereby improving their functioning and experience. However, an alternative interpretation and corollary of this notion exists. Specifically, if socially anxious individuals turn to the online environment for social support, while avoiding social interaction in the face-to-face environment, this might subsequently perpetuate their social anxiety (p. 106).

To me this feels like the "too much of a good thing is bad for you" argument. Too much reliance on online social networking could be a detriment to offline friendships if the person using social media is socially anxious. That individual may get their social needs met well at a distance and not build up the courage in person because there is no need to. Falling into the "comfortable" routines of social media.

Social media is rife with unfulfilled expectations. Through signaling theory, we can see that there are multiple layers to an interpreted behavior online. Through understanding reassurance seeking behaviors we can see that self-esteem highs and lows will be a common experience for the social media user. In spending time trying to understand the motivation for certain posts online we can start to understand the underlying psychology involved. It would seem careful balance is needed, there appears to be a feedback loop that you can get stuck in if your expectations are not met and you don't have the internal resources to manage the highs and lows. Too much of a good thing, it seems, can be bad for you, particularly if social media use and interaction online seems to dominate your methods of interaction with others. But how much is too much? And can social media use develop into something that cannot be controlled? This is exactly the concept that will be explored in the next chapter: Internet addiction.

CHAPTER

6

Internet addiction

Psychologist's Guide to Adolescents and Social Media
https://doi.org/10.1016/B978-0-323-91898-5.00022-9

As technology and connectivity have advanced, so to have the concerns related to excessive use. This concept of excessive and uncontrolled internet use, leading to psychosocial distress and impaired levels of functioning, has attracted growing interest worldwide. This chapter is going to delve into the debates, the research and the controversies surrounding the concept of internet addiction. But, before we get started, I want to briefly explore what addiction is, because then we can navigate better through the fog of adding "the internet" into our understanding of addiction.

Defining addiction

An addiction is a complex condition where there is an uncontrolled use of a substance despite the harm that the substance is doing to an individual. People with an addiction will often have an intense focus on using certain substances to the extent that there is a negative impact on that individual's ability to function "normally" in their day to day life. The Merriam-Webster dictionary has a detailed and specific definition of addiction:

> A compulsive, chronic, physiological or psychological need for a habit-forming substance, behavior, or activity having harmful physical, psychological, or social effects and typically causing well-defined symptoms (such as anxiety, irritability, tremors, or nausea) upon withdrawal or abstinence: the state of being addicted.

The Oxford English dictionary takes a gentler approach to its definition, like it's had a cup of tea after a long day:

> The condition of being unable to stop using or doing something as a habit, especially something harmful.

Both definitions are right, of course, but as this chapter continues you will come to realize that there are many layers to addiction. There wouldn't be textbooks written on the subject if it was simple to comprehend... and it only gets harder once you add "the internet" into the debate. Can the internet be a substance? Like alcohol? Or opioids? Instinctively, you might instantly land in the "no" camp, but let's explore some more before you resolutely decide.

Internet addiction

As research communities in various fields rally round to try and understand the overuse of the internet, various terminologies have been suggested to try and encapsulate such a phenomenon, these include:

- Internet addiction (Ghassemzadeh, Shahraray, & Moradi, 2008; Young, 1998)
- Internet dependence (Lu, 2008)
- Problematic internet use (Caplan, 2002)
- Pathological internet use (Davis, 2001)
- Compulsive internet use (Greenfield, 1999; Meerkerk, Van Den Eijnden, Vermulst, & Garretsen, 2009)

However, a detailed exploration and clarification of the boundaries between these connected concepts is currently lacking across the literature. The issues surrounding the concept of internet addiction do not stop there. In an article written by Amandeep Dhir in 2015 it's highlighted how several studies have reported similarities of internet addiction with substance-use disorders regarding its phenomenology (experience of individuals) and underlying neurobiological mechanisms (the mind–body connection). This suggests that internet addiction can be thought of in a similar way to substance related addiction such as alcoholism. However, the internet is not a substance that can be ingested, but seemingly can have a similar impact on us. These are what are referred to as non-substance related addictions.

This concept, of non-substance related addictions, has become increasingly popular in recent years. Across multiple studies internet addiction has been conceptualized as a non-substance related addiction akin to gambling addiction. Therefore, the term "Internet Addiction" has been proposed to describe the phenomenon of excessive, uncontrolled usage of specific online-applications (e.g., online-gaming, use of online pornography or social networking sites).

But, before we carried away and end the chapter on one page, it is worth mentioning that there are no universally accepted definitions for internet addiction. Do you sense a reoccurring theme? We had the same issue with defining cyberbullying. But think about it for a moment, to give someone a diagnosis is a serious matter, potentially life changing. I'll make up a disorder to prove my point. Let's say that Hyperzandualosis exists. From a clinical standpoint, in order for me to give a diagnosis of this, I should be able to recognize it, know it inside and out, be able to plan a treatment, but also, be able to recognize when it is *not* Hyperzandualosis. At this current time, in my view, there are too many variables surrounding the concept of internet addiction to be close to it being a diagnosable condition. Let's explore this further.

Martha Shaw and Donald Black, working out of the department of psychiatry at the University of Iowa, looked to explore the definition, assessment, epidemiology, and clinical management of "internet addiction." In their article they state that:

> Internet addiction is characterized by excessive or poorly controlled preoccupations, urges or behaviours regarding computer use and internet access that lead to impairment or distress.

This is a very broad definition. We have the "excessive," it has to be a lot. There has to be "poorly controlled preoccupations, urges or behaviors" involved with the internet use and it has to lead to "impairment or distress." As a definition goes, it gives us a good starting point. But there are intrinsic complexities of trying to encapsulate such a wide area of difficulty. One of the first difficulties in this area, particularly when working with teenagers, is the concept of the "problem owner."

The problem owner

This comes up a lot in my work, I would say that in most situations that I become involved with, I have the thought—"who is the problem owner here?" at least once. The problem owner is the person who "has the problem." Which seems simple enough, but when you throw in internet use or any non-substance related addiction, things can get really interesting, and the waters can become muddied quickly. Let's use an example to explore this further.

Jack is a 14-year-old boy who does well at school. However, recently at home Jack been getting into lots of arguments with his parents. According to his parents—when Jack gets home from school he goes straight on his tablet and then spends hours on his phone, meal times have been interrupted by this, he used to talk lots more with his parents and his siblings, but recently it seems all he is interested in doing is using his tablet and his phone. After school Jack spends at least 5h using his phone or tablet in one way or another. His schoolwork seems fine, his diet is good, he has friends and other than arguing with his parents when they make comments about his phone use, he doesn't get into conflict at home. When asked about his technology use, Jack doesn't see any issues with the amount of time he's on his phone or tablet.

So, who is the problem owner in this situation? Jack's parents are. Jack has no issue with his technology use, and it doesn't appear to be having an impact on his wider life. If Jack doesn't have "a problem" then he certainly can't be diagnosed with "internet addiction." Despite his parent's protestations that he is "addicted to his phone." If I had a problem with how much time you spent in your garden or walking on beaches, I would be the problem owner, and you certainly wouldn't be considered as being "addicted." This is where the "displacement hypothesis" which we explored in Chapter 2 seems to be rearing its head again... someone has a problem with the activity of choice.

Let's explore another example. Jamie is another 14-year-old boy who does well at school. Well, he used to do well at school, but things seem to have changed recently. And much like Jack, at home Jamie been getting into lots of arguments with his parents. According to Jamie's parents—

when Jamie gets home from school he goes straight on his tablet and then spends hours on his phone, meal times have been interrupted by this, he used to talk lots more with his parents and his siblings, but recently it seems all he is interested in doing is using his tablet and his phone. After school Jamie spends at least 5h using his phone or tablet in one way or another. His school work has deteriorated, his diet has become terrible, he has distanced himself from the people he used to be friends with and his behavior at home has really started to become a struggle, he has started to damage things around the house when upset. When asked about his technology use, Jamie doesn't see any issues with the amount of time he's on his phone or tablet.

So, who is the problem owner in this situation? Jamie's parents. It is still Jamie's parents because Jamie doesn't see any issues with the amount of time he's on his phone or tablet. The difference here is that Jamie's social, emotional and mental health seems to be deteriorating. Now there could be a whole host of reasons why this is happening for Jamie, who's to say that technology use is to blame for his current state? In fact, Jamie's use of technology could be, in his mind, the only good thing he's got going for himself. We would then end up in the murky waters of—can you be addicted to something and have no awareness of it? The answer is yes you can, but I would need to dedicate the rest of this book to exploring the psychology of addiction to give the topic justice. This isn't the space for that. But let's for a moment consider Jamie's closing statement, "he doesn't see any issues with the amount of time he's on his phone or tablet". What if Jamie did see he had an issue with his technology use? This would change things; Shaw and Black's definition of Internet addiction might fit Jamie. Jamie would be the "problem owner." And as is well known in counseling theory, until you recognize that there is something you wish to change, nothing will change.

So, a slightly different problem arises now in trying to understand the concept of internet addiction. Now we have two 14-year-old boys, with a good underlying academic ability, Jack who uses the internet for 5h after school and is "fine," and Jamie, who uses the internet for 5h after school and is a "mess." Two completely different responses to the same amount of internet use. It would seem that "time" cannot be considered a factor in determining if one can be addicted to the internet.... Because the same "amount of internet" does not do the same thing to Jack or Jamie. But, measuring the impact upon the individual might be a clearer area of exploration in order to determine the severity of the internet as a non-substance related addiction... we'll explore this further later in the chapter.

At present, no systematic survey attempting to differentiate aspects of internet addiction has been conducted, for example, investigating all of the potential "addictive" qualities of the internet, such as social networking addiction. However, there are several studies on internet addiction which have argued that social networking use is a predictor for internet addiction. I have a problem with such a statement. I believe it is difficult to grasp what can predict internet addiction, for example, to suggest social networking is a predictor, is a similar statement suggesting that being a runner is a predictor from suffering from leg cramps. There may be a correlation between social networking use and internet addiction, but that does not mean there is a causal link between the two.

For the moment, put aside the concept of "if" you can be "addicted" to the internet, and consider for a moment trying to understand who can be vulnerable to psychological distress due to their internet use. This may be a better route into understanding when things go wrong with internet use.

Who is vulnerable?

The question of vulnerability is an interesting one. Surely anyone could be considered vulnerable to psychological distress due to their internet use. While this is true, there is some research that points in the direction of adolescents being the "most" vulnerable to problematic internet use.

Panayiotis Panayides and Miranda Walker published a review in Europe's *Journal of Psychology* in 2012. This review explored internet addiction and adolescents and highlighted various studies examining the impact of problematic Internet use for this age group. In summary of the research, it is noted that:

- Adolescents are at a critical period of addiction vulnerability, based on their social and neurobiological factors. Essentially, adolescents are making multiple connections with people and their brain development is not at a stage where they make the most logical decisions.
- Adolescents are more vulnerable and at risk as they have easy access to the Internet and flexible timetables. This makes sense, I'm not sure that when I consider my work life and my home life that I would have time to become addicted to the internet.
- Adolescents tend to be less self-regulative… they find it harder to control and direct their time, attention, and emotions.
- Adolescents have less ability to control their enthusiasm for Internet activities. Which essentially means, it can be extremely fun and engaging.

So, it would seem that adolescents may have more vulnerability to excessive internet use than adults. There is another factor here to consider, and that is one of novelty.

One of the most well-known researchers in the field of internet addiction is Dr. Kimberley Young (1965–2019). Dr. Young was a psychologist and considered an expert on internet addiction disorder and online behavior. Dr. Young founded the Centre for Internet Addiction in 1995 and was a psychology professor at the University of Pittsburgh at Bradford with a PhD in Clinical Psychology. I feel very privileged to have spoken with Dr. Young when planning/conducting my doctoral research and organizing my thoughts for this book, her insights were invaluable. Research by Dr. Young in 1996 highlighted that participants who were classified as "internet dependents" were relative beginners on the Internet. Therefore, it may be hypothesized that newcomers to the Internet may be at a higher risk for developing addictive patterns of Internet use. It's interesting to consider novelty as a factor in excessive internet use, particularly as companies are regularly updating their software and new apps are being developed at pace due to the big business of social media. It pays to keep you interested, to give you something new to be obsessed with... the power of technology and its role in keeping you hooked will be discussed later in this chapter.

The internet is huge, there is no topic in which you wouldn't be able to find what you desire. Given that the internet is such a vast topic, considering "internet addiction" as a diagnosis seems to be quite a "catch-all" diagnosis... it would be like going to the GP complaining of symptoms and being told "you're unwell" as opposed to being given a specific idea of what might ail you.

In her research, Dr. Young had made attempts to try and break down the internet into categories for better understanding of specific addictions. Within the internet addiction phenomenon, five subtypes have been suggested and classified. Although there isn't widespread acceptance of these categories across the literature yet, it is an important step in trying to understand more. This is based on the understanding that people typically become addicted to a particular application that acts as a trigger for excessive internet use. Here are the suggestions:

- **Cybersexual addiction:** individuals are engaged in viewing, downloading, and trading online pornography.
- **Cyber-relational addiction:** people become overly involved in online relationship/s, more important than real life ones, with marital discord and family instability (chatrooms, social networks).
- **Net compulsions:** gambling, shopping, and trading online.
- **Information overload:** excessive web surfing and information and database search.
- **Computer addiction:** individuals are overly engaged with pre-programmed games.

Although categorization is an important step in trying to understand, we are far from being near to fully understanding internet addiction. Let's take the above categories and specifically bring social media back into the picture. When it comes to social media...What are you addicted to?

People? Connections? Relationships? Knowing what's happening? Showing others your life? Developing your identity? Attention? If I pick on my Facebook use for a moment I will look at people's profiles whom I'm friends with (cyber-relational), spend a lot of time on Marketplace seeing what's for sale in my local area (net compulsions- shopping), find out a lot of information (information overload) and play pre-programmed games (computer addiction). But I don't see myself as addicted, despite doing those things every day at some point, there has been no discernible negative impact on my ability to live my life. So how do we grasp measuring such an impact for an individual? And how do we separate the "addicted" from the "non-addicted"?

Measuring internet addiction

Most of the discussions and debates surrounding internet addiction have led researchers to attempt to develop an accurate assessment tool in order to diagnose and measure the impact of internet addiction. One of the pioneers in this area was Dr. Kimberley Young, who all the way back in 1996 developed an assessment tool to classify internet addiction in the form of an eight-item diagnostic questionnaire. This questionnaire was based on the criteria used to diagnose pathological gambling disorder. Dr. Young suggests pathological gambling is the most akin disorder due to the pathological nature of internet use. She stated that "by using pathological gambling as a model, internet addiction can be defined as an impulse-control disorder which does not involve an intoxicant."

Dr. Young introduced a diagnostic questionnaire for "internet addiction," with eight dichotomous items and it looked a little something like this:

1	Preoccupation with the Internet	Yes	No
2	Feeling a need to use the Internet in increasing amounts	Yes	No
3	Repeated unsuccessful attempts to control Internet use	Yes	No
4	Moodiness if restricted from Internet use	Yes	No
5	Staying online longer than intended	Yes	No
6	Lying about or hiding the extent of Internet use	Yes	No
7	Using the Internet as a way of escaping from problems or to cope with dysphoric mood;	Yes	No
8	Functional impairments or distress with respect to relationships, work, or other career opportunities.	Yes	No

The diagnostic questionnaire utilized a set of yes/no questions regarding preoccupation with the internet, the amount of time spent on the internet, and the negative impacts of the internet use. In Dr. Young's research she recruited 396 participants who took the questionnaire. If the participants answered "yes" to five (or more) of the above dichotomous items, then they were considered "addicted." Dr. Young highlights that the cut off score of "five" is consistent with the number of criteria used for diagnosing Pathological Gambling. Furthermore, it is seen as an even more rigorous criteria cut-off (5 out of 8) in comparison to what was used to diagnose compulsive gambling (5 out of 10).

After a couple years and following further research, Dr. Young modified the diagnostic questionnaire into a 20-item Internet Addiction Test (IAT). Participants using this test are asked to answer the 20 items on a 5-point Likert scale (scored from one to five) indicating the degree to which internet usage affects their daily routine, social life, productivity, sleeping pattern, and feelings. It would have looked something like this:

Example of Young's internet addiction test.

1. How often do you prefer the excitement of the Internet to intimacy with your partner?	1 2 3 4 5
2. How often do your grades or schoolwork suffer because of the amount of time you spend online?	1 2 3 4 5
3. How often does your job performance or productivity suffer because of the Internet?	1 2 3 4 5
4. How often do you fear that life without the Internet would be boring, empty, and joyless?	1 2 3 4 5
5. How often do you feel depressed, moody, or nervous when you are off-line, which goes away once you are back online?	1 2 3 4 5

Scoring key: *1 = Never; 2 = Rarely; 3 = Every Once in a While; 4 = Sometimes; 5 = Almost Always.*

And so on and so forth... Once you had circled a number for each question, indicating the degree to which the statement is true for you, it would be time to add up all of the circled numbers. With your total "internet addiction" number in hand, you would then refer to a "results key" to determine how much your internet behaviors could be indicative of an addiction.

These types of questionnaires should never be "an end in themselves" but should promote thinking and discussion, they are one piece in a puzzle. Since the introduction of Dr. Young's Diagnostic Questionnaire in

1996 and the Internet Addiction Test in 1998 several other assessment tools have been developed. For example:

- The Internet-Related Addictive Behavior Inventory (IRABI) by Brenner (1997)
- The Chinese Internet Addiction Scale (CIAS) by Chen, Weng, Su, Wu & Yang (2003)
- The Internet Addiction Scale for Taiwan High School Students (IAST) by Lin and Tsai (1999)
- The Pathological Internet Use Scale (PIUS) by Morahan-Martin and Schumacher (2000)

These instruments for measuring Internet Addiction have been developed in various formats, e.g., as criteria or as scales; with differing numbers of items; differing response sets to questions; and with differing "cut off" points to distinguish addictive behavior from normal behavior. This has presented major challenges for a consistent assessment of Internet Addiction across studies and across populations. This is one of the biggest methodological drawbacks regarding attempts to diagnose internet related difficulties.

There have been a number of critical reviews of internet addiction scales and their psychometric properties. Dr. Young's Internet Addiction Test is the most widely used measure of problematic internet use, has been translated into multiple languages across the world and has stood up to test re-test reliability, consistency, and validity measures. What that means, essentially, is that it is measuring the psychological factors that it was designed to measure, it has passed the test of being "worthy of use."

Any self-report questionnaire has its draw backs. You can never guarantee truly accurate information, people can struggle to self-reflect on their internet use and if the questionnaire is going to be read by another person, they might not be honest but instead want to project a certain image. For some, there could be repercussions related to completing it… "could this mean I have to "see someone" about my internet use?" then the person completing it could manipulate their responses to either try and receive support or avoid it. Methodology aside, Young's Internet Addiction Test is a step in the right direction in trying to look at the individuals experience in order to determine the impact of the internet on their life. What is important to remember is that screening tools should not be the sole strategy for any diagnosis, there needs to be a thorough investigation and discussion with individuals following their results to fully determine the nature of an individual's relationship with the internet.

Let's recap for a moment. There is no consensus surrounding a global definition of "internet addiction" yet there is a global recognition that some people seem to end up in psychological distress linked to their internet use, teenagers are considered particularly vulnerable. Efforts to understand this phenomenon have resulted in various terminologies and assessment tools to try and capture, measure, and understand the concept of "internet addition." Pathological Gambling has been used as a model to understand "internet addiction" as a non-substance related addiction and there is some research to support this. Efforts to try and categorize and break down the internet into various parts in order to aid the understanding of "addiction" have been made but no categorical "breakdown" has taken place due to the vastness of "the internet" and there will always be issues related to identifying "the problem owner" if behavioral change is a desire.

The difficulties surrounding reaching a consensus across the board regarding what constitutes internet addiction means that we are, as researchers, as diagnosticians, as parents, in a position of difficulty with regard to saying whether or not someone can actually have "internet addiction." It may be more accurate to describe someone as being cognitively occupied by their internet activities or experiencing various levels of difficulty regarding their internet use. This doesn't often help with responding to parents or professionals' queries when they want to know exactly what is wrong and want a label for it.

Conceptually, suggesting that the internet is the addiction could be questioned at the most basic level. This is a type of argument that posits that the internet is just a tool, a gateway, to reach your actual addictions. The same argument fits when responding to comments such as "he's addicted to his phone"—No he's not. The phone is the gateway to something else; more exploration is needed. Let's take the gambling addict—If you were to remove the internet, then the gambling addict would likely find another means to meet their addiction.

When asked, I take the position of the internet *not* being "the addiction," but merely a conduit to the actual addiction. This highlights an issue about identifying exactly "what" it is that people could be addicted to. I believe that "the internet" is the wrong focus, and instead, researchers should be looking deeper into what it is that the internet is giving someone access to. There is research that also contends that what is needed is a new psychometric scale examining potential addiction to a particular online application (i.e., social networking) rather than activity on the entire internet... this is what my research looked to explore further, with social networking being the focus—Section 3 of this book will go into detail regarding my research. I believe strongly that what we are looking at are behavioral addictions "on" the internet rather than addictions "to" the internet.

Behavioral addictions "on" the Internet

If you want to dive into the world of "behavioral addictions" further, then I would highly recommend Adam Alter's book: *Irresistible—The rise of addictive technology and the business of keeping us hooked.* Adam Alter is an associate professor of marketing at New York University's Stern School of Business. In his book, Alter illuminates the shadowy side of technology use, exploring why so many of today's products are irresistible and why it is no accident that they are so desirable. Alter brings the "hidden" into your conscious awareness so that if you desire, changes can be made. Because such a wonderful book exists, I'm only going to spend a few pages talking about the way technology has been programmed specifically to keep you "hooked."

The design of technology and the battle for your attention

By now you'll realize the vast amounts of money that these social media empires are worth, and why the time you spend on their sites/apps can increase or decrease the value of that company. In spending my time researching the design of technology, I recently read an interesting question, and the answer might surprise you:

> In America, what makes more money than movies, game parks and baseball combined?

The answer—Slot Machines. I was surprised by this; it hadn't even occurred to me as I reeled off a list of what I thought were possible answers. But how is this so? When Slot machines are traditionally played with one of the lowest denomination of coins? The answer lies in the design of the gameplay. Think about it for a second, put a coin in, pull a handle… then the joy of feeling "what am I going to get? Will this be the win?"

… Again, and again, pull the handle—what am I going to get? Rinse and repeat.

People will spend hours and hours at slot machines. Now think about how you refresh your feeds on your social networks… swipe down right? Swipe down…see what you're going to get, have a look through, get bored, swipe down… see what you're going to get, look through, refresh—swipe down. It is genius, the same psychology to keep people spending money at the slot machines is being used to get you to spend your time on social media, to spend your attention. In psychology this is known as "positive intermittent reinforcement." The intermittent part is important, if you reward the behavior immediately then not as much time would be spent on the device, because the reward would have been received, job done. But by making the rewards unpredictable, you end up triggering excitement and get a person to spend longer on their devices. The timing of certain content is planned and programmed to maximize your time online. There are many examples of this throughout various social media and technology service companies. I'm going to guide you through a few of them. Let's start with the "Autoplay" feature.

The "Autoplay" feature, simply put, is where a video will automatically play on one of your media streaming sites. Remember. We're dealing with the economy of attention… so this is a significant move. It started on YouTube with an "Autoplay of next video." Netflix responded, I mean that's big move to make, other companies in the battle of attention needed to respond. Netflix started with the "Autoplay next episode in 5, 4, 3, 2, 1"… what a move, I've been caught by that one—"just one more episode then, it's already starting, I don't have to move a muscle." Then Facebook got involved using "Autoplay in newsfeed" as people scroll down, the video automatically plays, you just have to tap to unmute the video.

All of this is designed to keep you there, to try and keep the time you spend on their sites to the maximum. While we're talking of automation, let's take a moment to focus on YouTube for a second. When you take an average of YouTube's watch-time per day for its users on mobile phones it averages out to just over 60 min per day. This is because of what the "recommendation engines" are putting in front of you. You may have gone on to have a quick look at a music video, or a cake recipe, or a "how to" video, but YouTube remembers, and based on your past viewing will throw a load of recommendations your way once your desired video has finished, wait too long and don't have control settings in place and they will automatically start to play and you will "fall into a YouTube hole"… emerging sometime later dazzled and disheveled with how much time has gone by.

Across the world 1 billion hours of YouTube is watched daily—70% of those hours are from recommendations from artificial intelligence engines designed to keep you on their site watching videos. Videos that have been selected specifically to try and keep you there. It's like through your whole YouTube using life it is creating a little digital version of you based on your online choices, so that it can target you based on your previous searches. YouTube is far from the only company that targets content based on your previous searches and viewing, Netflix is a key runner in this game. Entire rows of options will arrive based on your previous viewing…

> Because you watched Cloud Atlas you may be interested in these sci-fi classics.

Yes, I would Netflix, thank you. However, Netflix doesn't always get it right, to my wife's dismay the other evening…

> "Jeez, you watch one raunchy documentary and suddenly Netflix suddenly thinks you're a sex pest."

Auto suggestion doesn't have to be a bad thing, it can lead to new discoveries and great things. But to deny its capacity to keep you glued to your various screens would be naïve. Do you know who Netflix identified as their biggest competitor after YouTube and Facebook? Sleep! This brings us back round to the goal of such programming, the more time you're on it, the more money is made. I think that there is a bigger concern that is not often mentioned with regard to automatization, which is that of personalized news. Depending on interests, news feeds across social media are being personalized to individuals, which in many respects is narrowing people's view of the world. This type of narrowing and personalization can breed disconnection from wider society and what is happening in local communities as well.

Let's have a look at another popular social network and their attempts at holding you there—Snapchat. Snapchat is a social network popular for giving you the ability to send photos/pictures and augmented reality (face changing) video content to friends. It became popular partly because the content would disappear after a period of time, so a picture would be available to be seen, usually with a message and then it would vanish. Snapchat is particularly popular with children aged 16 and under. I'm going to talk about one particular aspect of Snapchat: Snapstreaks.

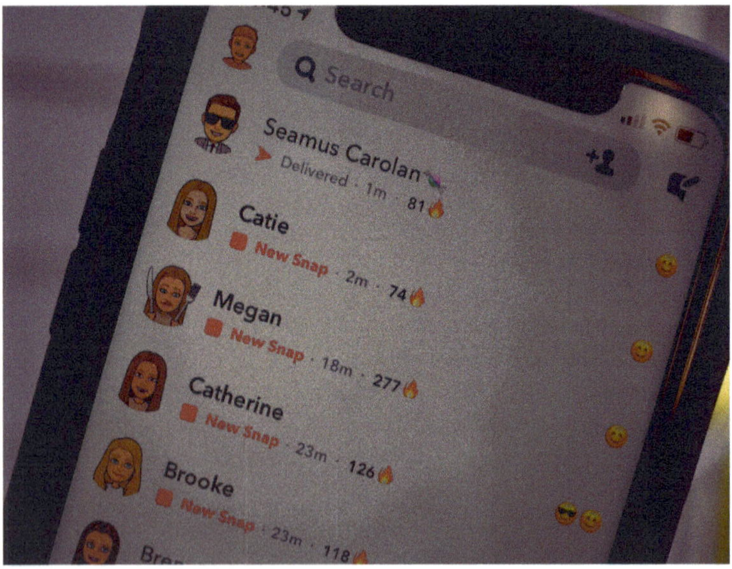

Simply put, Snapstreaks show the number of days in a row that 2 people have communicated with one another through direct pictures. It recognizes this with a number and fire symbol. In the picture above, this would show that Megan has sent pictures back and forth with a friend for more than 277 days. Therefore, Megan and her friend have a Snapstreak of 277. To keep a Snapstreak going, both Snapchatters must send a Snap (picture, not "Chat") back and forth to each other within a 24-h window.

It might seem harmless on the outset, but when you put yourself in a teenager's mind-set its appeal starts to show. What this is doing is giving 2 people something they don't want to lose, it's a numerical value that represents their friendship, it's a numerical value that can give a direct comparison to other people—"Megan and I are a Snapstreak 277 and she's only a Snapstreak 8 with Jessica." It helps a teenager feel valued by another, held in mind, daily. Snapstreaks build and if you do not send a Snap within a 24-h period, your streak goes down to 0. So, in reality what we have happening now is teenagers scheduling small slices of time in their minds where they have a "to do list" of social media responsibilities–.

> "I need to get on and do my streaks with A B & C, then check Facebook and like my friends posts, then get on Instagram and follow a few friends stories (all the way through or they'll see when you dropped out) then send a few memes that I like to my closest friends."

There are situations now where teenagers will be going on holiday with their families and they will give their passwords out to 5 other people so that they can keep their Snapstreaks going while they are away, the Snap doesn't even have to have meaning, it's not uncommon for these users to send a picture of a lamp, a table leg, the carpet, whatever… it is the Snapstreak number that matters to them. This is not dis-similar to the focus on a "number of followers" or a "number of likes" on different social media platforms—a numerical value that the individual will translate into "worth." The sad truth is that a "follower amount" ultimately makes you feel bad because it's driven by a comparison to others and you will always see more people who are "beating" your number. And if you get to the top? Well, then the struggle becomes staying at the top.

It is important to know this because a lot of focus seems to land on teenagers and adults for being at fault if they find themselves spending a lot of time on social media. It is important to remember that for every person who's struggling to curb their social media use, there's a hundred programmers that worked hard to keep people on it. Social media companies have a part to play in society's current behavioral addictions and with the psychology that they have utilized to hold its users to their devices. In fact, there are some lines of thought that suggest that behavioral addictions are not "addictions" at all and when you get to a scale that is as high as the "users of social media" you don't have an addiction, you have a societal problem. Let that simmer for a while… our whole addiction framework could be turned on its head when considering it society's problem. Because then it becomes societies responsibility, the government's responsibility, to shift the status quo.

So, who out there is taking a stand against the automation and behavioral design of these apps and tech? One such man is Tristan Harris. Tristan Harris is the president and a co-founder of the *Center for Humane Technology*. Earlier, he worked as a design ethicist at Google, and he studied extensively the ethics of human persuasion. The Atlantic magazine once referred to Tristan as the "closest thing Silicon Valley has to a conscience". What Tristan is doing is attempting to put conscious ethical choice back into the hands of the technology consumer… it's a huge step in the right direction and big companies are starting to listen. If you want to know more, and I highly recommend it, visit www.tristanharris.com

For now, before closing this chapter, we are going to take a side-step into some recent unpublished (at the time of writing) research. This side-step is done on purpose, because there can often be a level of "catastrophising" about social media use and it's important to bring balance to these discussions. This chapter has explored the concept of internet addiction, issues surrounding identifying the problem owner, how adolescents can be seen as vulnerable, how there have been attempts to break down the internet into its subsequent parts to better understand it, how researchers have attempted to measure the impact of internet addition and how what we might be looking at are behavioral addictions "on" the internet, not "to" the internet. We took steps to explore behavioral addictions and how the design of social media is programmed to keep your attention.

When it comes to understanding behavioral addiction, research points in the direction of narrowing down future focus away from "internet addiction" to become more nuanced and specific… to peer through the gateway of "the internet" and look at what an individual has become behaviorally addicted to. This is what my research aimed to do… but more on that later. A timely cautionary tale has recently been given in a tongue-in-cheek piece of research conducted by Liam Satchell from The University of Winchester and colleagues (from multiple universities). This research is titled: *Development of an Offline-Friend Addiction Questionnaire (O-FAQ): Are most people really social addicts?*

Offline. Friend. Addiction. Find yourself thinking about your friends when you're not with them? Have you ever ignored your family to spend time with your friends? Do you often find yourself spending time with friends in order to forget about personal problems? If so, then you might just fit the criteria for Offline Friend Addiction. Of course, the notion of being addicted to socializing with friends is ridiculous, right? We are driven biologically to be social beings; it is a fundamental human need. Which is exactly the point being made by Liam Satchell and his colleagues. They have taken the same route that many psychologists have done before in adapting the measure for internet addiction/alcohol addiction and inserted the behavior of interest... so in their questionnaire, instead of an item being "spent more time on Facebook than initially intended", they asked if participants had "spent more time with friends than initially intended". By repeating this process for multiple questionnaire points the team ended up with a 37-item questionnaire, which 807 participants completed.

What did the results say? In using criteria established over other social media studies as cut-off measures for classification of a "problem," their results suggested that 69% of participants were addicted to their friends. So... is this something new that we need to be worried about? Certainly not. The authors state that "Offline friend addiction is not an issue of concern for public health, but rather it is capturing experiences pertinent to social support, adaptation, and well-being across the lifespan." In other words, the results are capturing what people socially need in order to thrive in their life. This study highlights that multiple social media studies will be capturing this information, but not realizing so—the nuances of support that we give and receive through social media. The authors continue and state "What we have demonstrated here is that researchers can quickly produce farcical results when conceptualizing social media as a distinctive entity that is unrelated to any other social context."

Neither offline friend addiction nor social media addiction are formal psychiatric disorders. It is important to remember the social context when using scales that report on the impact of the internet and social media. Any questionnaire should be used as a small part of a wider exploration regarding someone's situation—otherwise we would end up in an awful situation of "diagnosing" everyday behavior instead of trying to understand a person's lived experience—which after all, should be the starting point of any "outside intervention." Questionnaires have their place, but they should not be an end in themselves when trying to understand something as complex as human experience, particularly under the microscope of "diagnosis."

The growing use of social media by adolescents is often accompanied by parental worry of the detrimental effect it has upon their academic achievement. Which is where this book is going to take you now, into the realms of "the educational impact of social media usage."

CHAPTER

7

The educational impact of social media usage

Psychologist's Guide to Adolescents and Social Media
https://doi.org/10.1016/B978-0-323-91898-5.00003-5

There is more to school than academic progression and getting good grades. In my day job I often find myself helping schools to reframe and understand why children may be struggling to make academic progress. Far too many times this is related to schools struggling to understand the multiple interweaving aspects that make up an individual... from home life, to emotional wellbeing to various adverse childhood experiences, there are often much more important things happening under the surface that need recognizing and supporting before a child can be in a "ready to learn" mind-set. Or, as a colleague of mine puts it much more eloquently:

> you never know how many rivers a child has had to cross before they've got to school that day.

I'm hoping by this point in the book you're realizing the multiple benefits that social media has to offer as well as the potential risks. Everything that has been explored thus far is relevant in an educational context, so bring it with you when reading this chapter. However, this chapter is going to spend a little time focusing on some research that has specifically explored how social media use has seemingly impacted academic progression and the cognitive abilities of those who use it. I say "seemingly" because in such research for as many studies that you can find to say that "social media is bad" you will find those that say "social media is good". Let's explore this in more detail.

Dr. Tracy Alloway is a professor of psychology at the University of North Florida. You may remember her from Chapter 2 and research exploring social connectedness. She has spent a considerable part of her career researching and highlighting the importance of "Working Memory" in education. If you are unfamiliar with working memory, it is the process of memory-in-action: the ability to remember and use relevant information while in the middle of an activity—to manipulate multiple sources of information, in your head, to produce an outcome. If you are told to "get out your criminal psychology textbook, turn to page 92, section 3 and answer questions 7–13" you will be using your short-term auditory and working memory to do so. Dr. Alloway has published 13 books and over 100 journal articles and book chapters on the topic. When she's not doing that, she writes blogs for *Psychology Today, The Huffington* Post and has had her research featured on various TV/news shows. Realizing I'm running the risk of sounding like what the teenagers I work with would call a "fanboy" about it... what all that means, is that Dr. Alloway is particularly good at her job.

In 2013, Dr. Alloway and her colleagues looked to explore whether or not the use of social media sites makes you smarter. In particular, whether or not using social media sites impacted upon the underlying cognitive abilities of adolescents (aged between 12 and 18). To explore this, participants were required to complete three things:

1. A questionnaire on their technology use.
2. A cognitive abilities test using the Wechsler Individual Achievement Test.
3. A Working Memory test using the Automated Working Memory Assessment.

Both the cognitive abilities assessment and the automated working memory assessment allow for standardized scores to be computed, which is comparable to children of a similar age. Facebook and YouTube were the main social networks that were explored in this study. The questionnaire allowed the identification of the amount of time someone had been a member of selected social networks.

The results showed that those participants who used Facebook for over a year had significantly higher working memory, verbal ability, and spelling scores than those who had used Facebook for less than a year. There was no difference in maths scores for either group and YouTube was not linked to higher cognitive scores for either group.

So, what is happening here? Dr. Alloway speculates that there is a similarity in the cognitive processes required in using Facebook and completing a working memory test. When you are using Facebook, you are processing multiple streams of information and actively manipulating it to navigate the site. Therefore, a "training effect" might be in effect which explains the high working memory score. Participants may essentially have been well practiced in what the assessment looks at and so scored higher. It is worth bearing in mind that no specific activity on Facebook predicted the higher score, just the length of Facebook use. With regard to verbal ability and spelling, Dr. Alloway suggests that this is due to the very nature of Facebook use, in conversing with others and copious amounts of writing and following different links to various websites, people are in fact increasing their literacy abilities. The fact that mathematical ability was not significantly improved for either group goes part way to support this, as Facebook/YouTube does not innately require use of any mathematical concepts.

In summary of Dr. Alloway's results, it is suggested that using Facebook for over a year improves some cognitive abilities... particularly with literacy and less so with working memory. However, I would view these results with caution as this was not a longitudinal study which could have strengthened the results.

Underlying ability, such as those assessed with cognitive assessments are one way to look at how social media can shift one's inner abilities. Another way is to consider if social media use is impacting the school grades of those who use it. Which is what researchers Paul Kirschner and Aryn Karpinski looked to explore back in 2010.

Kirschner and Karpinski found that Facebook users actually reported lower grade point averages than those who did not use Facebook... yet both groups reported a similar amount of time on the internet. This suggests that Facebook, and to generalize, any social media sites which are similar in design, may be negatively impacting school results for individuals. Their study, published in the Journal: *Computers in Human Behavior*, also reported some qualitative data which highlighted that some users actively use Facebook to procrastinate to avoid studying... which could explain the negative impact. I can certainly relate to that. In fact, checking my phone at random intervals during difficult (always admin based) work has certainly become a feature of my life... I don't even need to check it, I am actively distracting myself, actively procrastinating. But why do we procrastinate?

A brief psychology of procrastination

Procrastination, simply put, is the act of postponing or delaying something that you do not want to do. Procrastination to some extent is something that most of us are guilty of in one way or another. Some procrastination can be relatively harmless. For example, the fact that before I would sit down to write in an evening I wouldn't begin until I've washed the dishes, tidied up the lounge, vacuumed up and made myself (and my wife) a cup of tea - this is unlikely to cause significant delay in completing this book. Plus, it serves a benefit to what I would see as uncluttering my mind and working space. A familiar routine to get myself in the "working" frame of mind... and ultimately, less distracted by my environment. This type of procrastination is relatively harmless. However, there is procrastination that can be harmful... the type that leaves you staring at a blank computer screen for an hour, waking up in a panic during the night because of what you should have got done and leaving things to the very last minute, or past their deadline.

Being a student is a particularly important time when procrastination can become an issue. There is research to suggest that students are particularly vulnerable to procrastination and in a 2007 meta-analysis published in the *Psychological Bulletin*, it was found that 80%–95% of college students procrastinated on a regular basis, particularly when it came to completing assignments and coursework.

According to the book: *Procrastination and Task Avoidance: Theory, Research, and Treatment*, there are some major cognitive distortions that lead to academic procrastination. Students have a habit of:

- Overestimating how much time they have left to perform tasks.
- Overestimating how motivated they will be in the future.
- Underestimating how long certain activities will take to complete.
- Mistakenly assuming that they need to be in the right frame of mind to work on a project (which I do, all the time... and my wife does often when I suggest we watch a kung-fu movie and she's not "in the right kind of mood for a kung-fu movie").

If procrastination starts to become a more present and a more overwhelming experience, then that's when support might be needed. For some individuals, procrastination can be fear and anxiety based. In this situation the "just get started" school of advice wouldn't work at all, because it is not related to difficulties with time management. As Joseph Ferrari, a professor of psychology at DePaul University once said—"To tell the chronic procrastinator to just do it would be like saying to a clinically depressed person, cheer up." Realistically, what would be better would be helping this person to set tiny goals in an understandable way, with time carefully structured and blocked out for them, being mindful not to overwhelm them and ensuring that the "conditions" are optimum for avoiding unnecessary distraction.

One form of procrastination can take the shape of "task switching." Let's bring social media back into the picture and explore this some more. Looking further into the role of Facebook in the student's multitasking/task switching was Dr. Terry Judd, working out of the University of Melbourne in 2014. Dr. Judd examined comprehensive time-based logs of students' computer use during academic self-directed study tasks. 1249 students were analyzed, and the results showed that 99% of the sessions involved some form of multi-tasking. When students were multitasking/task switching there was a significant reduction in their focused behavior (the academic task they were initially engaged in). What we have here is a distinct inability to focus on one thing. For example, in having to write an essay, a student is likely to also have the internet at their fingertips, emails close by, a phone at the ready, perhaps the TV on in the background and music playing... opportunities for task switching and procrastination are abundant. A young person I worked with once described having social media as feeling like all their friends were in the room with them when they were trying to work.

There seems to be a growing body of research around the negatives of social media, the number of platforms one can "check-in" with their networks and the detrimental effect this can have on one's educational achievement. The "need" of adolescents to be in constant connection with their online networks can lead to various new and somewhat bizarre psychological phenomenon, for example: Phantom Vibration Syndrome.

Have you ever felt that your phone has gone off in your pocket, you've felt the vibration, but upon checking it you realize that that nothing had happened? Then you've experienced Phantom Vibration Syndrome. Essentially, what is happening here is that your body has become primed to expect to feel your phone going off, and your brain can sometimes misinterpret what it has felt, signaling to you that your phone has gone off. This highlights that there is a portion of cognitive function which is directed to your phone and message detection. It would seem that even our unconscious mind is distracting us from being solely present in the current moment or task. Unless of course there is some conspiracy that the social media companies are sending vibrations to your phone with no notification in the hopes that while you have your phone unlocked, you may as well check your socials? Thus, increasing your time on their apps and their worth as a company? Surely not? I have no idea… but there are some who believe so.

Overall, the pull of technology clearly has a detrimental impact on completing specific tasks which is applicable to there being a detrimental impact on academic performance. Research suggests it can take 23 min to re-focus and get back in "the zone" following being interrupted or distracted… and on average, we can self-interrupt every 3½ min. Add that to the knowledge we have about the pull of technology and it is a recipe for procrastination and task switching being a genuine problem for students. As time moves on and exposure to social media in various forms increases, this problem is presenting itself in some students as a kind of social media fatigue… in short, some people have had enough.

There are some schools of thought examining social media fatigue that take the position that as more people crowd social media, and more information gets shared and re-shared, people can show the tendency to back away from their social media. People are becoming overwhelmed with too many sites, too many pieces of content, too many contacts and too much time spent trying to keep up with what's going on. As social media evolves and new technology and apps are being developed to make it even more accessible, it remains important to pay attention to how people are coping with it. Do you know of anyone that has taken a break from social media for a while? You probably do… ironically, they probably posted an update telling people that they were taking a break from social media on social media.

To summarize, the educational impact of social networking may be in the improvement of working memory, verbal ability and spelling scores, yet this may lead to an overall reduction in educational levels/grades due to task switching, procrastination and cognitive distraction if the use of social networking interferes with educational tasks.

Part 2 of this book has explored the unintended consequences of using social media. Delving into the subjects of cyberbullying, unfulfilled expectations, internet addiction and the impact on education. Once I had gained knowledge surrounding the positives and negatives of social media use, I endeavored to construct my own research exploring the impact of social media on secondary aged pupils. The results were enlightening. Part 3 of this book will detail what I discovered and more importantly I feel, goes into a detailed analysis of the lived experience of teenagers who struggle with their social media usage.

PART III

Researching the impact of social media on UK secondary school students

CHAPTER

8

Delving in deeper

https://doi.org/10.1016/B978-0-323-91898-5.00020-5

There is an abundant amount of planning involved in setting up research. There are design considerations, participant considerations and ethical considerations to be made. Part 3 of this book will highlight the research I led, but I do not want to get bogged down in the philosophies of ontology (what is real) and epistemology (the nature of knowledge). I want to as quickly as possible get to the "core" of what my research uncovered. But in doing so I will need to lay the foundations of how I came to it otherwise we'll end up floating on a sea of random information. So, let's begin with where I began.

Research questions

Through leafing through multiple articles, books, and research I came to the following research questions that I wanted to explore further:

(1) **What social networking platforms are being used by secondary school aged young people?**
There was a distinct lack of research focusing on exactly what is being used by young people. Because of the availability and extent to which new apps, are being developed, and the fact that young people can use multiple social media apps simultaneously, researching this question is something which needs to be established often to add context to the findings.

(2) **To what extent do social media occupy the minds of secondary aged young people? Can they be considered behaviorally addicted?**
It is often taken for granted that young people are immersed in technology from birth, but what are the effects of this on their self and their relationships with others? Specifically, regarding social networking, there was a lack of research looking into this, it is often assumed but seldom explored.

(3) **What is it really like to be a young person using social media platforms every day? And what key themes are identified in the exploration of social media use?**
There is a lack of qualitative research looking into the in-depth lived experience of being a young person using social media platforms. Answering this question will allow for a detailed examination of the phenomenon.

How to find out?

There exists a long-standing debate within the psychological sciences about "the best" way to investigate phenomena. Traditionally, the two schools of contrasting thought were Quantitative and Qualitative researchers. In selecting how to approach this research I found it an important process to consider some debates in the field of methodological enquiry.

Quantitative purists suggest that social observations should be treated as entities, in much the same way that physical scientists treat physical phenomena. They would suggest that the researcher is separate from the entities that are subject to observation and make time and context free generalizations. In the quantitative school of thought, educational researcher should eliminate their biases, remain emotionally detached and uninvolved with the objects of study, and test or empirically justify their stated hypothesis. Like an invisible observer unknown to the object of study.

Qualitative "purists" suggest that there are multiple-constructed realities, that making time and context-free generalizations are neither desirable nor possible. This position would suggest that the "knower" and the "known" cannot be separated because the subjective knower is the only source of reality. There are multiple "truths" based on the individual and the context. This position in many respects is one of a "you are you; I am me, and our understanding will meet somewhere in the middle."

I refer to the above two quantitative and qualitative "purists" because those who follow what they may consider the "pure" form of their methodology, have advocated an incompatibility thesis. The incompatibility thesis posits that qualitative and quantitative research paradigms, including their associated methods, cannot and should not be mixed.

However, there is a third way, sometimes referred to as "the third paradigm," and that is one of mixed methodology. A mixed methodology approach recognizes both qualitative and quantitative data and methods as valuable:

> both methodologies describe their data, construct explanatory arguments from their data, and speculate about why the outcomes they observed happened as they did ***Sechrest and Sidani (1995, p. 78).***

In addition, both sets of researcher incorporate safeguards in their research to ensure that any potential sources of invalidity, that could call into question the "trustworthiness' of the data, is minimized. Research in the social sciences represents an attempt to provide warranted assertions about human beings, and the environments in which they live and evolve. I see this as a somewhat refreshing view of what can be quite a complex argument regarding paradigmatic orientations.

Mixed methods research is therefore defined and put beautifully by researchers Johnson and Onwuegbuzie in 2004, as "a class of research where the researcher mixes or combines quantitative and qualitative research techniques, methods, approaches, concepts or language into a single study." Which is why I choose it as a method to use. Because without a doubt it was the best way I had at my fingertips of exploring my research questions. I was going to mix large data gathering and personal experience to better understand social media. I believe that the psychology surrounding social media use are real and generalizable across the population and therefore can be measured using quantifiable ways... such as by questionnaire. However, with regard to investigating the meaning and experience of social media use, the experience is subjective and contextual and so qualitative methods of data collection are valuable, to gain a deeper understanding of the social media experience... such as by sitting with and talking to teenagers who use social media. I settled on having a 2-phase approach to my research... the questionnaires, following analysis, would identify a potential pool of children to interview.

Time to get to work: Designing the questionnaire

Questionnaires allow for the generalization of findings to populations and for statistical comparisons between individuals and groups. I decided to utilize paper copies of the questionnaire for convenience for the schools involved and because research has shown that online questionnaires have a significantly lower response rates than traditional paper questionnaires. Also, I've been in enough ICT classrooms to know that it would take 15min to get students logged on, then take time to get all the students to navigate to the right site for taking a digital questionnaire, while avoiding all distractions of the internet, it would be a nightmare.

Two large secondary schools were selected to take part in the study, one in the Midlands, and one in Devon. They had a combined population of approximately 3000 students, every pupil (present on the day of data collection) would receive a copy of the questionnaire to complete during registration time. From my experience of working in a secondary school, I knew that the registration period would be the best bet for getting anything "additional" completed. Teachers are always thrown things at them to "get done" during registration period, I felt guilty about this, sometimes there is only around 20min time in any registration period, there is a lot to cram in, so I knew it had to be relatively short, otherwise it would be ignored "by accident" or because there was already a lot the teacher had to be doing. So, I couldn't design anything too clunky, and I couldn't design anything too complex otherwise the students would be throwing questions galore at the teacher or would just choose not to complete it. Both schools have a diverse catchment area which should allow for a strong representative sample of British young people aged 11–16.

In order to explore Research Question 1—What social networking platforms are being used by secondary school aged young people?

The questionnaire incorporated multiple choice options of several popular social networks. To provide a deeper contextual answer to this question, the questionnaire also detailed multiple choice questions to report the technology being used, the days of the week and times of the day that participants accessed their social networks.

In order to explore Research Question 2—The extent to which Social Networking occupies the mind of secondary school aged pupils and can they be considered behaviorally addicted? My questionnaire incorporated an adapted version of Dr. Young's Internet Addiction Test (IAT). The IAT was adapted to focus in on social media and adolescents, rather than "all internet use." The overall structure and Likert scale remained the same. The brain regions and neural processes that underlie addiction overlap extensively with those that support cognitive functions, including learning, memory, and reasoning. Therefore, an adapted IAT is an appropriate resource to use to measure the extent to which social media occupies the mind of young people. Furthermore, out of all the assessments that are "out there" Young's IAT is the most studied and validated and so as tools go, it's a pretty good one to use. I am fortunate and grateful to Dr. Young for allowing me to utilize and adapt the IAT for my research. The adaptions made to the IAT were in the language presentation of the questions. This was done so that the students could better understand the question (due to their age) and to reflect social media use as opposed to all internet use.

In order to begin an exploration of Research Question 3—What is it really like to be a young person using social media platforms? The questionnaire contained a number of Yes/No options for participants to select based on a number of statements designed to explore if school experience, friendships and adult relationships were impacted by their social networking use. I also believe that in completing the full questionnaire, you start the process of understanding a wider context to answering Research Question 3. In gaining an understanding of the factors involved at Research Question 1 and 2, I found myself in an illuminated position to be able to answer Research Question 3. Which is why I chose to utilize the questionnaires to select some young people to talk with in detail once I'd analyzed them all… but more on that later.

There are always notes of caution when using self-report measures, such as those in questionnaires. The risks involved in relying too heavily on questionnaires have been explored already in the book. But what wasn't yet mentioned is that when looking at completed questionnaires, it cannot be assumed that the question is interpreted by the person completing it in the way the researcher intends, nor can it be assumed that the same responses mean the same for all people. The questionnaire eventually got turned into a social media assessment and reflection tool for use in working with children and adolescents, you'll find it in the last section of this book. For now, let' take a look at the results.

Results

I had 3000 questionnaires returned to me... more than I was expecting. That was almost two full school populations! I needed to find a way to narrow this down or I wasn't going to be able to write my research paper in time. When I sat down with my early 2000s laptop and the massive pile of questionnaires, I realized I may have bitten off more than I could chew... each completed questionnaire had approximately 90 different pieces of information for me to record for analysis. I first thought that I could narrow it down by ditching those questionnaires where a person identified themselves as "not using any social media." But here's the thing, there was none to ditch, absolutely every child in each of the schools used one form of social media. To narrow it down I selected all of the year 9's, 10's and 11's (13–16-year olds) for analysis. This was due to a position of feeling the selected participants would be able to reflect on their use of social media in Years 7 and 8 (for the next phase of my research). I also wanted to have a representative sample that covered Secondary School key stages 3 and 4. A total Years 9, 10, and 11 cohort resulted in 1245 questionnaires being selected for analysis. 97 questionnaires were rejected due to being incomplete. Therefore, 1148 were put forward for analysis. It took months, me, my dining room table and a lot of cups of tea and music. And here's what I found out:

Analysis

Year groups, participant numbers, and percentages.

Year group	Number of participants	Percentage (%)
9	463	40.3
10	446	38.9
11	239	20.8
Total	1148	100

The above table details the number of participants, the year groups they belonged to and the representative percentage of the total sample. The comparatively small number of Year 11's is due to GCSE exams taking place subsequently effecting the availability of that year group for participation.

The gender balance between participants.

Gender	Number of participants	Percentage (%)
Male	560	48.8
Female	588	51.2
Total	1148	100

The above table details the gender split between participants. This is a good split across genders. Therefore, the results will represent the views of both males and females accurately.

The Devon School and The Midland School participant frequencies.

School	Number of participants	Percentage (%)
The Midland School	514	44.8
The Devon School	634	55.2
Total	1148	100

The above table details the number of participants from each school. Due to GCSE exams in the Midland school, the Devon school has 120 more participants in this study.

What social networking sites and apps are being used by years groups 9–11.

Social networking site/app	Number of "Yes" responses	Percentage of cases (%)
Facebook	962	83.8
WhatsApp	400	34.8
Snap Chat	822	71.6
Vine	363	31.6
MSN Messenger	208	18.1
Twitter	527	45.9
Pinterest	292	25.4
Instagram	792	69.0
YouTube	1055	91.9
Spotify	571	49.7

Continued

What social networking sites and apps are being used by years groups 9–11—cont'd

Social networking site/app	Number of "Yes" responses	Percentage of cases (%)
Tumblr	204	17.8
Hootsuite	0	0.0
Tinder	27	2.4
Google+	461	40.2
Skype	602	52.4
Other sites	276	24.0
Xbox 360/One	489	42.6
PlayStation 3/4	298	26.0
Nintendo Wii	233	20.3
Other games	291	25.3

The above table details the results following the question; what social networking sites/apps do you use? The question was multiple choice, allowing participants to select from the above list of sites/apps. Please see the below graph for a visual representation of the above results.

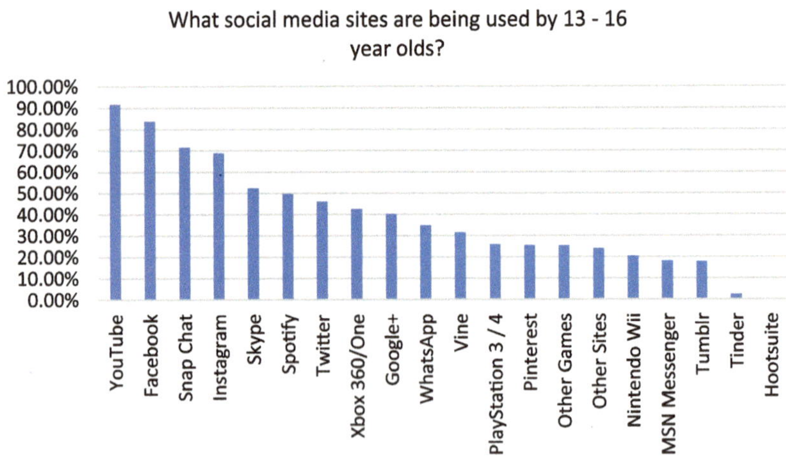

The above graph gives a visual representation of what social networking sites/apps are being used by 13–16-year olds. The results show that teenagers will often use a multitude of social media at any given time, the most popular being YouTube (91.9%), closely followed by Facebook

(83.8%), then SnapChat (71.6%) and Instagram (69%). Each of those sites has the capacity to work in a harmonious manner with one another. For example, a picture could be taken in Instagram, uploaded to an individual's Instagram profile, and then to Facebook and SnapChat. Likewise, an enjoyable video seen on YouTube, can be shared through Facebook and a number of different sites. The purpose of this explanation is that individuals who have multiple social media accounts, have multiple "audiences" to their online activity and multiple ways to interconnect via their networks.

No participants used Hootsuite, which was a relief, I put it in there as a validly-check for my questionnaire responses. Hootsuite is mainly focused for business users to be able to post to multiple feeds at once, it costs to use it and so would not likely be used by 13–16-year olds. If lots of people had selected it, I would have assumed they were not completing the questionnaire properly and I would have had to decide about disregarding their questionnaires. It's also important to bear in mind I collected this data in 2015… Vine doesn't exist anymore, being replaced in many respects by TicToc.

This data shows that young people use multiple social media sites/apps in order to select the right "tool" for what they wish to communicate. For example, an individual who only uses Spotify (a music streaming/sharing site) has chosen that medium to communicate their interests and seek likeminded "friends"/music playlists. However, an individual who only uses Instagram (a photo uploading site), has chosen pictures (and words to a lesser extent) to communicate with others online. Using multiple sites allows an individual to use a myriad of communication software to meet their particular needs on a particular day. This fits with and further reinforces what we explored earlier with *the uses and gratifications theory* suggesting people making active choices with particular media to meet their needs.

There is an importance in analyzing what specific social media sites are being used by teenagers. The importance lies within the fact that these sites have different styles and communities of users. Perhaps they should not be lumped together as "social media," because in understanding what young people are using and why, you may gain a deeper understanding of that person, and the communities in which they traverse.

I would expect that there would be changing trends in what social media young people use, within months of this kind of feedback other patterns may be evident…The Houseparty app is a prime example of the fluidity of social media as we explored earlier. I would anticipate these results as fluid, several interacting variables collide to help shape choices that young people make with their social media. Wilfred Trotter popularized the term "herd behavior" to explain the phenomena of large numbers of people acting in the same way at the same time, this effect is certainly evident within social media use.

What technology is being used to access Social Networking Sites and Apps?

Technology	Number of "Yes" responses	Percentage of cases (%)
Mobile phone	1048	91.3
Laptop/desktop computer	829	72.2
Tablet computer	777	67.7
Smart TV	267	23.3
Xbox 360/One	367	32
PlayStation 3/4	224	19.5
Nintendo Wii	131	11.4
Other games console	95	8.3

The above table details the results following the question, what technology do you use to get on to social networking sites/apps? The question was multiple choice, allowing participants to select from the above list of technologies. Please see the graph below for a visual representation of the above results.

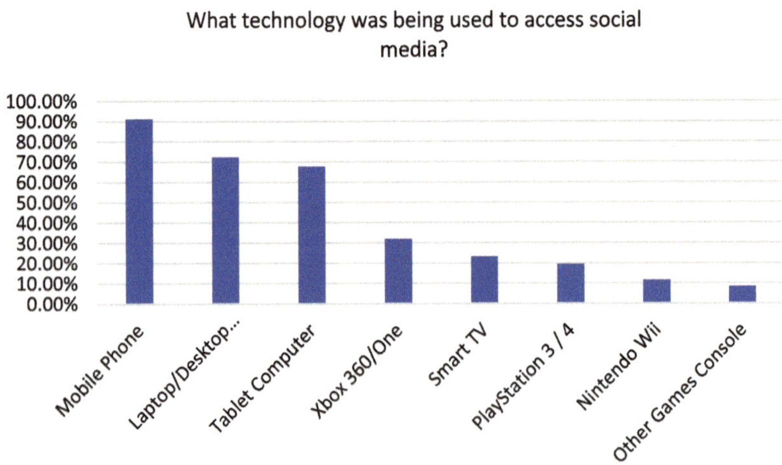

This graph highlights that a high percentage of participants would often use more than one technology to access social media sites. A high percentage of participants would combine the use of mobile phones, laptop/desktop computers and tablet computers to access their social media.

It is not surprising that the Mobile Phone was the most popular way young people chose to access their social media. Mobile Phones allow for instant access, on the move, at any time, with some level of privacy due to the size of the phone and that they are often "owned" by the users. The use of Laptops/Desktops/Tablet computers perhaps highlight that social media are used wherever a young person has access to the internet through compatible technology.

Being able to access social media through games consoles, and the relatively recent changes to how online gameplay can be linked to other social media, may go some way to explain why the percentage of use for accessing social media is quite low. Playing games (via consoles) with others online is a form of social networking, it may be that young people's conception of what they see as social networking did not take into account online console gameplay, but rather focused on the more popular sites/apps they use, dedicated to "traditional" social networking, for example, the use of Facebook.

However, the results may alternatively highlight a recent shift in gaming culture, being the ability to use online games through mobile technology, like tablets and smartphones. Perhaps, to get a clearer result of how many young people are using online games as a form of social networking, my study would have benefited from a category pertaining to mobile/tablet online games, oh the benefits of hindsight. There has been a massive shift in recent years with regard to footage of gameplay being added to YouTube, often with commentary and the ability to watch "live." I can only envisage this particular social media culture increasing over time.

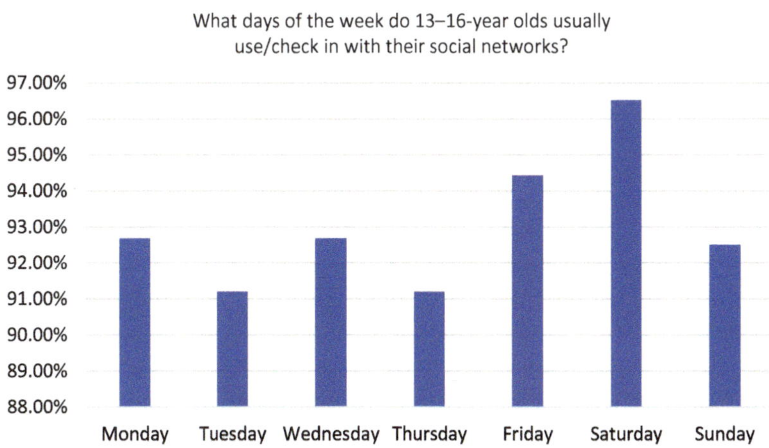

The above graph details what days of the week 13–16-year olds use/check in with their social networks. In exploring what days of the week young people access their social media, a staggering 91% of young people access their social networks every day. This highlights that social media use is an inherent day to day experience for a large number of young people. The percentage of use on Saturdays rises slightly to 96%, suggesting that for some young people, they may only indulge in social networking activities on the weekends, perhaps self-imposed, or perhaps parentally imposed. What does remain clear is a validation that social media is becoming an inherent element of young people's habitat. However, I would not necessarily state that it is solely inherent in young people's habitat and is becoming more evident in adults lives.

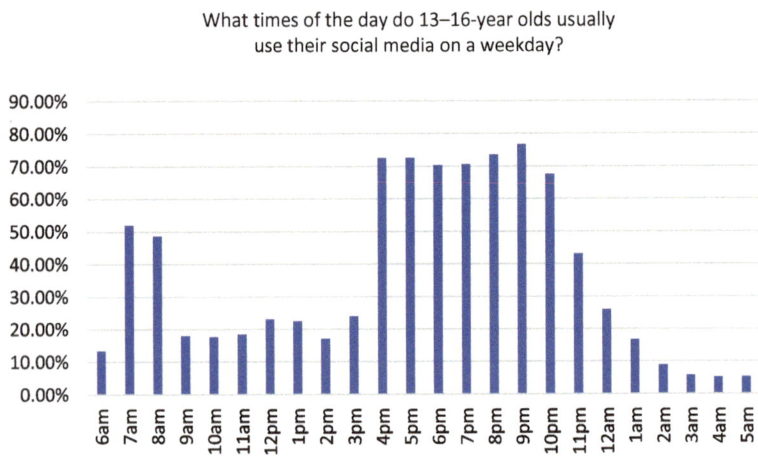

I love this graph because it paints a story. You can almost visualize the reality of it. 50% were waking up and reaching for their social media. School starts and there is a big drop of social media use. When school ends it picks up again and then reduces when it's bedtime... but not completely. It may be old fashioned of me, but I feel a lot of concern for those 13–16-year olds that are using their social networks from 1 am onwards. Let's take a deeper look at that data:

Between the hours of 9:00–16:00, there is a drop in social media usage, with about 20% of young people using social networking sites. It is noteworthy that this is during school hours. Small increases in use during what may be considered "lunch time," may show that young people, when given unstructured time, and if possible, will check their social media.

Social media usage spikes again between the hours of 16:00–23:00, with roughly 73% of young people accessing their networks. I'd say that this increase is due to there being fewer explicit restrictions to using social media/technology and because of the unstructured time available after school hours.

From 23:00 onwards there is a general decrease of social media usage, 26% at Midnight and between 01:00 and 06:00, it falls from a high of 16% at 01:00 down to 5% between 03:00 and 5:00. Although it is expected that there would be a drop in use overnight, it remains important to put some context and questions to the results. The participants are aged between 13 and 16 years old, which means parents still hold "responsibility" for them, how much social media use are parents aware of? If ¼ of young people are using social media sites at midnight, what impact does this have on them the next day? Do parents know that this is happening? and would they allow it if they did?

In the early hours of the morning, there is reported social media usage at 02:00 by 9% of participants, and between 3:00 and 5:00, 5% of participants reported using their social media. This shows that there are a number of young people who are either avoiding sleep to use social networks or are experiencing interrupted sleep by using social networks. This will inevitably have a knock-on effect to the young person the next day, lack of sleep will negatively impact the educational functioning of these children and have the potential to cause difficulty concentrating, defiant or opposing behavior and increased appetite. This has the potential for far reaching issues, poor sleep over the long-term has been linked to putting people at risk of serious medical conditions, including obesity, heart disease and diabetes and ultimately shortening life expectancy. Sleep is vital.

I think there is an important distinction to be made here, if a message alert tone goes off on your phone in the middle of the night, it wakes you and you look at the message, then go back to sleep, you have technically used your social media sites. In addition, if you are awake at this time and are spending conscious time using the site, for example, uploading pictures and looking through profiles etc., you are also using social media sites. The difference between these two "uses" of social media are in the intention of the user. The user who is "alerted to a message and so checks" then returns to their planned activity, for example sleeping, and the user who is awake and consciously using social media, because that is what they want to be doing, it is their chosen activity. This question on the questionnaire was not fine-tuned enough to separate those differences, it merely highlights usage, not the type of usage, therefore the results here should be viewed with caution.

To what extent does social networking occupy the minds of secondary aged young people? Can they be considered behaviorally addicted?

As a reminder, this is where I adapted Dr. Young's internet addiction test to focus solely on social media. 1148 thirteen to sixteen-year olds completed the adapted test. This is what the results showed:

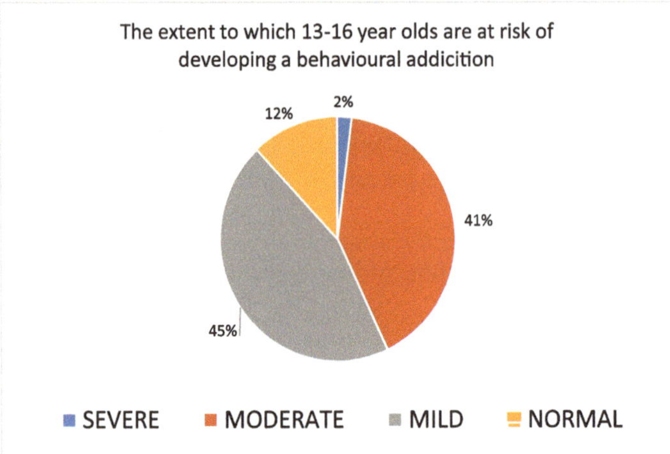

Percentage (%)	Result	Qualitative description
2	Severe	These individuals would be considered to be experiencing significant problems in their life because of their social media usage (occupies their minds to a severe extent) and would be candidates for consideration of a behavioral addiction.
41	Moderate	These individuals would be considered to be experiencing occasional or frequent problems because of their social media usage (occupies their minds to a moderate extent) and would be considered vulnerable to developing a behavioral addiction.
45	Mild	These individuals may use their social media a bit too long at times, but they have control over their usage (occupies their minds to a mild extent)
41	Normal	For these individuals, it is very rare for social media use to have any negative impact on their life (occupies their minds to a normal extent).

The above results capture the experience of the entire group. Now I'm going to split the results into males and females to highlight the slight variance in male and female experience.

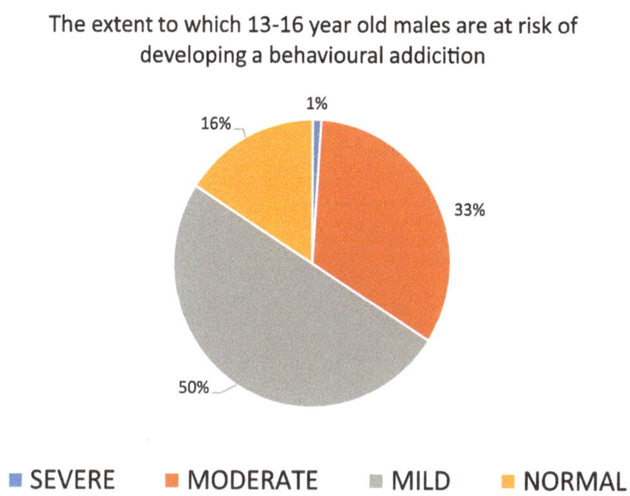

Male students aged between 13 and 16.

Percentage (%)	Result	Qualitative description
1	Severe	These individuals would be considered to be experiencing significant problems in their life because of their social media usage (occupies their minds to a severe extent) and would be candidates for consideration of a behavioral addiction.
33	Moderate	These individuals would be considered to be experiencing occasional or frequent problems because of their social media usage (occupies their minds to a moderate extent) and would be considered vulnerable to developing a behavioral addiction.
50	Mild	These individuals may use their social media a bit too long at times, but they have control over their usage (occupies their minds to a mild extent)
16	Normal	For these individuals, it is very rare for social media use to have any negative impact on their life (occupies their minds to a normal extent).

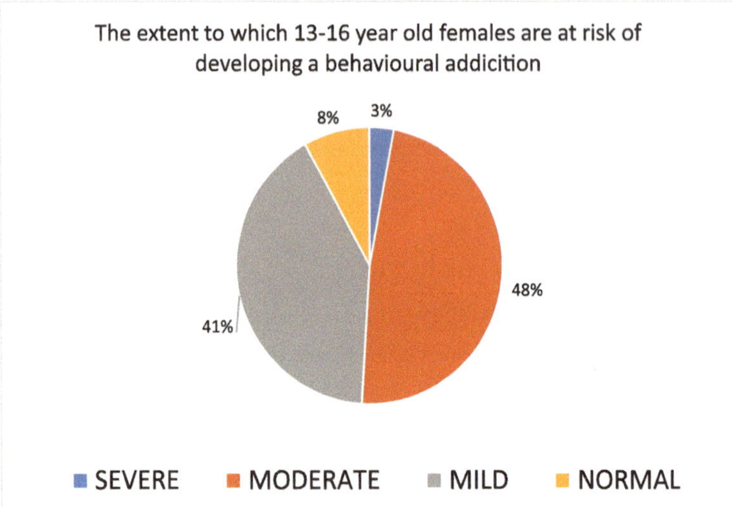

Female students aged between 13 and 16.

Percentage (%)	Result	Qualitative description
3	Severe	These individuals would be considered to be experiencing significant problems in their life because of their social media usage (occupies their minds to a severe extent) and would be candidates for consideration of a behavioral addiction.
48	Moderate	These individuals would be considered to be experiencing occasional or frequent problems because of their social media usage (occupies their minds to a moderate extent) and would be considered vulnerable to developing a behavioral addiction.
41	Mild	These individuals may use their social media a bit too long at times, but they have control over their usage (occupies their minds to a mild extent)
8	Normal	For these individuals, it is very rare for social media use to have any negative impact on their life (occupies their minds to a normal extent).

There were indeed gender differences across the school populations. The results indicated that 3% of female students are experiencing significant problems in their life because of their social media usage in comparison to 1% of male students. In addition, 48% of female students reported experiencing occasional or frequent problems because of online social networking, in comparison to 33% of male students. Possible explanations of this difference may be due to the inherent differences in social relationships for females and males. This position is concurrent with early research which highlights clear differences in the nature of interactions with friends between sexes. It is widely considered that teenage females seemingly show an emphasis on emotional sharing and talking; while teenage males reportedly emphasize activities and doing "things' together. It may be that female relationships between the ages of 13 and 16 are psychologically more intense than the equivalent for males. Therefore, the use and experience of social media during these friendships is also more intense.

The overall group results suggest that a large proportion of 13–16-year olds are experiencing difficulties while being members of social networks. The use of social media is having a fundamental impact for a large percentage of those that use it. The exact form and nature of how social media are occupying young people's minds would vary between cases, an in-depth exploration of individual questionnaire responses would give a more detailed profile of the impact for that person. These results show a broad overall experience of the impact of social media use for young people aged 13–16. Based on the factors that construct Young's (1998) Internet Addiction Scale, the difficulties fit across the following categories:

- Preoccupation with social media sites
- Feeling a need to use social media in increasing amounts
- Repeated unsuccessful attempts to control social media usage
- Moodiness if restricted from accessing their social media
- Using social media longer than intended
- Lying about or hiding the extent of social media use
- Using social media as a way of escaping from problems or to cope with negative mood
- Functional impairments or distress with respect to relationships

I was surprised by these results. In fact, my expectation was that the results would show lower percentages in the mild, moderate, and severe experience of social media use. Let me explain why. I narrowed the focus of Dr. Young's Internet Addiction Test to look at purely social media rather than wider internet use, yet maintained the original scoring framework. And despite doing so I found myself shocked with the potential number of students who would be candidates for having a behavioral addiction or at risk of developing one. You could therefore hypothesize that if the participants were to be retested and were completing questionnaires on full internet use, to include: social networking; catch-up TV; video/music streaming sites; online gambling; news; study; games and pornography (to name a few uses of the internet), then their scores would rise significantly.

What is clear to me is that the results highlight a distinctive cognitive impact of social media usage, further supporting the validity of Dr. Young's Internet Addition Test. Social media, as part of the internet is having a large impact on its users, some, whom are struggling significantly. There is a chance that social media usage may be the biggest contributor to the high scores of wider "Internet Addiction" if using purely Dr. Young's Internet Addiction Test. It would be interesting to see a sample of results of people being tested for "Internet Addiction" that did not include social media usage. Which brings us back to the fact that the wide uses of the internet need a more refined and tailored approach to measuring its impact on its users, that separate "the internet" into its contributing parts.

This above position is in line with a systematic review of the Internet Addiction literature by researchers Chang and Law in 2008, who identified four key facets common to most measurement and theoretical models of internet addiction: (a) impulsive use and excessive time spent on the Internet; (b) withdrawal symptoms when not online (e.g., moodiness, confrontations); (c) using the Internet for social comfort or mood regulation purposes; and (d) adverse consequences of Internet use (e.g., interpersonal, performance, health). If Internet addiction is indeed a multidimensional construct, then understanding the component parts and accurately measuring the impact on the individual, will help in understanding and treating any problematic behavior or areas of psychological distress experienced by internet users. It stands to reason that tools used to measure Internet Addiction should also reliably capture and reproduce this dimensionality of "the internet."

We need multiple assessment routes and tools to gather information, but only used when part of a wider assessment. I often find myself surprised when important decisions are made without speaking directly to people. It can't be ignored… the most valuable information is gained from hearing directly from people about what it is they are going through. It was, for me, transformative in my understanding of social media. More on that later. I want to leave behavioral addictions aside soon, but before I do, I want to show you some fascinating statistics from various items of the questionnaire that highlight the magnitude of social media in the lives of children:

> 25% of young people almost always spend longer on social networking sites than they originally planned
>
> 9% of young people prefer socialising online rather than in person
>
> 10% of young people think that life without social networking would be boring, empty and joyless
>
> 68% of young people have at some point tried to cut down the time they spend social networking but failed to do so
>
> 14% of young people almost always lose sleep because of social networking
>
> 73% of young people have at some point experienced losing sleep because of social networking

These statistics really drive home the reality of using social media and add a quantifiable edge to this book's earlier chapters. The experience of being held to social media, trying to cut down, failing to do so and loss of sleep. There is certainly a blurring line between "virtual" and "reality" and that there are clear "real-world" implications for use of the internet for social networking.

So far, this chapter has considered research into what social media young people are using, how they are accessing their social media and when they doing it—this is somewhat of a practical exploration of social networking. Then we continued to explore some of the psychological aspects of that social media use, the extent to which it occupies the minds of young people, risks of behavioral addiction and the behaviors that this might manifest. Now we're going to consider the impact that the practical and psychological experience of social networking may have on young people's school and home experience. This is based on the questionnaire responses to a number of "yes or no" questions.

Let's talk about school:

- 31% of young people have experienced something on social media that has made them not want to go into school the next day.
- 30% of young people have been worried in school, because of something that happened on social media.
- 10% of young people have taken time off school, because of something that happened on social media.

Firstly, there are positives in the above results, when considering their counterparts. There exist higher percentages of people that have not worried, not wanted to take time off or actually taken time off school because of social media usage. The balance here is in favor of a majority of young people not experiencing a negative impact in school because of social media use.

However, it would be an injustice to those individuals experiencing difficulty not to explore their situation further, as the reality of the above statistics highlight a concerning problem for schools in the UK. If you picture a secondary school having 1000 pupils (not uncommon in the UK), these results suggest that 100 pupils will have taken time off school because of something that has happened on social media. The results do not specify the exact amount of time that has been taken off. However, the impact that this absence from school has on the young people's education, and their emotional health and wellbeing, could be significant.

With 31% of young people not wanting to come into school, and 30% worrying while in school because of something that has happened on social media, it is likely that this also will have a dramatic effect on those individual's ability to access the academic material to their fullest capability, due to their current emotional state of mind. Essentially, how much are young people focusing on "schoolwork," in comparison to what's worrying them? There is an additional concern, regarding distractibility and attention to education, as 33% of young people access their social media during school hours.

The idea of distractibility and young people attuning to the education on offer should be an area of concern for schools, particularly when considering their pupil's use of social media. However, there is a flip side to this, that 70% of young people stated that use of social media has made their friendships stronger. In this example, social media is a positive force for social support and connection to one's peers. This adds to the balance of evidence showing the use of social media supporting some young people's experiences of school and their emotional health and wellbeing and thus being ready to learn.

When it comes to experiencing difficulties on social media sites, 65% of young people would comfortably speak to a member of staff at school about it. In addition, 68% of young people would comfortably speak to their parents about social media difficulties. What is not clear, is if these results represent the same people who would talk to both, and therefore, if it means that there is a group of around 30% who would not tell anybody. It is positive to see a high percentage of young people who would seek adult support but concerning that there is such a high percentage of those who would not. Perhaps, if there were specific routes for reporting social media difficulty in schools, then pupils would seek staff support more often, do they even know that they can seek help with it? And are teachers willing to hear about it? It is also not clear why young people would/would not seek support, understanding the "why" of this area is important in trying to respond to young people's needs regarding social media. Without a doubt having someone who is willing to listen will be the most important start to support.

When asked if their parents use social networking sites, 83% of participants responded that they do. This is an interesting dynamic between children and their parents, it is likely that some parents have a detailed understanding of social media sites. There may be a generation of parents who are in an informed position to understand the difficulties, and positives, that their children experience online. This idea that parents understand the world of social media leads to a positive position in being able to attune to, support and connect with their children via their networks. This could lead to common language use, and effective parental monitoring, which could in turn support the parent—child relationship. There is also a chance that the opposite could happen, in that the child could "learn" a lot about their parents via social media, which could lead to challenges regarding parenting their child. For example, it is somewhat hypocritical to tell a child that they should not be using social media, or not using it as much, if the parent is themselves a regular user… an example needs to be set.

I took all this data, all this information, and selected eight young people to talk with further. Four Males, four Females, all of whom were considered as to have a severe risk of becoming behaviorally addicted to their social media. The next few chapters of this book are going to introduce you to these individuals and delve deeper into the experiences that they have with social media.

CHAPTER 9

"Tell me more about that"

Psychologist's Guide to Adolescents and Social Media
https://doi.org/10.1016/B978-0-323-91898-5.00012-6

It is time to hear about the experiences of living with social media from the children directly affected by it. For reasons of geographic convenience, the interviews I conducted took place with students from a mainstream secondary school in Devon. These students had already taken part in completing the social media questionnaire I put together and were, following analysis, considered as being high risk of developing a behavioral addiction due to their social media use.

Year 10 students (14–15-year olds) were selected for interviewing. The highest scoring 4 Year 10 males and the highest scoring 4 Year 10 females were selected for an interview, which would allow me to gather a gender balanced participant group. The selected participants were then approached to begin discussions regarding if they would consider being interviewed by me about their social media use. They all agreed.

In psychology there are multiple different ways to conduct interviews, as well as multiple different avenues to take when considering an analysis of the gathered information. Before we dive into the interviews and what was uncovered, I'm going to take a brief detour to set the scene of the approach taken during the interview and the method of analysis used. Some people can find this kind of information difficult to digest, let's be honest, it's not the most fascinating of things to write about either. But I wanted to include it so that there was transparency to my work and the conclusions I made. Plus, it can give those who would like to conduct research themselves a path that has been trodden that they may also like to take, build upon, or trash and pave a new better way.

Semi-structured interviews

In order to elicit a rich and detailed account of the participants' experience of social media, I decided to use semi-structured interviews as a method of data collection. Semi-structured interviews allow for a level of consistency about ensuring the same area are covered in each interview but does not fix the interviewer to a set order of the questions. This allows the participant and interviewer to explore areas for discussion that arise based on the interviewee's experiences. Semi-structured interviews also allow for a comparison across participants, as the same areas were covered in the interviewing, leading to a more accurate analysis of differing and comparable viewpoints.

Interview design

There were 2 phases to the research I designed, linked by how the students completed the questionnaires—enabling selection for interview. The questionnaires gave a context to social networking use, the qualitative interviews allowed the questionnaires to be brought to life by the participant's dialogue surrounding their experiences. The interview questions were then, in many respects, an elaboration on the quantitative data provided by the students. These were designed to allow the participants to articulate and explore their thoughts and experiences with social media. Across the world, there is a lack of qualitative research surrounding young people's lived experience of social media. Therefore, the constructed interviews, linked and alongside the questionnaire, resulted in a robust data gathering process and a great design. Not that I'm blowing my own horn or anything, but it's true.

In order to generate a rich and detailed account of the students' lived experiences of social media, open ended questions were utilized alongside narrative questioning techniques. These allow people to tell stories about their experiences in their own way and from their own perspective. The open-ended questions allowed the students to express their experiences and views unencumbered by restrictive or limiting questions. This was designed to allow me to develop an understanding of the participant's experiences, at a person-centered level.

Interview schedule

This is what my original set up of questions looked like, alongside aid memoirs should certain paths be taken by the interviewees.:

1. Tell me about the social networking sites that you use?
   a. *Do you have a particular favorite?*
   b. *Why do you use social media?*
2. When did you start using social networking sites?
   a. *What was it like when you first started using social media?*
   b. *What is it like now using social media? Has anything changed?*
3. What are your thoughts about how much you use social media?
4. How would you feel if all of a sudden you were no longer able to use social media?
5. What do you think your parents think about you using social media?
   a. *No problem—do you think they should be concerned?*
   b. *Problem—can you give me an example of when they've shown they have an issue with you using social media?*
      i. *How do you handle your parents trying to tell you when/how to use social media?*
      ii. *How do you feel about your parents trying to control how you use social media?*
6. How do you think social media impacts what school is like for you?
   a. *Do social media interfere with schoolwork?...tell me about a time when this has happened*

   b. *Do social media interfere with homework?... tell me about a time when this has happened*
7. Would you tell me something about how you feel social media has influenced your relationships with your friends?
   a. *Has social media ever been the cause of any friendship fall-outs?...tell me about a time this has happened?*
8. You mentioned in your questionnaire that something had previously happened on social media that had:
   a. *Made you not want to go into school the next day*
   b. *That had resulted in you taking time off school*
   c. *Had made you worry in school*
      i. *Would you be willing to tell me about what happened?*
9. What do you think life would look like if social media no longer existed?
10. How often would you say social networking is on your mind during the day?
    a. *What is that like?*
11. What is the best thing that has ever happened to you while using social media?
    a. *Can you tell me a little more about that?*
12. What is the worst thing that has ever happened to you while using social media?
    a. *Can you tell me a little more about that?*
13. What advice would you give someone who had never used social media before and wanted to start?

These questions aren't perfect, and if I could do it all again, I would change them, adapt them. But that is the gift of research, you can build, adapt, and look again to be sure.

Qualitative analysis

In order to reach a deep level of understanding, my research took a phenomenological perspective, which explores how our experiences are informed by the contextual and personal meanings they hold for us. It sounds fancy, it's not really. Phenomenology is embedded in a philosophy that for understanding, it was necessary to examine the bedrock of everyday experience. It is in everyday experience—in our emotions, actions, perception of things and relationships, that true understanding can be gained. This is not an easy task, because for one it is using language to describe what is beyond language. There are just some feelings and connections so complex that words aren't a good enough medium to explain them. A regular criticism of phenomenology is that it is attempting the impossible—that what can be "known" is what can be "said".

There was chance that the people I would be speaking to would not be able to take such a meta-perspective on their own experience. Therefore, in order to reach an understanding of the participants lived experience of social networking, it would be my job to make interpretations on the participants' verbalizations of their experience.

Such a technique of analysis concentrates on mental experience rather than behavior. This is known as an Interpretative Phenomenological approach—probably the most widely known approach to phenomenological psychology used by psychologists in the UK today. Johnathan Smith and Mike Osborn are well known psychologists and researchers who have written textbooks on qualitative psychology. They describe that Interpretative Phenomenological Analysis (IPA) puts the participant and the researcher in a unique position - in a double hermeneutic:

> The participants are trying to make sense of their world; the researcher is trying to make sense of the participants trying to make sense of their world.

Within IPA, the researcher does not simply use tools, they are the tool. There are benefits and difficulties with using this approach, especially when considering that it is "interpretative". To make interpretations, requires the ability to analyze tacit knowledge, that which is implied but not spoken. On top of this, as an integral part of the process of analysis, there may be biases to what is being looked for within transcriptions, even down to the questions being asked. I had to be careful that I wasn't guiding the participants down conversational alleyways that I wanted to go down beyond my research questions.

There are criticisms surrounding qualitative approaches in general. For example, for this part of my research I had 8 participants... some would therefore argue that I would lose the ability to generalize the results to the larger population. However, the more controlled an experiment, the more the findings are limited to their context. Therefore, a balance must be drawn between generalizability and practical relevance. Qualitative study is a lengthy process, yet if this time is taken to focus on individual accounts, arguably eventually there will be an element of the generalizability of knowledge claims—doing research in this field is like adding a small puzzle piece to a massive puzzle. Eventually, we'll get to the full picture, it just takes time. I always seem to forget how long it takes to transcribe interviews word for word. But I do believe that it is the best way to start the process of analysis, doing it yourself, you hear things that you would miss if you paid a transcription service to do it for you.

I came to select IPA as my research method because of the underlying assumption that the words used by participants, when exploring their experience of social networking, give an understanding of the phenomenon of social media itself. In doing so, I become immersed in the research process as the tool for interpretation and the final analysis can be seen as an amalgamation of the participant's exploration and the researcher's engagement and interpretation with the data. The data in this case were recorded and transcribed interviews.

The process of interpretative phenomenological analysis (IPA)

Following the stages outlined in Jonathan Smith and Mike Osborn's textbook on conducting this type of research, I engaged in a 6-step process:

(1) Reading and re-reading the transcripts from interviews/achieving immersion in the data.
(2) Initial noting of my interpretations
(3) Developing emergent themes regarding what was said and my interpretations
(4) Searching for connections across those emergent themes.
(5) Moving on to the next case.
(6) Looking for patterns across cases—the generation of superordinate themes—what appeared across the experience of all participants?

Results

A number of superordinate themes (group themes) and emergent themes were gathered from the interview analysis that took place. I will guide you through each of these themes along with verbatim extracts from the young people who gave up their time for me. All the names have been changed to protect the identity of the participants. You are about to be introduced to Jack, Jenny, Lacy, Mark, Brendan, David, Emma, and Imogen. If you have concerns about a young person's social media use, then you may recognize some of the experiences that these 8 young people are about to share. My commentary and analysis from an IPA framework may help you to better understand their experiences.

CHAPTER

10

Connection to others: Social connection, relationship maintenance, the monitoring of others

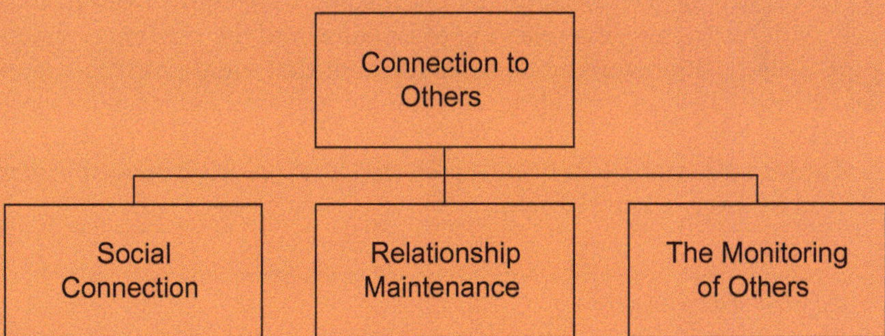

https://doi.org/10.1016/B978-0-323-91898-5.00002-3

All 8 young people noted the use of social networking sites and apps for the purpose of experiencing a connection to others. From this superordinate theme, the following emergent themes presented themselves: Social Connection, Relationship Maintenance and The Monitoring of Others.

Social connection

The experience of socially connecting to others was felt by all participants. The concept of using social media, to connect socially with others, is well established in the field of social media research. The use of social media to socially connect to others was experienced by all. However, these experiences vary in a subjective way as to the participant's experience of that connection. A particular experience of social connection was commented on by Mark who stated:

> It's the only way to communicate with people, like I would go on and I would message my mates and be like 'I'm stuck can you help me out' and they would.

Interestingly, Mark seemingly forsakes all other forms of communication with this comment, thus highlighting the importance social media has for him, without it he would be isolated from his friends. In the example he gives, Mark is seeking support from his friends, and receiving it. So not only does Mark use social networking for socially connecting with his friends, but through the seeking and receiving of support. For Mark, social connection via social media encapsulates the "only" way to connect with his friends, the relieving of isolation and the receiving of support. This position supports earlier research that highlights the use of instant messages as providing an intimate and private space to share worries.

The idea of social media being a preferred form of social connection was echoed by Lacy, when she said:

> Umm just like, to get hold of someone I would go through social networking to do it, I'm not too sure, I just use it.

The idea of being able "to get hold of someone," reverberated throughout the group's response to why they used social media. Lacy highlights the use of social media as a key resource in connecting socially to another, but with a sense of it being akin to a physical contact if you consider her use of language. Therefore, social media contact may produce a similar psychological response as physical contact does.

The social connection for some moved beyond their geographical location to wider destinations, this was highlighted when I was speaking with Jack:

Dr C: *"Why do you use social media?"*
Jack: *"It's mainly down to my friends who moved away, so I'll talk to them over the Xbox and things like that. One of my best friends moved to Manchester."*
Dr C: *"So other than the Xbox and Facebook, do you have any other social networks that you use?"*
Jack: *"Yeah, I've got 'steam' on my computer"*
Dr C: *"When did you start using social networking sites?"*
Jack: *"I think it was when I was 8 or 9"*

For Jack, social media has allowed him to connect to one of his best friends, whom he may have lost touch with without social media to support the relationship. Jack started using social media when he was still in primary school, and the use of social networking here may have helped Jack deal with the physical loss of a best friend. However, Jack does not consider it a loss, his language highlights a presence, he did not describe how he "used" to have a best friend, but they moved away. Jack's friends may have moved away, but he remains socially connected to them. The feelings of being socially connected seem to traverse locality for Jack, and indeed for Jenny who described a developing friendship over distance:

Dr C: *"What is the best thing that has ever happened to you while using social media?"*
Jenny: *"Umm I met a friend that lives in America on there that I skype a lot now and talk to."*
Dr C: *"How did you meet that person?"*
Jenny: *"On Instagram, he started following me and then messaged me."*

Jenny experiences an international social connection here, which she uses "a lot." Interestingly with Jenny you get the sense that for her that social media is a destination in itself, she met someone "on there," as if "there" is a place. Perhaps, then social media sites are becoming more like a place to hang out and meet people, replacing the streets of your neighborhood, with the internet connected world. If we follow this line of thought through, then this is also allowing people to be more selective about who they socially connect with, there are no limitations to whom you can "meet" online. The concept of meeting someone is no longer isolated to a physical presence, but I am left wondering about the "quality" of such a meeting, and indeed the risks, and if what is "present" in person can ever be replicated online?

From the distant social connections to the more practical and local ones, social media seems to be used for both. David highlights a use of social media to facilitate a face to face social connection:

> Some of my friends, just getting hold of them has helped me meet them a lot more easier than trying to find them, using Facebook has helped me a lot in finding my friends.

Here, David shows an elaboration of Lacy's previous sentiment, to "get hold" of another. However, in this case David is using social media to locate and then physically connect socially with his friends. David described in his interview, a failure in previous attempts to find his friends. Yet, with the use of social media he has been able to succeed in finding them. Social media have facilitated in transforming something that was hard, into something that is "a lot more easier." David experiences social networking as the catalyst to overcoming difficulty. The idea of connection being made easier via social media is only true if those with whom you're close to, are also members of the same social networking sites. If all your friends are a part of a site, and you are not then, then you become disconnected from an aspect of that social connection. This was particularly evident for Imogen, when she was considering her use of social media sites:

Dr C: *"Do you have a favorite social network?"*

Imogen: *"I think Facebook is one of my favorites, because I've got all of my friends on there and know what everyone is doing, umm and then Instagram and snapchat…mmm…I can get Facebook on my laptop but Instagram and snapchat are the main ones that I really want to have, so yeah I quite like those."*

Dr C: *"Why do you use social media?"*

Imogen: *"I don't know, because everyone does don't they? So, you don't want to be the odd one out, and then everyone's talking about something and you don't have a clue because you don't have it."*

Dr C: *"So it's useful to stay in the loop?"*

Imogen: *"It's a way of staying in the loop when you're not face to face, with someone."*

Dr C: *"When did you start using social networking sites?"*

Imogen: *"Umm maybe since I was 12/13, I wasn't allowed in primary school, I wasn't really allowed to in secondary school…"*

Dr C: *"Did you do it in secret?"*

Imogen: *"Yeah, but then, obviously people talk, people find out and then my mum was like 'I want you to delete it', and my little sister did as well, but she's kind of become immune to it now, so, she doesn't mind now."*

There seems to be an element of pressure in Imogen's account, a level of social conformity to fit in with her friends for fear of not fitting in. For Imogen, the pressure was enough to go against the rules set by her mum. The idea that if she was not a part of the online social world then she would be without information, that she would be left out. The fear here for Imogen relates to remaining socially connected to her peers, to be able to socially connect and remain on "the same page" as her friends for fear of missing out.

This all firmly supports the concept of the internet becoming a principal venue for social interaction for teenagers and that social media is being used in an attempt to "connect" socially with others. What is becoming clearer is the differing complexities of social connection online—the importance of isolation reduction; receiving of support; the management of distance; social inclusion and social conformity. This is indeed one of the greatest fears expressed to me by parents I talk to about social media "if I don't let them have it, they will end up being left out, I don't want that for my child".

The idea of remaining socially connected leads into the next emergent theme under the banner of "connection to others"—which is the theme of relationship maintenance.

Relationship maintenance

The experience of relationship maintenance was evident for all the young people I spoke to. In highlighting the variance of the use of social media for relationship maintenance, a deeper understanding of how relationships are maintained, or not, becomes apparent. Brendan expressed his experience of using social media and relationship maintenance when he stated:

> I've fallen out, with not many people, but that has been online, I'll realise 'they're not my friend, so I'm not going to talk to you'. But there's a few people that I've like become closer to because of it, like I know more about them now, I talk to them.

Here we notice Brendan having some turbulence in a friendship over social media, to the extent that he comes to the realization that they are not his friend anymore. This realization leads to Brendan not talking to that person any longer. Communication, for Brendan, is a fundamental aspect of friendship, and to remove communication, is to remove the friendship. Brendan continues and highlights that through using social media he has become closer to other friends, that he "knows more about them." This may suggest that Brendan is using social media to maintain and develop deeper bonds with certain people, either through talking, or even though access to their information on their chosen networks. For example, he may browse the personal information someone has shared detailing their likes and interests etc. For Brendan, knowing more about someone is likely to mean becoming closer to them emotionally.

This idea of gaining some deeper friendships and the diminishing of others was also experienced by Jenny:

Dr C: *"Would you tell me something about how you feel social media has influenced your relationships with you friends?"*

Jenny: *"It's made me lose some and gain some, I guess because you get a couple of people that message you that don't live around here, and you sort of just talk to them and you get friends that make you fall out over them."*

Dr C: *"Would you be able to tell me a little more about the friends that make you fall out?"*

Jenny: *"Umm I don't know, there could be something like they would make a group chat about you and you would find out and that can make you fall out over Facebook."*

The above excerpt from Jenny's interview highlights a form of jealousy expressed over social media. Her friends do not like the fact that she is connecting with other people, perhaps strengthening her bond with them, and thus feel threatened about their position as her "friend," which starts an issue that leads to a "fall out." In this situation, a strengthening or weakening of the relationship will ensue. There is a level of detachment evident for Jenny—"it's made me"—as if she is not responsible for what happens online, absolved of responsibility. Emma uses social media in a different way with regard to friendship maintenance, this was expressed clearly when she said:

> Umm, now you can, on Facebook, you can add people to the top of your lists, so you can see their posts before anyone else's.

In the above example, Emma is electronically ranking and positioning her friends by level of importance to her. Emma is selectively choosing who she wants to know better, know more about and what she wishes to see. There is a second level to this, as the posts by people with whom she selects, will appear first "before anybody else's." This type of relationship maintenance and selecting of important friends allows Emma to show people how much she likes them. By "following" someone online she is letting them know that she values them, that she's interested, that she cares and that they are an important part of her life, quite the compliment and an efficient way to maintain friendships through social media.

The above example for Emma highlights a tangible piece of evidence of her friendship with others, especially if the arranging of a "top list" is reciprocal in her friendships. A further example of where social media provides evidence of friendship was stated by Lacy:

> I'm not too sure, like umm, like when I'm with my friends we take a lot of videos of each other and photos, and we're all like laughing and stuff, and when I look through like after I've been with them, and of me with them and it's all laughing and stuff, it's just nice to see you've got good friends and stuff.

What a great example, it shows on a personal level the use of pictures as a form a reminiscing about enjoyable times and having good friends. Additionally, the sharing of these pictures online means she's sharing with the world that she has friends, that she is sociable, and they enjoy each other's company. It is a bold statement about the social connections she has, for the world (or at a minimum those she is connected with online) to see. In this example the pictures are used to maintain an ongoing relationship with friends, or after time, to look back and reinforce said friendship—if only social media was used more like this.

Emma gave the example of socially meeting up with friends in person, and then evidencing that friendship online. Therefore, using social media to help maintain that friendship when not in face to face contact. This concept is also evident in research we explored earlier on in this book which identified the use of social media to maintain and strengthen already established "offline" social networks. There's more flavor to add to that now, because we can see the use of social media to strengthen friendships externally, by the use of "evidence" of friendships being posted online, but also internally, by using social media as a digital photo/experience album to reminisce about time spend with friends. One of my personal favorite features of Facebook is when it shows you "8 years ago today" and I can take a moment to reminisce... often, prompting me to contact friends I haven't for some time to re-connect.

There is another example of friendship maintenance via social media that does not involve meeting face to face, which was provided by Jack:

Dr C: *"Would you tell me something about how you feel social media has influenced your relationships with you friends?"*

Jack: *"It's probably helped because when we're playing online we can still actually do stuff together, even when I'm not actually there, because some of my friends do live quite far away, so if I didn't have social networks then I couldn't talk to them, and we'd probably just lose contact."*

Here Jack provides a useful insight into social networking via online gaming—the idea that connecting over online gaming leads to a deeper connection to those friends. This connection is more valuable to Jack, than textual or picture based online networking. Therefore, Jack is using online gaming to "do something" with his friends, there is a story, an event, the virtual spending of time together, focused on completing an activity, or engaging in a story. This helps Jack maintain his friendships despite him not being physically present in their lives.

Social networking via gaming, gives a narrative and activity hitherto not present with traditional social media and allows for a much richer experience. With online gaming you can become more than yourself, you can virtually save your friends' life, defeat enemies together, or even battle against one another. This allows for a rich tapestry of experiences that Jack would not be able to engage in during his "normal" life offline. Perhaps, this level of engagement is enough to maintain the friendships that do not happen face to face. Online gaming can be a useful resource in maintaining relationships hindered by distance and face to face contact. There is one thing clear, if Jack did not connect with and maintain these friendships over online gaming, he feels he would likely lose contact with his friends, risking feelings of isolation. The comradery that develops playing online games with a group of friends should not be underestimated, these online stories often traverse into real world conversations about time spent together—"do you remember that motorcycle heist mission where we were all trying to get to the helicopter and..."—Joint activities, memories made and friendships strengthened, all through the medium of digital online gaming. It is powerful stuff.

The next emergent theme that became apparent following the 8 interviews was the use of social media for the monitoring of others.

The monitoring of others

As the analysis of the transcripts began, a sense of using social media sites to monitor others emerged as a distinctive theme for all participants in one way or another. Anecdotally, the idea of using social media to monitor others seems commonplace in society, the phrase "Facebook stalking" didn't just appear out of nowhere, it fits as a way to describe a seemingly commonplace behavior that was developed over time. However, there is very little research into the use of social networks to monitor others, and where there is reference to it, it is usually in the context of criminal usage. The use of social media to monitor others was particularly evident for Imogen:

Dr C: *"Tell me about the social media sites that you use?"*

Imogen: *"Umm, Facebook, Instagram, snapchat, I don't really use twitter but I have it, but it bugs me, umm, I think that's it."*

Dr C: *"What bugs you about twitter?"*

Imogen: *"Just pointless tweets about people just having random rants that no-one's ever going to see, I don't know, I just don't like it. My sister is addicted to it, all the time, just random tweets, she tweets about me, and I'm like what? That's the only reason I have it, just to see what she's writing."*

Imogen is referring to the use of social media site Twitter, for those readers who don't know, if someone is posting messages through twitter you are making "tweets." Imogen refers to her sister as "addicted" to social networking, revisiting the concepts of what we have explored in Chapter 6—a sense of social media being a substance or an activity that can be pleasurable, but with continued use becomes compulsive and interferes with daily life.

Imogen's primary reason for using Twitter is to monitor her sister's posts, particularly about her. There is a sense of shock and betrayal that her sister would be writing about her online, and a need to monitor such behavior so that she can be fully aware of what information is "out there" about her. Therefore, Imogen's use of Twitter is a defense mechanism against the behavior of her sister, and in having an account she is letting her sister know, that she knows, what her sister is writing. Doesn't this convey the sense of social media being a dangerous place to be? That there are risks and responsibilities in its use, and that perhaps in using it you are arming yourself with information to protect yourself if needed. People may end up having social media accounts just to be socially aware of their surroundings.

Another form of the monitoring of others emerged with Jenny, Lacy and David's experience of social networking. This is evident in the following excerpts from their interviews:

Jenny: *"To talk to friends, to see what people are doing"*
Lacy: *"To talk to my friends, to know what people are up to and stuff, just talking to people and stuff, knowing what they're doing"*
David: *"So I can get hold of my friends quite easily and just see what's going on"*

The commonalities in the above quotations lie within the monitoring of others. Jenny, Lacy and David are using social networking to "See" and "Know" what people are doing and "what's going on." Social media is allowing a connection to others without the need to directly contact others. It is allowing a monitoring of a social group, or individuals, for the purpose of staying informed on all aspects of one's friendship or social group. In using social media sites to monitor others, you also become aware of the sense of being monitored yourselves. Therefore, you could hypothesize that people are very selective with what they choose to post online, because of the "audience." This concept of there being an "audience" online was captured well by Imogen:

Dr C: *"What do you think life would be like for you if Social media no longer existed?"*
Imogen: *"I think it would be quite hard, it would be like being back in primary school, where you would have to ring on the landline, and get their number and stuff, it would be quite difficult, but I think*

there wouldn't be this negative... you know, nothing would get ramped up, you know, it would stay in school, so it wouldn't be on social media, no one could 'screen-shot' it, no-one would know exactly what you have said or other people have said. I think it would be better in a way..."

Dr C: *"You'd get a break from it... does that kind of thing, screenshotting and shared with a large group of people, is that quite common?"*

Imogen: *"Yeah, all the time. That's why you have to be really careful what you say, to a certain person, because nothing is private anymore."*

For Imogen, the realization of the loss of privacy online is a constant presence, impacting what would normally be an easy conversation into having to be "really careful." This realization highlights that once something is written online, it can be read, re-read, passed on, and to some degree represents you as a person, a digital footprint. In joining a social media site, you are putting yourself on show to others. Imogen catastrophizes to some extent—"nothing is private anymore"—as if her privacy has been lost that she used to cherish in her past. There is a sense of the hidden now being out in the world for all to see, and although difficult, I feel that Imogen misses the times before social media, that friendships used to be more positive without it.

Previous research that highlighted the use of instant messaging as providing adolescents with an intimate and private space to share worries, is perhaps not entirely accurate. Privacy online, or the concept of a private space, is no longer experienced in a complete sense of it. Young people remain at risk, of whatever they post online, being shared with the masses. This risk is something that seems to be an ever-present aspect of online social media use.

A further experience of the monitoring others was described by Jack when he stated:

> Yeah, when like I've run out of things to play, I'll just watch people on that.

Jack's comment was in reference to online social gaming. In his watching of others playing online, or in watching videos of gameplay that have been uploaded, Jack is aiming to improve his skills and abilities by the monitoring of others. Jack is taking what he has learned and employs it in his use of online social gaming. For Jack, social media is allowing enjoyment of gaming and the improvement of himself, as he learns from others when he spends time watching "how they do it." Perhaps, this self-improvement allows Jack to raise his social standing in his online community, alongside his self-efficacy and self-esteem when he is successful or shows he has the knowledge needed to solve something difficult.

The idea of there being a connection between social media and a change in one's self leads us on to the next superordinate theme for the group, one well established in research surrounding social media, that of Identity and Construction of the Self.

CHAPTER

11

Identity and construction of the self: Change over time; A part of you; The role of parent

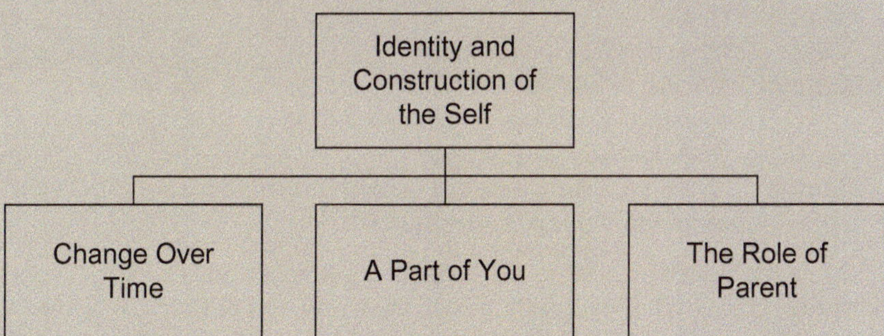

https://doi.org/10.1016/B978-0-323-91898-5.00015-1

All of the young people interviewed experienced the use of social media with regard to their Identity and Construction of the Self, concurrent with previous research in the field. From this superordinate theme the following emergent themes presented themselves: Change over Time, A Part of You and The Role of Parent.

Change over time

The experience of there being a change over time with social media use, was present for 7 out of the 8 participants, with the exception being David, who was relatively new to social media. This idea, of the changing use of social media at different stages of life, is not yet represented in previous literature. Therefore, may be a relatively unexplored area of social media research. Jenny reflected on what social networking was like when she first started using it, in comparison to what she experiences now:

Dr C: *"What was it like, when you first started using social media?"*
Jenny: *"Umm, it was alright, it was just talking to friends and putting pictures up and that, it was alright."*
Dr C: *"What is it like now using social media? Has anything changed?"*
Jenny: *"It's worse, umm people can message you and start arguments and post horrible things and that."*
Dr C: *"Does that kind of thing happen?"*
Jenny: *"Not to me, but the arguments do, but yeah that's it."*
Dr C: *"Do you see quite a lot of arguments happening online?"*
Jenny: *"Yeah."*
Dr C: *"How do they usually start?"*
Jenny: *"Uh people will fall out and they will message you to start an argument, sometimes to start one with you or to pull you into one."*
Dr C: *"Has that happened recently?"*
Jenny: *"Yeah, I fell out with a girl called Vicky and then she started an argument on me and all my friends."*

Note the use of past tense for Jenny at the start of this excerpt, "it was alright," immediately suggesting that presently, it's not alright. There is a sense of innocence in what social networking used to be like, an innocence that has been lost by the exposure to "arguments" and "horrible things." However, arguments and horrible things have always existed, people have always had the capacity to send horrible things. This could be a reflection on how people have changed over time. Perhaps then, in growing up, the use of social media has changed over time with the change in the development of its users. This position was echoed by Imogen:

Dr C: *"What was it like when you first started using social media?"*
Imogen: *"I didn't really have many friends on Facebook at the time, so it wasn't as crazy as it now but, I don't know, quite weird, because obviously I'd never experienced anything like that before, like, knowing where everything is, it's a bit confusing at the start."*
Dr C: *"What is it like now using social media? Has anything changed?"*
Imogen: *"The sort of stuff that you see now is completely different to what you saw like 2 or 3 years ago. (sigh) it's like everyone's always having a go at each other, it's not a nice thing anymore. Before, everyone was like in year 7, you were putting photos of your friends up and where you went, and now everyone is posting rants and you know, like, just being really horrible, people are always 'calling each other out' and I just see these statuses and people are being horrible..."*

Imogen describes a complete shift in social media use, she sighed when considering it, perhaps reminiscing to when friendship was simpler, and when social networking was "a nice thing." Much like Jenny's account, Imogen highlights a shift in social media use. With this shift, the tool of social media changes its function, from celebrating friendship, to challenging others and expressing one's voice (posting rants). A similar experience was described by Emma when she commented:

> Now you can add people in a group and other people won't know. It just different, like now there's all these new meanings for things, where in year 7, when you say it you just mean it. And it's not sarcastic or anything because you're just like an innocent year 7.

Here Emma is describing a shift in uses of social media to include, and by the very nature of including someone...excluding someone else. In describing "new meanings for things," now that she's older, she eludes to sarcasm, complexity and subtlety of what people "say" online. Emma's experience suggests an innocence and honesty of being younger, something which now she may have lost. Over time Emma's use of social media has changed from innocent and honest to more complex and interpretable on multiple levels. It seems, that as relationships change with the developing child, the uses of social media shifts alongside. This change was captured well by Lacy:

> ... like now everyone is about pouting and trying to get the best lighting, it's like, back then you'd pull the weirdest poses and put like effects on them and stuff, it's really embarrassing. There's this thing going around not that long ago where you nominate someone to put their first profile pic up again, and it was really

> embarrassing. Now people are trying to get the best photo, and lighting, and 'likes' and stuff.

Lacy's reflections show the adaptation of social media use to display your best self, the pouting, the perfect lighting, all in an attempt to shape and construct the "you" that you want others to see. This is in stark contrast to Lacy's earlier uses of social media, to the extent that to look back at what she used to look like, to what she used to post online, as embarrassing. The nature of earlier pictures may come into conflict with Lacy's current "self," that she is trying to portray online. Lacy highlights the use of pictures to express a sexuality, a value in beauty, and showing others such value. If we were in the animal kingdom this would be the "displays" put on to ascertain ranking/importance within a group and attract a mate—a display of dominance and what is seen as widely socially desirable.

What Lacy is describing above is the use of social media to construct an ideal version of one's self, at a particular time. The first chapter of this book explored how the self is relative, it is a social construct and thus we define ourselves in part by using others as a benchmark. Therefore, there are links here to the previous emergent themes of social connection, as Lacy's social connections will have an impact on her self-image and vice versa. When we think about identity evolving over time, so to, does the use of social media to represent such changes. I remember hearing it described that "user profiles" on Facebook are a stage to make presentations of your "self," to follow this metaphor through, I would say that the stage stays the same, but the show changes regularly.

Mark comments on a different change in his self over time:

> A lot of people nowadays can't cope without a phone for a couple of minutes, and there's other people who can cope without a phone for like half a year, and that used to be me.

Mark has noticed a change in his ability to cope without access to social media sites via his phone. The sense for Mark would be that he needs his phone, like "a lot of people," in order to cope. He reflects about how he "used to be," perhaps, that he used to be stronger without social media and now has a reliance on it in order to function. Mark describes a further example of change over time when he mentions:

> You just know what to do, you know where everything is, each icon and that, what they mean, and so 'just there you go' pretty easy.

This elicits a familiarity with social media, perhaps like a well learned instrument or your local town, you know where everything is and what it does, and there is comfort and ease in that familiarity. However, this familiarity can take another form over time, as discussed by Emma:

> It was fun, it was like really exciting, just the build-up of when you're a child, you suddenly felt so grown up getting to use it, but now it's just boring.

For Emma, there was a long anticipation of using social media, a coming of age tale where she was suddenly allowed to use it, a transition from being a child to feeling "grown up." However, now the excitement has worn thin, "it's just boring." For Emma, the use of social media has moved from the novel to the mundane, perhaps more like a routine than an event in itself, it has become a normal part of her life. This leads on to the next emergent theme of social media use for the interviewees, a sense of it becoming a part of you.

A part of you

The theme of social media as being "a part of you" developed across the interviews for all participants. For some, it was in response to the following question; what would life be like for you if you suddenly you could no longer use social networking sites? For others, it seemed to develop just in conversation around their use of social media. Jenny expressed what she thought life would be like is she could not use media anymore:

> I dunno, I wouldn't be able to do anything, like, message my friends to meet them, so without it, I don't know what I'd do. I would be devastated.

For Jenny, a sense of being unable to do anything emerges, a breaking down, coming to a standstill, in a sense that she uses it to keep going, to move forward. For Jenny, the removal of social media would remove her ability to function, with her experiencing a sense of helplessness—"I wouldn't know what do to" and the emotion of feeling devastated. Losing the ability to use social media would be an akin to an emotional bereavement for her. This was also the case for Mark:

> It would be terrible, uh, cor, it would be literally manic, I don't think anyone would live, it is such a helpful resource in a way... It would bother me quite massively.

With Mark's experience, another picture of life without social networking emerges, highlighting how much a part of him it is. His language use clearly sets the scene of fear, as if losing a piece of him, and the idea that in losing social media, you would be losing life. For Mark, social networking is tied to his ability to live. A further example of social media being tied to life was expressed by David, when he stated:

> I spent quite a lot of time on their, to be fair, yeah, it's basically my heart.

For David, social media is directly compared to the most important organ of the body, the heart. To follow this line of interpretation through would see social media as a life source for David, it keeps him going, fuels his muscles, responds to his needs and metaphorically is the location of emotion (love). The heart is also constant, with a natural rhythm, this continuality was expressed by Lacy when she commented:

> I use it all the time, like I'll go home and I'll go on it, but the first thing I do when I wake up is go on it, and when I'm doing my homework I'll go on it, it's just all the time.

For Lacy, we find social media as a continual process, seemingly a part of her everyday life and experience. Checking her social media is the first thing Lacy will do when she wakes up, so arguably the first thing on her mind, even while she is "doing" other things she'll still be using social media. For Lacy, the lines between using social media and not using social media are blurred. Lacy is a part of a continual process of being connected to her networks. There is a merging of the technology-based connection to others and her "self." This concept adds to previous explorations suggesting that online and offline worlds are psychologically connected. Imogen reflects on a time where her use of social media was taken away for a short period of time:

> It feels so weird, because you've all of a sudden gone from… it's almost boring, because you've almost got nothing to do but your school work, and then you can't check anything, it's like a habit, a routine, at the times I check it, when I'm on it, when I'm at work, when I'm on my way to school, it's just so weird, it's like your routine is just changed, and it's weird.

Imogen is struggling to describe the exact feeling of being without her social media, a "weirdness," as if something is not quite right for her, like something is missing. Imogen's routines are changed, and she is somewhat muted and dulled, as if an excitement and enjoyment is no longer available to her. Perhaps then, the use of social media for Imogen transforms her into a better version of herself. Emma describes how the experience of social media continues even when she is not using her networks:

Dr C: *"How often would you say social networking is on your mind during the day?"*

Emma: *"Umm well it sort of depends, but quite a lot of the time I'll be thinking about it, like what someone's said or done recently, and be like thinking, why? And it's funny though sometimes. But other times there's just really serious things, like one of them was one where quite a lot of people shared it and it was where this person had* *died cause he had his phone in his hand in the car, and his head was in the back seat, cause he was driving using his phone, I remember that quite a lot."*

Dr C: *"That's quite a shocking thing to see online and then remember, does that pop up in your mind quite a lot?"*

Emma: *"Not all the time but sometimes."*

Emma seemingly carries her experiences online in her thoughts during the day, a plethora of experiences, emotions, and questions. But alongside those, a more concerning experience, one harder to move beyond, the witnessing and recalling of something traumatic. Emma cannot "un-see" what she has seen, it is now a part of her thoughts and has gone some way to shape her current experiences of social media.

A position of placing social media in such high importance was reflected on by Brendan, when thinking about what advice he'd give to someone who had never used social media before and was going to start. His advice was to only use a few:

> Because it's just too full on, your life becomes dedicated to them, you become very dependent on it, and forget to talk to people face to face, you're always just texting or snapchatting or whatever.

This is a cautionary tale from Brendan, expressing the dangers of allowing social media to become a part of you, and in essence, replace your natural communication ability. This fear of becoming dedicated, and dependent on technology to communicate, seems to be something that Brendan holds close, drawing a balance to what he sees as the "right" way to be.

Research has already shown that social media is used for expressing one's "self," but for certain users, in regular connection to others via social media, those networks seem to become a part of the self. It's not difficult to see how this can occur if you consider the amount of time people are spending with this technology.

An interesting avenue of discussion emerged with Lacy, in regard to the use of "likes" on the social media site Facebook. If you are not familiar with Facebook, this is a function to which you can "like" someone's status, comments, pictures etc. by a click of a button, which then tally's the "likes" alongside a list of the people who also "like" the post online. Lacy described:

> Yeah, especially like, I don't know, like one of my friends she's in the popular group, and she's always had loads and loads of likes but it's never bothered her, but she must secretly like it, but my umm, other friend she umm, a lot of people find her a bit weird, but when she got 100 likes she was going mad, umm, she obviously cares a lot.

Here Lacy explores her friendships online and the experience of receiving "likes." A hierarchy of popularity is mentioned, suggesting that receiving "loads and loads" of likes is linked to one's popularity with others. In addition, there may be some secrecy in enjoying it, because it would not be "cool" to be overly excited about it, which could inadvertently decrease one's popularity. A contrast is given to another of her friends, who "was going mad" when she reached a certain number of likes. In this situation "likes" seem to correlate to one's feeling of acceptance, and links to one's sense of self-esteem. In further exploration of this Lacy confirmed that she thinks:

> It makes them feel good about themselves, that people like them, but just because they 'like' it doesn't mean they like you as a person. I've liked people's pictures that I don't like.

Interestingly, "likes" are being used by Lacy with people that she doesn't actually like in "real life." Thinking more analytically about her reasons behind such behavior online Lacy reflected:

> I don't know, just because I've liked it, probably because, people just... just I guess I have liked them just to be neutral with them, so they know that I don't hate them or something.

For Lacy, the use of the "like" function on social networking sites is used as a form of social capital. She lets people know that "she doesn't hate them," this is likely to impact the offline environment Lacy lives in. She is surrounded by people that she's not "friends" with, but they know that she "likes" them and their posts. Lacy is consciously constructing the social environment in which she operates. It seems that for Lacy and perhaps others online, that even in not communicating with people, something is being communicated. Lacy can "like" some things, it will be seen online, and if Lacy does not "like" something, that is also seen, with purposeful and perhaps unintended consequences on one's social relationships and environment.

This paints a complex and multifaceted nature around exactly what is "communicated" to others online, as to "not communicate" something online can indeed send a message which is received a certain way. The functions of social networks are being used by people, intentionally, and unintentionally, to carve and mold their social landscape. A lot can be communicated at the click or not click of a button.

Throughout the interviewing, and in light of the group's age, the role of the parent began to emerge as a distinctive theme with regard to the participants' use of social media.

The role of parent

Parents hold an important role in the developing identity of their children and in allowing access to technology. This is a relatively new branch of research—concerned with how parents interact with their children using technology and the resulting implications for their relationships. The "role of parent" theme was evident for all participants. In particular, there were multiple experiences of the parent setting the boundaries to social media use, as shown in the section of transcript below, taken from the interview with Emma:

Emma: *"I'll be on Facebook until like 10:00pm and she'll come upstairs, and she'll take my phone away and say I'm using it too much."*
Dr C: *"If your mum didn't come and do that, would it keep you up?"*
Emma: *"I'd just carry on"*

In this example, Emma experiences her mother removing her connection to others, so that she can sleep. For Emma, this is both a positive and a negative. It is good as it allows her rest, however if her mum did not remove her "connection" then she would carry on. This is perhaps what she would ideally like to do. The parent here is making an executive decision for the wellbeing of her daughter. However, Emma does not always appreciate this role:

Emma: *"It's a bit annoying, she'll look through all my messages, and I won't have done anything bad or anything but… I'm a little more technical than she is so I know how to change things and I can change like her name on it and the color and she doesn't know how to change it back."*
Dr C: *"How does that feel when your mum is going through your phone checking? What goes through your mind?"*
Emma: *"I just feel really annoyed, because if I were to do that to her she would go absolutely crazy."*

Emma experiences an intrusion of her privacy here, with her mum going through her Facebook account. In addition, a sense of unfairness arises with a misbalance of power. Emma would not be able to do to her mother what she has done to her. Emma regains a sense of power via her technical ability and knowledge, likely being able to shape the landscape of social media that her mother has access to. These small wins for Emma help her to cope with the boundaries that her mother has put in place regarding her social media use.

Emma was not the only individual to experience the imposing of boundaries with regard to social media use, Brendan explained:

> Yeah, sometimes, they like, sometimes they get home before me and so would get hold of my phone and put it in one of their drawers or something. I'll come home and

be like 'where's my phone?' and they'll be like 'we've got it; you've got to do your homework first. So, I'll do it for an hour and a half/two hours and then I'll come down and get my phone, so you know.

Brendan's situation highlights the use of social media as a privilege, which he has to earn the right to use. The boundaries in place are accepted by Brendan and he seems to take a rather holistic view to the experience of having his phone taken off him:

I know because mum and dad just want the best, for me to be able to do my best, and if that means taking my phone away, that's what it is, so yeah.

This situation is echoed and experienced by Imogen in a similar way:

Yeah, if we have to do something (homework), so like if we're at the dinner table she'll ask us what we've got to do and stuff, and we'll tell her, obviously, and sometimes she'll turn the Wi-Fi off, or she'll just take our phones if we have to do something, or we'll go downstairs and she'll watch us do it.

For Imogen, the turning off of the Wi-Fi, the taking of phones or the monitoring of work, are all examples of her mother monitoring and placing boundaries on her social networking. This allows Imogen a distraction free task, suggesting that the use of social media is interfering with her work… and we all know what procrastination can do to us. Parents seem to emerge as the gatekeepers to social media usage, as expressed by Jenny:

Yeah, I was too young, my mum wouldn't let me… (But eventually), all my friends were using it and so she let me in the end.

This example shows a hesitance from Jenny's mum to allow her to use social media, based on age, yet eventually, for fear of socially isolating her child, allowing her to use it. There was a point for Jenny where permission was needed, which gives social media a desirable quality for Jenny, it is a treat, a privilege, awarded to her by her mother. This is by far one of the most common points of debate for parents when considering social media use for their children… They want to protect their children from it, they don't want to "lose" their children to technology, but also, they don't want their children to be left out and seemingly different from their peers.

Lacy's experience of the role her parents take in her social networking, is in line with the groups experience. However, she explores a slight variation on the above examples:

My dad doesn't really mind, he says 'everyone on Facebook is a fool anyway', but my mum she like checks that I'm ok on it, like I'm friends with her on Facebook and stuff. If something happens then I would tell her and stuff.

Lacy describes being "friends" with her mum via her social media, and an open communication with her mum if "something happens." Lacy's mum has a presence online and in person, this acts as a form of safety for her, a guardian watching out for her well-being. Interestingly, Lacy's dad's perspective does not appear to phase her, despite its meaning that he views both her and her mum as a "fool" for using social media. I wonder whether or not this resonates on a deeper level for Lacy, or whether she justifies this position as one simply outdated and therefore invalid.

There is an example of conflict between Mark and his foster dad, this was expressed when Mark said:

> Umm it depends on my mood really, if I'm in a happy mood, see my foster dad comes in and is like 'hey you have to turn it off now'. . .fair enough yeah, but it all depends on the time, obviously, my internet goes off at 10.30 and if it's going round near 10.30 and my foster dad is like 'right the internet is going off early tonight' yeah that's fine but if I'm in a really angry mood like, I'll want to keep it on, and me and my foster dad will get into an argument.

Mark's experience centers on his "mood," he lives with parental boundaries and is comfortable within them and can even allow for variance if he is in a good mood. However, if his mood is bad and social media is taken from him, he responds negatively which can result in an argument. The Uses & Gratifications Theory would suggest that Mark is actively deciding to use social media in order to satisfy his needs. For Mark, social media likely allows a form of relaxation or enjoyment to help calm his negative mood, with the cessation of use causing emotional upset.

***

The findings above have expanded on previous research that parental use of social networking centers on communication with their children, their children's friends, and the parents of their children's friends. It has done this by highlighting by that there is much more to the role of the parent online. What we see developing is the role of the parent firstly as a gatekeeper to social media, then, a continual safeguarding of the well-being of their child online & offline, to monitor their use for fears of what they could be exposed to and support during any social difficulties—if the child-parent relationship allows. It should not be underestimated that the conditions of agreed boundaries, and open communication in the parental relationship, is a powerful protective factor for children.

The third superordinate theme that was uncovered following analysis of the interviews is one of Cyberbullying.

CHAPTER

12

Cyberbullying: Group judgment & reaction; A venue and channel for negativity; The use of "blocking" as protection

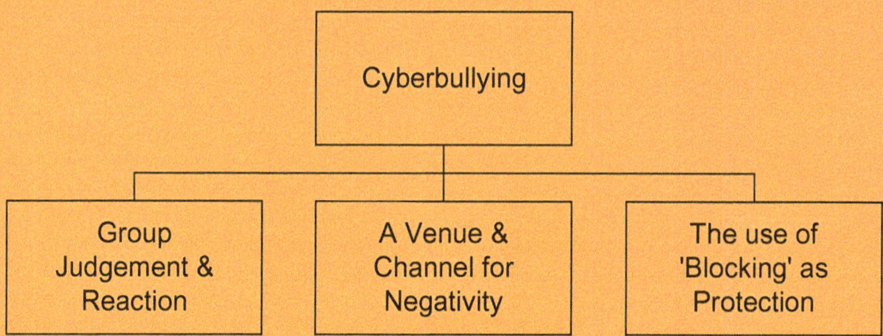

Psychologist's Guide to Adolescents and Social Media
https://doi.org/10.1016/B978-0-323-91898-5.00007-2

All the participants experienced the use of social media with direct, or indirect, involvement in cyberbullying. There is an abundance of research on cyberbullying and the negative impact this can have on victims, we've explored this in a previous chapter. Now we get to hear about some of the direct experience of cyberbullying from those who have been involved. From this superordinate theme, the following emergent themes presented themselves: Group Judgment & Reaction, A Venue & Channel for Negativity and the use of "Blocking" as Protection.

Group judgment and reaction

Experiencing a sense of group judgment and a "reaction" online emerged for all participants in similar ways, but under different circumstances. With several social media platforms, there is an inherent "group" element, with the entirety of your chosen connections being able to message, share and/or comment on something. There is also the capacity with certain social media platforms to invite a few selected people into a dedicated group. The discussion that takes place in the group involves only those "invited," rather than in the more public forum with all connected. I note the distinction because there are examples in the following interview extracts that have occurred across both the public and the more private forums. Brendan shared an experience he had:

Dr C: *"What is the worst thing that has ever happened to you while using social media?"*

Brendan: *"Dumping my girlfriend, that's it, I didn't dump her over social networks but it's just the repercussions of dumping her that spilled onto group chats and everything. And then she put this status on Facebook saying 'single' and all her friends were like 'he's and idiot, he doesn't know what he's missing,' and they were tagging me in everything."*

Dr C: *"That must have been very awkward?"*

Brendan: *"Yeah, the next day I had to avoid them, if they came near me, I'd just walk away. They tried to; they're very involved in school as well as on social media. But I just walked away really, couldn't be bothered with it…"*

Brendan's decision to end his relationship with his girlfriend resulted in "repercussions" online, much like the ripples of a pebble being dropped in a pond, the initial event sent waves through his social connections. Brendan became a witness to people's reactions to this decision via social media. The changing of his ex-girlfriend's online status to "single" acts as flag to signify the end of the relationship, visibly informing all connected instantly. There is no slow pace of the news leaking out via word of mouth. Through this experience, Brendan feels the full force of his girlfriend's support network responding instantly, and a wave of negativity and group judgment (of his decision) directed at him through the use of tagging and in school over the following days. This must have been a difficult experience for Brendan and may have resulted in a reinforcement of his decision to end the relationship, or the experience of regretting the choice he's made.

David has been a witness to this type of group reaction before. He was invited into a private group for the sole purpose of targeting someone else:

> I've been invited into one of the groups being mean about someone and had to remove myself from it, because some of the things are quite horrible.

David highlights his experience of witnessing something that has come into conflict with what he considers acceptable behavior toward another. David has to "remove" himself from the group because he feels strongly about the "horrible" things being said. This removal means that he is not a part of the problem. However, he is also not part of a solution to help the other person, despite how strongly he felt about what was happening. Another example of witnessing a group reaction to an individual was given by Imogen:

> like, just being really horrible, people are always 'calling each other out' and I just see these statuses and people are being horrible to this one person, and sometimes there's 80 people reading the comments, and they're liking the comments, so they're not actually commenting, but they're reading it and, I would just hate to be the person who people are having a go at.

Imogen highlights another experience, witnessing a group judgment and reaction and then the aftermath of negativity online. There is also the element of passively supporting the event via witnessing and not intervening. The individual, experiencing such a large group reaction, or lack thereof, must feel the impact of such an event on their sense of self-esteem and self-worth. Imogen highlights an area of danger in social media and a fear in what it would be like to be a victim to such group judgment. What becomes evident is that there is a "bystander effect" taking place, in which individuals do not offer any means of help to a victim when other people are present, perhaps assuming that someone else will. One of the young people I worked with, Jenny, has been a victim of group judgment in the past:

> When I fell out with Vicky, they made a group chat, but I left it, because they were all bitching, it was pure bitchiness, so I just left, it was boring.

Jenny describes leaving a group chat, which was made for the sole purpose of discussing her, following a fall out with Vicky. Notice how Jenny ends the sentence with "so I just left, it was boring." There's not a chance that Jenny found it boring, but rather, this is a defensive response to the situation. Jenny shows that she does not care about the opinions of those "attacking" her, but more so, that they bore her and that their comments hold no interest. It's highly likely that this did emotionally upset Jenny, but that she did not want to show it to anyone, she wanted to remain strong in the face of her attackers. Jenny is not alone in her experiences, Lacy was very open in discussing her experience of a group reaction towards her:

Dr C: *"What advice would you give someone who had never used social media before and wanted to start?"*

Lacy: *"Just don't try and get involved, don't put things on to try and get attention and stuff, just use it for what you need to use it for. As long as you're using it in the right way and you don't like try to get involved and... the worst thing you can do is get in an argument on social media, because you never know how it is going to turn out, like if I had an argument with my friends they would come into school and not talk to me, but if it was someone who I wasn't friends with then they wouldn't do anything because they don't know me as well."*

"I would say be careful because it's very easy to try and get things the wrong way, and it's easy to start things, for people to get at you. Say something happened, and they needed to tell you it - that they weren't happy, they wouldn't come to your face, that wouldn't be their first resort, their first resort would be to go on social media and message you. And on there they can say whatever they want, they can call you every name under the sun on social media they can just type it... but to your face they wouldn't say it."

Dr C: *"What do you think it is that makes it so easy to send messages?"*

Lacy: *"No-one can see your face when you're typing it, conversations and arguments and stuff, they can go on for ages, but in school someone can walk away from it. On social media you can't walk away. That's probably the hard bit from before, you couldn't walk away from it. Until my mum told me I shouldn't go on it. Like the messages just keep on coming up, as much as you mute it, the vibrations keep coming they still come up. You know that they're there as well, even when your phone is taken away, you know that it's there, that people are sending you stuff."*

Dr C: *"What does it feel like when you know people are saying stuff, but you can't see the message?"*

Lacy: *"You assume stuff, and normally when you assume it's not always the same or right thing, but it's not very nice at all."*

Dr C: *"And I suppose you know they'll be there when you get your phone back?"*

Lacy: *"That moment I got my phone back, I didn't want to look at it, I didn't change accounts or anything, and I just didn't look at them. They died down as soon as I wasn't replying so..."*

Dr C: *"So you think that was a useful thing to do, for you, to ignore it and not reply?"*

Lacy: *"Yeah, umm, because I was on a group chat and all my friends were on there and because I was in a big group, there was like 15 people in there, in the chat, and they stopped after a while and it was fine."*

Lacy strongly feels a sense of being trapped, cornered without an easy escape route, and without respite from the messages. That the perpetrators feel powerful hidden behind their technology. Her phone even vibrates, as if the messages have a physical force trying to break free from her phone. It takes her mother's intervention to remove her access to the social media, so that she may get some resemblance of a break from the messages. Yet, even with the removal of technology, the knowledge of the unread messages haunts her, the knowledge that the abuse and negativity is ongoing, in her absence. There is a sense of helplessness when connected and when disconnected. On the one hand, she does not see the messages and so is safe from the hurt, on the other hand she cannot defend herself or know what is being said. Lacy can only ruminate on the situation, trapped in her thoughts about the possible content until she regains access to her networks, until the storm has passed and she can review the damage… or in her case, ignore it in the hopes it will go away and be alright again.

Some situations emerged where the limited nature of using technology to communicate led to a fallout within a friendship group, this was the case for Emma:

Dr C: *"You mentioned in your questionnaire that something had happened on social media that had made you not want to go into school the next day, can you tell me more about that?"*

Emma: *"Yeah, umm I remember me and my best friend, I commented on her photo, saying like nice hair and that, and she thought I was being sarcastic, and then she messaged me saying are you being sarcastic? I said no, but before she got my answer she had told everyone else and everyone else thought I was being sarcastic, and I had to explain to her that I wasn't, and then everyone else sort of thought it, and then we had to go around saying to everyone that I wasn't."*

Emma's message was misinterpreted by the receiver, who then shared concerns with her friendship group. The group began to formulate their own opinions on Emma's intention. Emma's difficulty was one of intonation and body language, something that can be easily picked up on face to face. However, written text can be misinterpreted, and once seen, cannot be undone. It took a lot of reparation across her friendship group to reaffirm her position in the group and reinstate her temporarily tainted reputation with her peers.

Being ostracized from a group is a distinctive part of cyberbullying. But what isn't often included is the idea and concept of "group judgment," which as seen above can be a highly anxiety provoking experience for young people.

Across everyone's experience of Group Judgment & Reaction, a sense of social media being a venue began to emerge, much in the sense of it being used like a courtroom. Your character can be called into question, a sense of helplessness, to be judged by a group of your peers, the need to defend one's self, all the while being witnessed by a galley full of spectators. This idea of social media being a venue is explored further in the next emergent theme which became apparent for the group. Social media becoming a venue and channel for negativity.

A venue & channel for negativity

Imogen: *"Last night, literally, before I went to bed the last thing I saw was someone calling someone out on something…'oh she did this'… it's just twisting stuff, it just makes things so much worse when people go back to school. Because I know what that's like."*

Imogen shows us the use of social media as a channel to challenge others, to express an opinion, to incite someone to respond, or support their position. Imogen feels that there is a lack of truth within this, the idea of "twisting" the truth to suit one's need. Imogen also eludes to real world impact this has had for her in the past, and the empathy she feels towards others experiencing difficulty. Perhaps experiencing this difficulty online strengthens Imogen in some way, like a veteran soldier who has experienced battle and become stronger for it.

This "twisting," as Imogen would describe it, has been experienced by others, with social media becoming the venue for the ensuing arguments associated with misinterpreted messages. As Lacy described:

> Umm, things can, instead of like talking, like face to face, listening to someone's voice, having it written down, it can sometimes be interpreted differently, and that can sometimes be very hard, like with your friends, like they might take it the wrong way and stuff.

Similarly, Emma detailed:

> Yeah, I mean like my friends Tess and Jade, they were best friends and then Tess sent something to Jade, and Jade took it wrong and misinterpreted it and she thought it was something completely different and had a massive falling out over it, and they

weren't friends for ages, like a month or two, and then when finally, they realised, they both misinterpreted it, and then they were friends again, but not as good friends as they used to be.

For both Lacy and Emma, social media has been used as the place where the seeds of negativity have been planted, often through a misinterpreted message. This has resulted in "real world" difficulties for both of them, be it through things being "very hard" with their friends or though the long-term damaging of a previously close friendship. Further experiences of the use of social media as a venue/channel for negativity were described by Jenny:

Uh people will fall out and they will message you to start an argument, sometimes to start one with you or to pull you into one.

For Jenny, social media has been a landscape where you can be targeted for an argument or be pulled into one. There is a lack of control over both situations, to be targeted or pulled takes the choice away from Jenny initially, but how she responds will remain in her control. Jenny elaborated on the idea of being "targeted":

I basically have this other (social media) account that is for my personal stuff, but she (a girl Jenny does not get on with) found it and tried to message me so she could see my stuff but I wouldn't let her, she made 5 accounts to try and find it so I deleted all my accounts.

For Jenny, it was more important to delete all of her accounts than to allow someone she dislikes to gain information on her. Information that she feels would have been used against her in some negative way. Jenny values her choice of "friends" and the information she shares with them, information is valuable to Jenny, and protecting her privacy of paramount importance. At the time, I wish I had asked Jenny more about her other accounts. Jenny seemed to be displaying online a sense of her true self, an honesty, or a vulnerability that she does not want the "wrong" person to access. The experience of vulnerability and the vast openness of social media was experienced by Jack and his online gaming:

... you've got people saying 'newb' and then there's other times when you'll join a game and there will be people shouting and swearing because they got killed, or if you kill them a really annoying way.

Jack describes online gaming and the meeting of people who are insulting him. From the use of "newb" as an insult into his ability to play the game well (newbie), an insult to his skill, to the swearing and shouting in response to frustration in the game. However, arguably this is not something that would be seen in the street, or face to face. There is something about the online social media spaces that is allowing people to express their unfiltered emotion or views. David and Mark highlight the specific use of social media for cyberbullying when they comment:

David: *"Be careful of the friends you pick, because there's people making fake accounts and doing some disgusting things, so there's a boy in the school that's made a fake account in my year, he's made a fake account and just starting putting loads of nasty stuff on Facebook. Which I disagree with."*

Mark: *"... but I've seen videos of people making fake accounts on YouTube and cyberbullying and that, and it's pretty sick to be honest, I don't like it, but that's the way people are like."*

David and Mark both experience the risks of social media - as a tool it can be manipulated and used to spread hatred, to make people feel bad. This does not sit well with David or Mark. However, Mark seems to have a specific viewpoint about the capacity of people to be unkind—"that's the way people are." The venue of social media is not seen as a pleasant place to be, it is risky, with dangers lurking in all the same places where enjoyment is experienced. There is a function on social networking sites to protect one's self from the negativity of others, usually through a form of blocking the individuals or the messages from being received. The use of "blocking" as protection is the next emergent theme that presented itself following analysis of the interviews.

The use of "blocking" as protection

Six out of the eight young people had experience of using the "blocking" feature across their social media, doing so in order to protect themselves from others. In fact, previous studies have shown that many young people know how to end or restrict cyberbullying, harmful and hurtful messages. This is often done by using blocking or restricting access to their personal spaces on social media sites. People can be hesitant to do so however, like taking your eyes off a predator. When I was working with Imogen, she described that her "block list is huge" and showed frustration with how difficult it is to truly block someone out:

Dr C: *"Would you ever block anyone?"*

Imogen: *"Yes, my block list is huge? If I get fed up and think that it's not going to stop, there's no point, I don't really want them seeing what I'm doing, so I'll block them, I've got so many people that are blocked."*

Dr C: *"What leads to you deciding to block someone?"*

Imogen: *"When people are, obviously they'll gang up on you for something that someone said to them, but they'd never say it to my face, so it's always on social media, and umm, they just non-stop message you, and you try to defend yourself, and they're screenshotting it and sending it on to other people, and in the end you just have to stop, or it's not going to stop otherwise and so I just block them, that way they can't get hold of me, and I can't get hold of them. And if their friends message me, because obviously I blocked that person, then I have to block them straight away I don't even reply, I have to stop it then and there, otherwise it will just carry on and get worse. And I just hate coming into school and feeling scared."*

Dr C: *"It sounds really difficult to get away from it..."*

Imogen: *"It is, especially when you have so many, like it's not just Facebook, it's everywhere, they'll get hold of you on Instagram, they'll message you on snapchat, so you have to block them everywhere, you have to cover all your bases, it's really annoying....exhausting, endless, and sometimes they get your number and I'm like 'how the hell did you get my number?' and they text me and I have to block them on there as well, and it's just so annoying."*

Dr C: *"It sounds so stressful; does it take up a lot of your thinking during that time?"*

Imogen: *"It does, it's all I think about."*

Imogen uses the phrase "cover all your bases" regarding blocking another person who is trying to message her. Her language use describes a defense, which shows how she's feeling - under attack. In a similar stance, like a sport, she needs to block her attacker and mount a defense across all her social media accounts, in order to win this battle. I got the sense that this takes a toll on Imogen, moving beyond it being annoying, to exhausting and endless. It seems that for Imogen having to guard herself online is an ongoing task, because people can find a way to get to you if they really want to. A similar experience was reported by Jenny:

> She made a fake account on Instagram and started messaging me like a big paragraph, so I blocked it and she made another one.

Jenny also experiences the persistence of others, to try and get their message delivered to their target. "Blocking" only seems to be a semi-effective measure, because as detailed above the sender of the message made a completely new account to bypass the "block" and try once more to send the message. Much like a strategic game, social media is being manipulated to deliver messages and some in-built security features are not as concrete as might be hoped. For example, in "Blocking" Sadie (to pick a random name), you are only blocking her account, not the person, the person can make a new account, use a friends account, find other means of contacting you, e.g. through your phone number. The experience for Jenny is one of a game of cat and mouse, finding ways to evade and hide, to restrict someone's access to her in any way possible. There is a sense of being hunted, a sense of having to survive or win in the social exchange. When I was speaking with David it was notable that his experience of "Blocking" varied from the other participants, as it involved messages that were not initially targeted at him:

> …my family that live up north, they have been saying some quite horrible things to my mum, and I have had to block them, so they don't start saying it to me.

David's mum is targeted by other family members and in order to protect himself from the potential of having "horrible things" said to him, he "blocks" the family members pre-emptively. For David, this serves two functions, one of protection, but also one of loyalty. In "blocking" family members, David solidifies his relationship with his mum, in choosing her, and it sends the message to his family that their behavior has lost them contact with him. Such a simple function on social media can send a very powerful message to others. The "blocking" of someone online also had an impact on the real-world relationship between Emma and a friend in school, as described by Emma:

> Yeah, umm I blocked this one girl because we had this major falling out and we used to be in this big group, and we blocked each other because she blamed me for something and then I retaliated and we both fell out. So, we're still being civil but we're not friends or anything, we're in the same tutor. I was in year 8, I don't really speak to her properly now and she doesn't speak to me.

For Emma, a "major falling out" online ended up with blocking being used. Unable to move past their fall out, the blocking also translated into an in-school change for both parties. Although "civil" to one another the friendship did not survive and they now, in many respects, "block" one another in person. This is seemingly a transference of the online relationship to the in-person experience. This is an example of a symbiosis between one's online self and their offline self. What happens on one, impacts the other. The behavior one experiences online seem to clearly impact one's offline life. I would say that there is more than a simple psychological connection between online and offline worlds but that in reality the lines between online/offline are becoming increasingly blurred resulting in "real" change within relationships, should we even be considering them separate? I'm not sure the young people I work with consider "offline" and "online" when discussing things that have happened... I often find myself having to clarify with young people whether something happened online, offline, in person, in a physical location, in a group, or witnessed by others. The young people I work with don't add such clarification to their autobiographical stories, they speak through everything as one experience, regardless of "the internet." When I met with Brendan, he also described people he's had to block:

> ...I think about 1 or 2, if someone's just annoying me on Facebook, I'll just umm either block them or go up to them in school and say, 'just leave me alone'.

Brendan's example is also one of highlighting a symbiosis of online and offline worlds. He will either use the social media site to "block" someone or he will challenge that person in school. Thus, having the same impact online, with the other person receiving the message that they have "annoyed" Brendan, to the extent that he needed to react to it. This concept of the online world impacting on the offline world, or the blurring lines between the two, leads us to the next and final superordinate theme for the group I interviewed—when social media moves from "online" to "in-school."

CHAPTER

13

From online to in-school: Interference of work; Threats, intimidation or violence

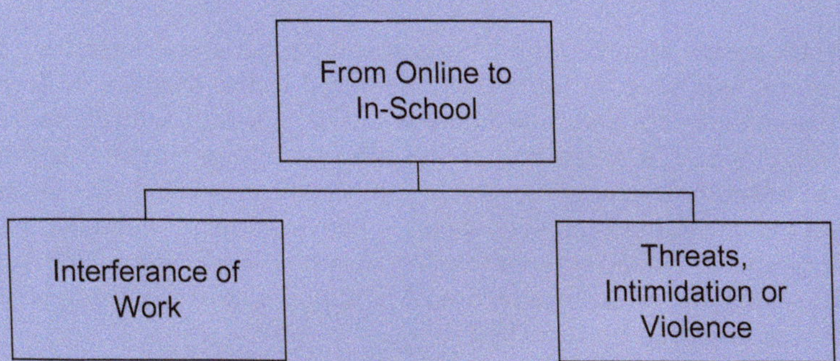

Psychologist's Guide to Adolescents and Social Media
https://doi.org/10.1016/B978-0-323-91898-5.00001-1

All of the young people I spoke with experienced that the use of social media having a direct impact in-school. From this superordinate theme, the following emergent themes presented themselves: Interference of Work, and Threats, Intimidation or Violence.

We have already explored the educationally relevant impact of social media use in Chapter 7—highlighting the improvement of working memory, verbal ability, and spelling scores. Yet, that this may lead to an overall reduction in educational levels/grades due to task switching, multitasking and cognitive overload. There is also growing research body exploring the correlation and factors involved with in-school bullying and cyberbullying, highlighting a complex relationship between the two. In order to expand upon the understanding of the online/ in-school experience we are first going to look at the theme of interference with work.

Interference of work

I remember when I was working with Mark that he gave a particular example of how social media was having a large effect on the completion of his homework:

> … it does affect me quite a lot, because obviously I'll have my laptop open, and go onto quite a big website called MyMaths, which is used for homework, umm, I'll go on it, have it open and have another tab open for Facebook and I'll switch between the two, but I do it really often, so it's effecting me even more than normal. I'll keep switching. It's easy enough to get the homework done while it's there, that's how I've always learnt, get home, get the homework done, but with Facebook, it gets in the way.

Mark seems to have found himself trapped in a task-switching loop, where he will have multiple tabs open, and rather than solely focusing on one activity, for example homework, he will find himself switching between them. His reiteration of "I'll keep switching" highlights the fine line of where he's struggling with his ability to control his behavior, to the extent that it's going against how he's "always learnt." Facebook for Mark has become an obstacle to completing his homework, one which he currently seems powerless to overcome. The experience of switching between tasks was mirrored by Brendan:

> … for me, yeah, a lot, because I'm always talking to my mates, even when doing homework, I'll have the iPad on. Even listening to music and talking to friends as well.

Brendan describes a glorious recipe for distraction—music, homework and talking to friends all at the same time. As the importance of the final school year approaches, some of the young people I worked with reflected on the social media "distraction" with regard to their GCSE schoolwork:

Imogen: *"I use it way too much, yeah, especially doing my GCSE's I always find myself side-tracked, like if I've got my laptop out, I always got Facebook open on a tab, and then something will come up and I'm distracted, I use it way too much, I'd rather be on social media than do my school work."*

Lacy: *"Yah, like, I go on it whilst I'm meant to do homework, especially now that I'm in year 10 and I've got to start revising for my mocks and stuff, umm, it's a bit of a distraction."*

For Imogen and Lacy, the idea of social media being a preferable activity and distraction, in comparison to schoolwork, seems to side-track their efforts to complete work. And for others, the experience of social media seems to dominate their thinking space:

David: *"Sometimes yeah, because I'll get carried away with it, and forget to do my homework."*

Emma: *"Yeah, cause I just won't do it if I'm on Facebook, or Instagram or Snapchat, I'll just be messaging my friends or something and I'll forget that I've got homework to do, so I'll have to do it later, or in the morning, which just doesn't work."*

For David and Emma, the use of social media seems to fill their attention span to the extent that they forget the work that they are supposed to be completing. Much like I was once told—being connected to one's friends via social media is like having them all in the room with you, and it is difficult to focus on homework with so many people in the room. I also get the sense that our old friend procrastination is rearing his head again—being tethered to your friends and seeking the connection to distract from the task at hand. Procrastination and avoidance of work were captured succinctly by Jack when he stated:

> Yeah, it'll be, I'll get home, say I'm going to do homework and just go on the Xbox.

Well said Jack, clear and to the point. This outright deception with his parents serves to meet his apparent need to play online games and connect to his friends online. For the whole group of young people I spoke with, there seems to be a mix of choosing to avoid schoolwork, or attempting it, and being uncontrollably distracted by social media. Jenny made a distinction between what she was meant to do, and what she actually did:

> Yeah, yeah, I was meant to do my child development homework and my business homework, but I didn't because I was on my phone. So, I haven't done that.

Such a matter of fact approach with Jenny, it's wonderful, I love honesty like this... as if for her, it is a perfectly good excuse as to why her work was not completed. The counterbalance to this would suggest that if she was not on her phone then the work would have been done. So, the priority, for Jenny, on the evening that she refers to, was in using her phone to access social media. This was the choice that she made, or perhaps like some of her peers, there was a pull towards her using it, and a cycle of use that is difficult to break once started. We know that the pull of friendships is strong, and the design of social media will likely hold Jenny in there for a while. The cost of this is the detriment to whatever task Jenny should be doing.

Previous research highlighted some educational positives of using social media, in the improvement of some cognitive abilities in line with using technology and the practice of using language to express thought. However, these results have shown a negative impact of social media on the completion of homework in line with Judd's research on the detrimental impact of task switching.

The second emergent theme, nested within "From online to In-school," has a connection to Cyberbullying—Threats, Intimidation or Violence. However, this is distinct from Cyberbullying in this analysis because with Cyberbullying, the location remained online and for the following examples, there was a distinct shift of location between online and offline worlds.

Threats, intimidation or violence

All of the participants experienced threats, intimidation or violence that seemed to stem, or shift from a purely online situation, to a "real world" event. One particularly shocking example was given by Imogen:

> ...Something happened over snapchat, you can see when people 'screenshot' people's stories, apparently according to her, I screenshotted something, and I didn't, and she kind of went nuts, and she's not well in the mind, I think anyway, and she was talking to my sister trying to get information out of her, and my sister is like the type of person who would do anything to get more popular, to get herself out there, she's 14, in the year below me, and pretty much threw me under the bus and lied to her, and she went psycho and she threatened to stab me with scissors, and she had scissors in her pocket, and I was so scared and so I went to talk to someone, they got her in an isolation, she left the isolation at lunch and she actually attacked me and yeah, punched me in the face, I had a nosebleed and everything.

Sadly, more and more of these events are becoming common place in and out of schools. Imogen is describing being accused of collecting information on another person, for the sole purpose of using it against them. Imogen's sister corroborates the accusation. This for Imogen is obviously a huge betrayal, look at the language she uses; "threw me under the bus." She feels like this betrayal is going to have serious ramifications for her and she is right, with a serious threat, the fear she felt in school, and despite school intervening, a physical assault against her. To pull this example to its foundations, an online accusation, of something that may or may not have happened, led to a serious physical assault in school. But this event was not contained as a "one on one" incident, as Imogen elaborated:

> There were a load of girls involved as well, it was horrible, there was like 30 girls, behind her, and they were all following, trying to find me, and then I'd obviously left because I wanted to be somewhere near the teachers, so they couldn't get to me because we've actually had altercations before, umm, yeah and they were all there, they were dragging me, on the floor, it was just horrible.

Imogen felt hunted by a group of people, intimidated, scared, she wanted to retreat to the safety of teachers but was caught by the group before she could escape. Imogen is not the only person to have experienced a serious in-school incident because of something that started online, Emma gives an additional example, about a Year 7 girl who posted an insult on a Year 10's photo:

> ...and this year 10 that did it, is really popular and will like beat you up, she's that kind of person, and they were all ganging around the year 7 area and Miss Fletcher had to go in and like stop them, but, like they had to be escorted to and from places for ages by the teachers because of what they had done.

This young girl's school experience has been jolted by her online comment, she needs escorting to and from places, for fears of what will happen to her if unattended. A few words online have resulted in intimidation and fears of being assaulted. And what were those fateful words that caused such a backlash? Two simple words... "Nice Eyebrows." That was it, think of the emotional turmoil it caused in school for that 11-year-old child. The problem with such a comment is that it can be taken either way because there's no tone or intonation—is it an insult? Sarcasm? A compliment? There's no way of telling. What we do know is that it was "received" as an insult. That Year 10 girl eventually got hold on the Year 7 and broke her nose. She was excluded from school for the assault and the Police became involved. Her response to those 2 words has now impacted her reputation with the Police, her GCSE's (moving school mid-term) and her friendship support group... all starting with social media and 2 simple words—"Nice Eyebrows." Brendan also described an in-school reaction following an online post about his breakup with his girlfriend:

> Yeah, the next day I had to avoid them, if they came near me, I'd just walk away. They tried to; they're very involved in school as well as on social media. But I just walked away really, couldn't be bothered with it.

You get the sense with Brendan, that he has the capability to stand up to any intimidation tactics, but he chose not to, he chose to avoid it, perhaps for fears about the situation escalating. Brendan is also of athletic build, is tall for his age and has a gentle disposition to his voice—he's not an easy "target" in the traditional sense and so has that on his side. His comment highlights the idea that people can be "very involved" in both online and in-school matters. Think back to when you were at school—there is always certain people being overly involved in other people's business, enjoying the drama of it all. Brendan is above such behavior, painting himself as perhaps better than those who behave in such a way. Lacy reflected on her thoughts about the impact of social media on school life:

> People get scared to come in if something's happened, and then they won't learn as well at school. I think that most bullying happens on social media as well, that's why so much happens in school, after leading from that.

Lacy touches upon a disabling fear that can be experienced with negative interactions on social media, leading to schoolwork suffering. She feels that social media is the catalyst for a lot of in school problems. When I was working with Lacy, she explored some of the reality of the online altercations. Particularly about what school can be like the next day:

> Sometimes you get stares and stuff, and you just don't talk, but a lot of the time they just forget about it, or they don't, they sometimes act like nothing's happened, it's like they're keyboard warriors, they say what they can there, but in real life they're just wimps, they won't say anything.

A lot can be communicated with a stare, a lot can be miscommunicated also. Lacy has perceived attempts of intimidation through being stared at but highlights the difference for some people with regard to online vs in-school. The phrase "keyboard warriors" show social media as a battleground, that she has faced people online, that they are comfortable fighting from behind their computer screens, but when it comes to being face to face, they are not as powerful as they are online. Jack experienced a similar situation with receiving threats online, but with them not manifesting in-school:

> Well some of my friends have got annoyed and some have said 'oh I'm going to beat you up' but then apologise as soon as they are in school.

It's interesting to think on the internal experience of Jack in this situation, or for any of the young people I interviewed when having to face school the next day following an altercation. Jack would experience the fear of friendship being over, and the fear of physical violence, but not the reality of it coming to pass. Interestingly, Lacy refers to "real life," suggesting a disconnect of what is online as "not real." For other participants, there doesn't seem to be such a clear divide. This is the case for Jenny, who described:

> ... I've been in an argument with a girl called Misha, and she is on about how she threatened to punch me and stuff, and so I refused to go to my lessons that day and I went home instead. I came into school, went into one lesson, then I'd seen her... so I left school, I just walked out.

For Jenny, the reality of seeing Misha in person brought forth all the threats she'd received recently online. This led to fear of what might happen when meeting Misha in school, a fear that must have been quite emotionally strong because it resulted in a refusal to attend school. A blatant breaking of school rules to retreat to the safety of her home. For her, social media interaction acted as the catalyst to non-attendance at school.

***

It's important to add these young people's voices, their experiences, into the wider field of social media research. Kwon and Skoric's research into the correlation of in school and online bullying is backed up by these young people, which further explores the extent to which the online and in-school worlds can merge with regard to bullying (threats, intimidation, or violence).

Importantly, their voices give a detailed account of the experience of cyberbullying, leading onto in-school incidents, and vice versa. It is important that the views and experience of users of technology remain central, to further expand knowledge in such a complex area of research.

CHAPTER

14

"A cup of tea and a notebook"

https://doi.org/10.1016/B978-0-323-91898-5.00023-0

I am often in awe of the power young people wield at their fingertips when using social media, often without conscious awareness. This is a power to genuinely impact the experiential lives of others by how social media is used. A power in using social media to be the catalyst to bring enjoyment, or to bring upset into the lives of others. I am reminded of a quote from JK Rowling's superb character—Albus Dumbledore, taken from Harry Potter and the Deathly Hallows:

> Words are, in my not so humble opinion, our most inexhaustible source of magic, capable of both inflicting injury and remedying it.

Let's take a moment to look at the overall map created using these fantastic 8 young people who gave up their time… I say gave up; I have to say they did seem quite pleased to get some time out their lessons to speak with me about social media.

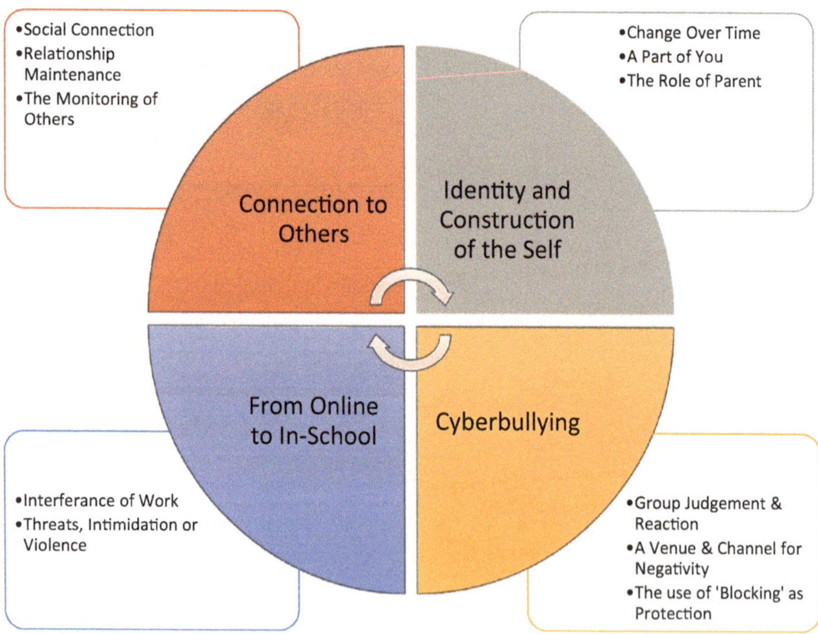

I started my research drowning in questionnaires and being fascinated by the results… results which made it possible to find Jack, Jenny, Lacy, Mark, Brendan, David, Emma, and Imogen—young people at risk of becoming behaviorally addicted to their social media. These findings were based on an Interpretative Phenomenological Analysis of interviews with a small number of participants. Therefore, the results must be viewed within that context. It was not the aim of the interviews to achieve a representative sample in terms of population. But, to provide an account rich in experiential content. Although the interviewee's transcripts fit within superordinate themes and emergent themes there is movement and connection between them all.

The young people I worked with used social media to socially connect to others, to maintain relationships and to monitor others. The use of social media also emerged as changing over time, becoming a "part" of its users and involving parental moderation. While connected, young people were exposed to group judgment and reaction, social networking as a venue and channel for negativity and the use of "blocking" for protection. The impact of using social media resulted in the interference of schoolwork and in experiencing threats, intimidation, or violence.

The holistic experience of using social media does not solely stay in these identified themes; there is an interweaving and connection between all the emergent themes. By socially connecting to others, you gain the ability to maintain your relationships online and monitor the people you are connected to. Over time, social networking use changes as you develop emotionally and physically, becoming a part of you and your routines. Parents have a role in monitoring their children online as they would offline, supporting and protecting them. In using social media and connecting to peers, young people are joining a large community and can become a victim of group judgment and positive or negative reactions to their behavior. Young people may be a participant in the judgment of others, determining the space of social media as one of negativity, positivity, or both. Interacting via social media at any of the above levels can result in an interference of work commitments and in opening the possibility of experiencing threats, intimidation, or violence. But I ask you this… isn't all the above also possible without social media?

Take social media out of the picture for a moment… By socially connecting to others you can still maintain those relationships and monitor the people you are connected to. Over time, socially connecting with others does change you as you develop—pruning some friendships and cultivating others. Parents have a role in shaping children's friendships as they always have. And in being a social individual, or not, as part of a larger community there is always the chance that you can become a victim of group judgment or a participation in it. Spending more time with friends has always had the risk of interfering with work commitments and being a part of society runs the risk of being on the receiving end of threats, intimidation, or violence.

The difference is that social media has made all of the above much easier, it's like life with an injection of adrenaline, everything twice as fast, the risks twice as evident and the technology advancing faster than our ability to acclimate to it. As Edward O. Wilson once put it:

> The real problem of humanity is the following: We have Palaeolithic emotions, medieval institutions and godlike technology

When I had finished my research, I sat down with a cup of tea and my notebook and began to write. It was time to consider it all, everything that I had learned before about social media, and everything that I had come to learn following my research.

The overall aim of my research was to explore the experience of using social media for children in UK secondary schools. The research methods employed in collecting and analyzing the data, allowed me to explore these issues in breadth and depth. The analytical process which was applied to the data, revealed a story of a vast number of young people using multiple social media sites, through multiple devices, for large proportions of the day, every day, and a measure to which this use cognitively occupies young people highlighting some at risk of developing a behavioral addiction.

The analysis of the "lived experience" of young people, who are at risk of developing behavioral addictions, painted a detailed and connected picture of the landscape that young people are a part of and the complex social and psychological environment of which they are members. I started with several research questions, it's time to answer them.

Research Question 1: What social networking platforms are being used by secondary school aged young people?

The young people who took part in this study would often use a multitude of social media sites at any given time. The most popular being YouTube (91.9%), closely followed by Facebook (83.8%), then SnapChat (71.6%) and Instagram (69%). Using multiple social networking sites allows an individual to use a myriad of communication software to meet their needs on a particular day.

Research Question 2: To what extent does social networking occupy the minds of secondary aged young people and can they be considered behaviorally addicted?

Exploration of this question yielded the following results: of the 1148 participants who took part: 2% of them are experiencing significant problems in their life because of their social media usage (that's 23 young people)—a severe risk of developing a behavioral addiction. 41% (470 young people) reported experiencing occasional or frequent problems because the social media use (occupies their minds to a moderate extent, which is a moderate risk of developing a behavioral addiction). 45% (516 young people) may use their social media bit too long at times, but they have control over their usage (occupies their minds to a mild extent—a mild risk of developing a behavioral addiction). 12% (137 young people) report that it is very rare for social media use to have any negative impact on their life (occupies their minds to a normal extent—no current risk of developing a behavioral addiction).

Research Question 3: What can be understood about the experience of being a young person using social media platforms every day? And what key themes are identified in exploration of social media use?

A number of themes were identified during the second phase of my research, which painted a rich and complex picture of what it is "really" like for secondary aged pupils who at high risk of developing behavioral addictions to their social media:
Superordinate themes of: Connection to Others, Identity and Construction of the Self, Cyberbullying and From Online to In-School were highlighted as prominent. Participants used social media to socially connect to others, to maintain relationships and to monitor others. The use of social media also emerged as changing over time, becoming a "part" of its users and involving parental moderation. While using social media, participants experienced group judgment and reaction, social media as a venue and channel for negativity and the use of "blocking" for protection. The impact of using social media resulted in the interference of schoolwork and in experiencing threats, intimidation, or violence.

An interesting reflection was noted in discussion with several teachers following their students' completion of my questionnaire. The process of completing the questionnaire allowed a number of student's time to think about their social media usage. Some were quite shocked about their own use of social media. It was something that no-one had asked them about in detail before. It was this reaction that prompted me to develop the questionnaire further into a self-reflective assessment resource that can be used in schools and at home—more on this later in the final section of the book.

Previous literature and research have explored several psychological impacts that social media has upon its users. To summarize: the purposes and positives are in expressing one's identity and the construction of the self, social connectedness, and emotional regulation. The consequences of using social media can be being on the receiving end of Cyberbullying, or perhaps worse, actively bullying others, to not getting the anticipated responses/social support of fellow social media users and the potential of developing a behavioral addiction.

Various studies have shown that there may be educationally relevant impacts of using social media in the improvement of working memory, verbal ability, and spelling scores. However, this may lead to an overall reduction in educational levels/grades due to task switching, multitasking and cognitive overload if the use of social media interferes with educational tasks.

When I conducted my research, it expanded the field of research into young people's uses and experiences of social media. Highlighting that a vast number of young people use multiple social networking sites, via multiple devices, for large proportions of the day, every day of the week. Importantly, showing a large percentage of young people being cognitively occupied by their use of social networking and at risk of developing behavioral addictions.

The analysis of the "lived experience" of young people painted an interweaved rich picture of the landscape that young people are a part of. Social media is a complex social and psychological environment, of which, many young people are members and actively embroiled. Parents and professionals need to be aware of the influence of social media and how it is shaping young people's communication and relationships for the positives and the negatives. And importantly, parents and professionals need to get alongside the young people they are connected to so that they can be able to support them to navigate their world. Online or offline no longer seems to be relevant, there is a seamless transition between the both for the young people of today and to ignore it would be akin to ignoring the body language or facial expressions of someone you are speaking to… you'd only get half the message.

When I started delivering training in schools and giving talks to parents on social media and teenagers, I was inundated with questions about "what can be done to help those who are struggling with their technology use?" This is one of the difficulties with relatively new fields of research and enquiry… there isn't a lot of "evidence based" approaches to support young people, or adults for that matter, who are struggling with their technology and social media usage. But what I will attempt to do, in the following and final part of this book, is guide you, the reader, through various levels of thought and intervention that could be considered when responding to the psychological impact of social media.

PART IV

What can be done to help those who need support with their social media use?

CHAPTER

15

"You can lead a horse to water…"

https://doi.org/10.1016/B978-0-323-91898-5.00017-5

The final part of this book is going to explore several thoughts related to what can be done to help those who are struggling with aspects of their social media use. I'm going to start wide and then narrow the focus down to the individual level as the chapter continues. There's a reason for this and it's because that very often I find that there isn't something "wrong" with an individual and that if time is taken to make changes to the conditions that a person is living in, or growing up in, this can often make the most profound and positive impact for them. A good friend of mine uses the following metaphor when discussing how to support someone in need:

> if a flower is failing to thrive you don't do anything directly to the flower, you first consider the conditions that that flower needs in order to thrive, the water, the plant food, the position it's in, the soil, the lighting... in doing so, you provide the right environment for growth.

The final pages of this book will give you the ability to reflect on social media and the impact it can have on young people and also leave you with the tools and resources to actively engage in exploring and supporting those who need it.

What is society's responsibility?

I used to live close to Exeter. Exeter is a small city with a population of approximately 130,000. It is nestled in the countryside of Devon in the southwest of England. In the early 2000s Exeter was facing a regeneration of its high street and much like many cities across England plans were drawn up for the design of a shopping center. If you are a high street shop owner, the knowledge of a shopping center being considered is often met with dread. When malls or shopping centers open people flock to them, they are often self-contained with shops, restaurants, and parking. High streets and their shops often end up neglected and closing because the customers no longer "walk the high street." People park at the shopping center, shop and eat within and then return home. A loss of connection between shoppers and the wider shops available to them. People's behavioral and shopping patterns change due to the design of the shopping districts within cities, which can result in many businesses failing to thrive. However, this was not Exeter's story.

On Thursday 20th September 2007 the Princesshay Shopping Quarter officially opened. This was no Mall-like container for shoppers, but new streets, interweaved with the high street, weaving through the city center like veins from a muscle, connected to the landscape, the history, and the "old" well established shops. It was a regeneration that promoted connection between the old and the new, the independent and the "chain" shops, the restaurants and the cafes, the historic architectures and space for public art, 122 new apartments and a heritage center. You might be thinking that I get commission from the Exeter Tourist Board… perhaps I should, alas, I do not. But what Exeter has done is promote connection that serves the wider community. It was a socially responsible design that served the longevity of the city, its inhabitants, and its business owners.

Some people are becoming overly attached to their phones and their social media that their other relationships and connections are suffering. Their connections to the wider world, the environment, their families, their metaphorical "high streets" are becoming damaged—so then who holds responsibility for the ethical design of this technology? Left unchecked, social media becomes the mall that devastates a high street. This is where the government steps in (or they should), and in the UK there is evidence of this starting, the government, alongside their faithful friend Ofcom. Ofcom is the regulator for the communications services that are used in the UK—making sure people get the best from their broadband, home phone and mobile services, as well as keeping an eye on TV and radio and as technology advances, to police social media. This move is supposed to make the companies protect users from content showcasing things like violence, terrorism, cyber-bullying, and child abuse. Social media companies will have to ensure that "harmful content" is removed rapidly and take steps to prevent it appearing on their sites.

Previously, social media companies have relied on an argument that is essentially the same as "we've made a playground, we have nothing to do with how people use it." However, things are starting to change, YouTube and Facebook have their own set of rules or "community guidelines," about what is considered unacceptable and the way people are expected to behave towards one another… and in other places across the world laws have begun to arrive to police usage, but more on that later.

Self-governance

When it comes to social media companies and self-governance, YouTube relies on various teams around the world to review "flagged" videos and remove content that violates their Community Guidelines. Between April 2020 and June 2020 YouTube removed 11,401,696 videos from their site:

- 10,849,634 removed by YouTube's automated flagging system
- 382,499 removed by individual users
- 167,318 removed by YouTube's individual trusted flagger program
- 2220 removed by Non-Governmental Organizations
- 25 removed by Government organizations

YouTube employs approximately 10,000 people in monitoring and removing content from their site. And they're not alone in their commitment to managing the content posted on their site. Facebook & Instagram also publish data on the content that they have removed from their sites called their *Community Standards Enforcement Report*. A quick online search on either of the above reports will give you the full statistics.

So, it looks like social media companies are taking more responsibility for the content posted on their sites. This, alongside the work of people such as Tristan Harris and the center for humane technology is a good indicator that ethical cogs are turning when it comes to social media. But there is no such thing as 100% protection, there will always be a chance that those who use social media will see content that is not appropriate for them to see or not desired. I have spoken to a lot of young people who have seen things that are not age appropriate for them, or legal for that matter, through social media.

If anything that is posted online breaks the law, such as revenge pornography, threats of violence or extremist material, it has previously been the person who posted that material who was at risk of being prosecuted... not the social media companies. Things, however, may be changing. Let's take a wider look at what has been happening around the world in policing content on social media:

Germany

The NetzDG law. From the beginning of 2018 this law forced companies to set up procedures to review complaints about the content they were hosting on their sites (if their sites had over 2 million registered users). They would also have 24h to remove anything that was illegal and publish 6 monthly updates about this process. If these requirements were not adhered to under the NEtzDG law, then individuals could be fined up to £4.4 million and companies up to £50 million.

The German government issued its first fine under the new law to Facebook in July 2019. Facebook were instructed to pay £1.7 million for under-reporting illegal activity on its platforms in Germany.

The European Union (EU)

The EU is clamping down on extremist content posted online. Giving social media platforms 1h to delete extremist content or face fines. The EU has also introduced the General Data Protection Regulation (GDPR) which set rules on how companies, including social media platforms, store and use people's data. European Union member states have until 2021 to implement the directive into their domestic law.

Australia

In 2019 Australia passed the "Sharing of Abhorrent Violent Material Act" introducing criminal penalties for social media companies, which includes possible jail sentences for tech company executives for up to

3 years and financial penalties worth up to 10% of a company's global turnover. This followed the New Zealand: Christchurch shooting in which a gunman live-streamed for 17 min an attack on to mosques that killed 50 people (viewed 4000 times before it was removed).

China

Twitter, Google, and WhatsApp are blocked in China. Their social media and search engine services are provided instead by Chinese providers such as Weibo, Baidu, and WeChat. It is my understanding that China have thousands of cyber-police, who monitor social media platforms and screen messages that are deemed to be politically sensitive.

It would appear on the surface that social media companies are responding to the content on their sites and countries are also taking a stand. However, these responses tend to be tailored towards content that is deemed to be "breaking the law" or "illegal" in some way, shape, or form. There doesn't seem to be anything that is being done to address the "culture" of social media or the impact that social media is having on day to day lives... it would seem that responsibility rests with us, the users, the parents of children who use social media and the professionals who work with young people directly impacted by social media.

What can parents do?

In short, plenty. But it needs to start at a young age to be most effective. One thing parents need to consider in their households is "relational health." How is everyone going to be around one another? How are they going to live and communicate well together? Parents should be finding any options possible for increasing family social interaction—These moments over time are buffering children from the inevitable adversity that they will experience in their lives—and in doing so, children will be better regulated, better capable of learning, of sharing and of being creative. As professionals working with young people, there are times where we will need to be supporting parents in their role to try and achieve this.

The importance of face to face connection cannot be underestimated. There was once a meta-analysis study into empathy in American college students over time. This study showed that there had been significant drops in "perspective taking" ability over time. These are young adults aged 17 years and above who are showing empathy abilities of much younger children. Empathy, using body language in communication and perspective taking are all skills learned as you are exposed to social communication over time. It's not so different from language, the more language you are exposed to, the more words you start to build in your vocabulary... hear half as many words and your vocabulary will end up half as developed. There is a risk that the more technology takes the attention of children, the less developed their social skills will be. Julian Treasure is an international speaker on sound and communication skills. He feels that as a society we are slowly losing our "listening" abilities and advocates that we need to be teaching children how to receive, appreciate, summarize, and ask. Children need to be explicitly taught the skills of communication because, as Julian would put it—"the art of conversation is being replaced, dangerously, by personal broadcasting."

At the end of "formal education," when people find themselves in interviews for jobs, the qualifications no longer matter. Qualifications are what get you to the interview, from that point on it is the "soft skills"—the ability to work in a team and to communicate effectively in person that will matter when it comes to actually landing a job.

In the UK there has been a cultural shift over time. There was a time where it was commonplace for multiple generations to live together in a house. Over years there has been a developing shift away from social connection and community, of living together—into cognitions of I want my own house, to I want my own room in my own house, to I want my own screen in my own room in my own house. Mealtimes have been punctuated by phone use and disconnection... McDonalds Restaurants even have tables set up with rows of tablet computers down the middle. Is this ok? Have we fallen into this state of being by accident? We need to consciously be making decisions and choices with a mind-set to relational health when considering technology use and social media memberships. As Professor Andy Przybylski from the University of Oxford once put it—"A discussion of screen time that is divorced from a discussion of family life in general is pointless."

Even though each child could have their own room, could they share? Even though you could each have your own TV, should you? One position is to say that TV's need to be out of children's bedrooms—"if we're going to watch TV were going to do it together, as a family."—This also gives an opportunity for negotiation of what is going to be watched, a useful skill to learn. I know of some families who will take it further, they will have a 1 screen rule in the lounge, if the TV is on, no phones are allowed. It's time to start helping parents question things they may not have questioned before.

There will come a time in parenthood when a child asks a parent for their own smartphone. They'll probably be specific with it as well; they'll probably name the phone they want. This will not be the first time in parenthood when a child has requested something that they "really really wanted forever." But this may be the first time that they have requested something that is as advanced, with monthly costs and real-world dangers and consequences linked to it. As professionals, we have a place in supporting parents to think around the decisions they make for their children.

A good analogy to use with a parent when they are considering if their child is ready to have a phone is one of swimming. Just because a child wants to go in a pool doesn't mean they should, they need to learn to be comfortable in the water first, start in the shallow end, use floats, practice, and over time they can start moving towards the deep end, all the while under supervision of parents... it is a long time before a child is allowed to swim unsupervised by a parent. The same should be true of smartphone ownership. This is normally when a parent leans around the corner with a comment like:

> Oh, but I need my child to be able to contact me because they are starting to walk to and from school by themselves, what if something happens and they need help? I need my child to be safe, are you trying to put my child in danger?

To this, I often respond with "you don't need to give them a *smartphone*." There are many phones that have minimal functions that are cheap and can only make and receive calls/messages... suggest one of these to start with, consider this their arm bands in a pool, the shallow end. There are even watches that can be worn which can make and receive calls to a select number of contacts and have GPS tracking included so parents can monitor their children's whereabouts. You can even buy individual GPS tracking clips to attach to school bags linked to parent's smartphones... There are multiple ways to keep children contactable and safe that doesn't involve buying them a smartphone. A child should show that they can responsibly use this type of phone/watch for a long period of time before parents should consider upgrading them to a smart-er-phone. And even then, this decision should be made in consideration to the individual child's development and needs... not because "everyone my age has one."

Decisions need to be made by parents about if they are going to let their children have access to social media and certain technologies. Steve Jobs, one of the founding fathers of Apple, the creator of iPads, refused to let his kids use them... and he's not alone, there are numerous tech giants who limit their children's access to the technology that they design and sell. As Adam Alter puts it in his book *Irresistible:*

> it seemed as if the people producing tech products were following the cardinal rule of drug dealing: never get high on your own supply.

This should be a huge red flag to those of us that buy their products... especially when considering children's use. It should not be taken for granted that children "should" have access to technology and social media, it should be a privilege to have access to such things.

IV. What can be done to help those who need support with their social media use?

There will be parents that have already decided that they do not want their child to have access to social media, there will be parents that have decided that the benefits outweigh the risks for their child. There will also be parents who have taken no part in the decisions surrounding social media and let their children decide. So, let's say that a parent has made the decision to give their child access to technology and social media and go further down this rabbit hole.

They're in, so now what?

Let's take a social media detour and start with tablet computers and let's start young. I personally don't think a young child should have "their own" tablet computer. I'm not saying that a child should not be able to use a tablet computer, in fact, in learning how to navigate one while young you are giving a child some useful skills in using technology. What I'm saying is that it should not be "their property." Let me explain why. If you give a child their own tablet (computer), it is the same as giving them a set of coloring pencils or a doll... it becomes their toy, their property. At some point the parent will want them to not be using the tablet and it will spark an argument, because it will be seen as unfair, it's their toy and the parent keeps taking it away in an unpredictable manner (they won't understand why)—there will be meltdowns galore. However, if the parent "owns" the tablet then the child will have to ask permission to use it, at that point you can set the conditions for use... "Yes, but only for 1 hour and I'll let you know when the time is almost up"; "no, because I haven't charged it"; "yes, but only when you have tidied your other toys away"; "no, because my tablet is only to be used on long car journeys." I can guarantee there will be fewer arguments this way around.

While we're on this diversion and discussing young children and tablet computers—one of the major problems is that young children will often spend hours on a tablet computer by themselves, often on YouTube, or KidsTube. I say by themselves because even if others are in the room the activity is very much a solitary one—a child and their personal screen. And I get it, when my daughter was a baby I would often put her in the "jumperoo" because I knew she would be safe and contained and finally I could have a slice of time to do the thing I needed to do... usually tidying up. Tablet computers slow and quieten our children down, suddenly they are on the sofa mesmerized, you know they are physically safe, and you can get on with something else, you can finally cook dinner, you can finally close your eyes for a moment. The problem is we're letting children work out everything by themselves. And as we know, the video they start watching on YouTube often changes into something else and something else (thank you, prediction engines) until they end up watching some weird stuff... endless videos of toys being unwrapped and strange voice-over acting with toys and home-made cartoons. A big issue while watching these videos online, is that children are not getting "counter-messages" and their world views are being shaped by this time, their interests are being shaped by this time.

What needs to happen is simple—adults need get alongside children while they are using tablets, to ask them questions, to make it a social activity, to give counter views and expand their thinking. This doesn't just have to happen with tablet computers, this should happen with TV shows as well. I can't tell you how many times I've been watching Peppa Pig and taken a moment to ask my daughter—"do you think that's a nice thing Peppa has said to her friend? How do you think they feel now? Do you think it's alright to make fun of someone for being overweight?" Peppa Pig needs an attitude adjustment! For the families that we work with, we need to be instilling a counter-message culture early so that balanced views become a part of the norm. Starting early, and getting some foundations of technology use instilled young makes dealing with technology and adolescence much easier.

How long is too long?

There is a lot of talk in the media about "screen time" and the impact that this can have on people. But we don't talk about "food time" or "book time" when discussing diet or literacy. "Screen time" is a phrase that has arrived and is embedded in what we explored earlier in Chapter 2 with the displacement hypothesis—the idea that every moment in front of a screen displaces a more wholesome moment that would have led to something better for you. In an Article written by Jon Sutton (for the British Psychological Society) he highlights that the evidence simply doesn't back this up—"It's nearly all correlational work, and even the best evidence (from large-scale social data) shows only very small effects on sleep (duration, onset), health (activity, general), functioning (social), and behavior (aggression)." But where there is new technology, there will always be new worries—the concept of "screen time" is exactly that, a new worry. Don't get caught up in it. Ask the families you're working with: Does your child have balance? Do they have friends? Time face to face with people? Time to use technology? Time away from technology? Time for physical activities? It's not terrible to start considering the use of technology and social media like a diet... Chocolate isn't inherently "bad" for you, but too much of it is.

Help parents to practice what they preach

What children will need to see in their households is consistency and fairness. If parents are setting up rules surrounding technology and social media use, then they also need to follow them. If there is to be a "no phones at the table rule" then the parents had better be ready to ensure that they don't break that rule. If there is a "no internet use after 10pm" rule then parents need to stick to it themselves... without consistency and fairness across the family these types of situations will quickly fall apart.

This comes from a "parent setting rules" position, and let's face it, that can sometimes only promote a rebellious streak and a boundary stretching effort from children and young people. There is another way. One thing many children crave, particularly as they are getting older but also evident when they are young, is autonomy. To be able to make their own decisions about situations is very powerful for young people and can have its place when working with social media. I would go as far as to say if you can get a young person to agree their own boundaries to technology and social media, you are far more likely to succeed long term than in comparison to forcing a child to adhere to a certain way.

This type of approach has to start with a little bit of education—young people need to be taught about how this technology is designed to hold their time and attention, and so the young person is going to need to actively plan how much time they will spend on such tech, explore the values that a young person has... what type of person do they want to be? What is important to them? Where do their commitments lie? How will they schedule their time? How will they monitor their time during such activities? By giving a young person's autonomy, the parents are giving them the responsibility over their technology use. By giving young people responsibility for how they use their free time, the parent will be in-directly also be giving them responsibility for how this impacts upon other things. There is a risk here of course, many parents will not want to delve into such waters. Lacking a parent-bound rule system could mean a child doesn't complete their homework, or perhaps fails a test in school through lack of revision? But here's the kicker, sometimes, a child needs to fail and feel that failure. It's a risky position to take but I think in the long term the risk can pay off... what we're looking to do here is instill a work ethic—"if you put time into doing homework and into revision you get better grades, if you don't you might fail." Sometimes young people need to fail in order to learn and as Nir Eyal puts it in his book *Indistractable:*

> Maybe they (young people) need to know what failure feels like sooner rather than later... empowering children with the autonomy to control their own time is a tremendous gift. Even if they fail from time to time, failure is part of the learning process.

This isn't one of those "oh we just let our children roam the world" positions, this is about autonomy over "free time." Morning routines, breakfast, school attendance, dinnertime, bedtime, etc., are still the realms of parents, household flow and the need for consistency and boundaries to protect children and create the conditions for them to flourish. But within that, giving children autonomy during free time is important.

I was recently asked if I could summarize advice for parents about social media in under 3min. I instantly said "No, it's not possible, I've got too much to say." But once I'd taken a moment to breathe and recover from that request, I realized that if I was unable to do it, then that's more a reflection of my limited thinking than the subject being "too big." I now think that any information can be boiled down into 3min so that some "take-aways" can be gained to shape parents' efforts. If you can have in-depth discussions with parents, then that is great, but if you can't, then consider the below for the parent's you come into contact with.

Three minute take-away

There are four things that need to happen if parents are considering introducing social media into their child's world:

(1) Have conversations from a young age

Talking about the internet and social media should be as normal as talking about something you've seen on TV or read in the newspaper. Make it something that is normal to be talked about, that way if your child comes across something they don't understand or have been shown they are more likely to talk to you about it. Teach children how to use technology—It's important to help them to use the online world in a way that's safe and positive for their mental health. These conversations should not feel like interrogations, children will clam up quickly if they think you will take their technology away from them, but giving the opportunity to talk and checking in with them about their technology/app use for a few minutes can make all the difference if questions arise.

(2) Lead by example

Talk to your child about your experiences of the online world and Apps that you like to use, show them the internet in a positive way. I remember sitting with my daughter and showing her "the night sky" App that I use to look at the stars, constellations and planets which are visible in the night sky. She was fascinated by this and it prompted a fascination in space that lasts to this day. Show your child how to use the internet in a positive way, to research the world, to speak to the family. If you are constantly on your phone, so too will your child. Talk to your child about the less positive things that appear online... the before and after photo-shopped images of models are a good source of discussion about the reality of "the perfect way to look" and how what you see online isn't always "real."

(3) **Ask your child about the apps and websites they want to use**

Technology is moving at a fast rate and it can be easy to feel that you are out of the loop or wouldn't understand the latest apps and technology, but don't let that be an excuse to not get involved. Ask your child to tell you about their favorite Apps or the ones that they want to download and why... keeping the communication pathways open about these things is important. Recent research has highlighted that taking selfies may not be bad for self-esteem, but editing them is... if your child is downloading a lot of photo editing software to their phones—to shrink noses, whiten teeth and thin their bodies this should ring alarm bells about your child's current self-esteem and their need to portray a certain image online. If you want to know more about the Apps that your child is using then look them up online, if you feel they are not appropriate then be ready to explain why and where possible make a joint decision about the "need" of this App on their phone.

(4) **Set the boundaries**

You are the parent and you are probably paying for the phone/contract/tablet/laptop and allowing it in your house, so it is your responsibility for setting the boundaries. The boundaries will no doubt change depending on the age of your child, much like "bedtimes" change and how your child doesn't have to hold your hand in high street when they are older. You may want to set up times where tech will not be used—in bed at night, at the table etc. This is easiest to put in place at the beginning of inviting this technology into the home and harder (but not impossible) at a later date.

Three minutes... and a rough guide that could really help give a framework for parents that might not have considered it before. As far as I'm concerned, that is time spent well.

The minefield of apps

Facebook, YouTube, WhatsApp, Snapchat, Instagram—world famous apps for social networking... all of which carry risks of using and benefits. There are a lot of Apps out there designed around some form of social networking. Often these will be free at the point of download and then have in-app purchase options. There are also some which are extremely risky for teenagers to be using, hell some of these detailed below are risky for adults to be using. So, consider asking any parents you work with this question—Do you know what Apps are on your child's phone? If they don't, it's time to find out. Young people have access to a world of digital spaces, and much like "the rough parts of town," parents need to know where their children are spending their time in order to keep them safe and remain connected to them. Below is a list of a few social media apps which are available to download that, as professional working with parents and young people, you may want to be aware of. This list isn't exhaustive, in fact, it took a short amount of time to cultivate from having discussions with young people and looking through the various online app stores:

HOLLA: Live random video chat

Live & instant video chat with people from all over the world! This app has more than 30 million users from 190 countries around the world, people can meet new friends from different cultures and backgrounds worldwide. Sounds lovely right? However, this app is all about connecting with strangers, you get matched with a stranger almost instantly once signed up, you can even enable location tagging to be paired with someone nearby. But what parents and professionals need to know is that video chatting with strangers is extremely risky for teenagers—If you search online for user reviews it will highlight that there are instances of masturbation, fake identities and nasty comments becoming commonplace.

Yolo: Q&A

Yolo is an add-on that works with Snapchat. This app allows users to ask anonymous questions and get feedback. The choice is then whether or not to make the feedback public. This is a nightmare in schools, and you can imagine why, imagine being able to canvas an entire year group's opinion on one person and then publishing the results. Teenagers love anonymous feedback apps because they want to know what people think and like the idea of "being real"—despite the emotional consequences of such actions. This type of app can easily be used for bullying.

IMVU: 3D Avatar creator and chat

Through the website or through having the app, users get to create and interact with others using 3D avatars. You choose the clothes, take them into public or private online rooms and chat with other people who have made avatars. There is no specific "goal" of this game, it is primarily for chatting, and collecting new items which can be bought with money, or time—by watching adverts. One particular thing that parents will need to be aware of is that the avatars can have virtual sex and there are of course risks of talking with strangers. The outfits that can be bought/ earned are often skimpy and the avatars often overly stereotypical of "ideal" physiques which gives the app a sexualized undertone.

Likee—let you shine

Formally known as "Like—Magic Music Video Editor." This app is similar to TikTok and allows users to create short videos often involving music and lip syncing. What parents need to know about this particular app is that there is a leader board system that encourages users to get "likes" and therefore post more and gather more followers. The risks of this app are related to strangers interacting and the in-app costs if sending "gems" to other users to show you "like" them.

Calculator%

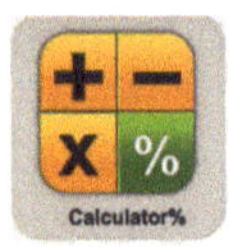

This app looks like a calculator on a phone but is actually a secret photo, video, and files vault. Only being able to be viewed when a PIN is entered into the calculator panel of the app. There seems to be a lot of pressure on young girls to send nude pictures of themselves to boys and vice versa... to keep these photos out of the traditional gallery on a phone, this app is often used. If a child is using this app then they have content, pictures, or videos on their phone that they wish to hide.

Burnbook

Burnbook allows users to post anonymously in their community. And for teenagers, that means schools. It is not uncommon for this app to be used for posting rumors, profanity, photos, voice notes or text about other people. This app, much like other "anonymous" apps is a recipe for cyberbullying.

Wishbone

This app is designed for comparing social content. Within the app you'll get sent some "pop culture" questions and you have to vote between two distinct choices and get to see how your friends voted. That bit seems fine, the company generated content. However, this app also gives you the ability to create your own Wishbone to share with your friends and that's where the problems arise. This app has been known to be used by school aged children to compare two people in a school population, "who's the hottest?" Then the voting begins.

Chatroulette

Chatroulette is an in-browser video chatting service that pairs two people at random. You can type messages as well as video chatting to strangers quickly being able to jump from one chat to the next at random. The risks are obvious, nudity being commonplace. I know of groups of teenagers who used to go on Chatroulette at sleepovers to see how many naked men they could find over an evening using a laptop. There are a number of random video chat apps that exist and if they are on your child's phone or computer (check the history) then you need to be aware of them.

This list could go on and on, the point is that as parents and professionals we are aware of the neighborhoods of our cities, towns, and villages that we would not want our child or children we work with to walk down alone... the same is true of unknown technology. Support parents to metaphorically walk with their children or to do their research in order to keep their children safe.

Parents using technology to their advantage

If parents invest some time getting to know the technology that children are using, then they will be in a better position when supporting them to use it and talk about apps without feeling absolutely lost. There is an additional level to this that some parents may wish to take. Some parents may wish to take advantage of the technology that is available to them in order to make the task of running the household and monitoring children's technology use much easier. There are a number of apps that can be downloaded and features already linked to phones that can be utilized to broaden technological-parenting and increase specific information available to parents. Currently, two of the most popular mobile phone operating systems are Apple's iPhone and Android.

If parents and their family members have an Apple iPhone, then there are a number of ways in which they can track their child's location using the built-in software of their Apple products. Let's face it, if a child has an iPhone then it's likely that it's always going to be on them or close by, and so this feature is a useful one for parents to know about. And the name of this feature? Family Sharing. You may need to practically help a parent to set this up or just having the instructions may be enough. See below:

To track a child's location using Family Sharing, follow these steps.

1. On your child's phone, navigate to Settings
2. Tap Location Sharing
3. Tap Share Your Location

For Apple devices parents can also download the "find my friends" app from the Apple store. Find My Friends allows parents and young people to easily locate "friends and family" using their devices. This app also lets parents set up location-based alerts that can notify them automatically when their child leaves school, or a family member arrives home safely. There are other ways that parents can check up on their child's location quickly using this app that can bypass opening up the app itself, to do so they could:

1. Go to a text message thread with them and their child
2. Click the ⓘ button at the top right of the screen

Their location will now be shown. If you find yourself talking a parent through various apps or features they that they can use within their parenting arsenal, don't forget to remind them that they can always just trust that their child will be where they say they'll be. There's nothing wrong with that, let's face it, trust is vitally important in the parent–child relationship. These features are designed to give peace of mind, not to stifle children with "over-parenting" so caution parents to use them wisely.

When you are working with parents they may come to a realization that they do not know how much time their children are spending on their devices. Or, they may have a general response of "too much" or "all the time." If a parent wants to get an idea of how much time their child is spending on their phone, then there are a number of apps available that can do this accurately. Some parents may want to insist on this as a pre-requisite to getting their child a phone or have put something like this in place as a point of interest to see how much time their child is spending on their phone. If a parent and their child have an Apple iPhone, then they will need access to their child's device. Then, if they follow these steps they will see a full report:

1. On the child's phone, navigate to Settings
2. Tap Turn On Screen Time
3. Tap Set Up as Parent

There is also a way parents can set up "Screen Time" through Family Sharing... this way they can get weekly reports and set limits from their phone as the parent. Outside of the parent phone's operating system there are a number of separate apps that can be downloaded on iPhone's or Android devices through their respective app stores. These are often free or incur a small cost. For information, I have included below a selection of apps currently available followed by a description of what they can do to support parenting in a technological age:

RespondASAP
If a parent is ever getting frustrated with their child ignoring their messages or calls, or of the excuse "my phone was on silent" then an app like RespondASAP might help. This app freezes the child's phone by taking over the screen and sounding an alarm—which forces the child to call the parent back to unlock the phone.
Qustodio
If a parent has concerns about their child's web browsing, then this software might give them peace of mind. Available for Windows PC, Mac, iOS, Android, and Kindle devices this software provides a "dashboard" to help parents monitor their child's online activity, including search engine use, social media logins and can set time controls for computer use. There is a "premium" Qustodio, which gives more control and more options for a cost.
Checky
If parents would like their children to become more aware of the time they are spending on their phone, then an App like Checky may be a good starting point. This App keeps a tally of how many times a day a child (or adult for that matter) has checked their phone. A similar App for the iPhone would be "Moment." In general, these Apps are designed to support "healthier smartphone habits."
Screentime
Screentime lets parents monitor the amount of time children spend on their mobile devices. With this App daily limits can be set, tasks can be assigned for children (do homework, take out bins, tidy up), parents can also see what features of apps their child spends the most time using. This app can be used as "parental control" and also for self-use. What makes this App particularly powerful is the "instant pause" feature—allowing parents to instantly pause their children's devices... which makes dinner without phones much easier.
Forest: Stay focused
Forest is an app that is designed to help people stay focused. If a child (or adult) has something to focus on and does not want to be distracted, by opening the Forest app a virtual tree is planted... and will grow

slowly, if you leave the app the tree dies. By successfully growing a whole tree and remaining undistracted you earn virtual coins and can even spend them on having a real tree planted in the world. It's amazing how well this can work to keep procrastination at bay, particularly when working to deadlines.

There are many more downloadable apps out there to help in supporting self-recognition of phone use or in adding a layer of parental monitoring/control over technology use. I don't endorse any particular one over another, but what I would say is that with many of these types of apps if a parent can support a young person to monitor their own use of technology, they will be giving them the skills needed in adulthood when they have to independently direct their own time and work.

One of the most useful tools in supporting children as they navigate the world of technology and social media is the parent. It is through the parent–child relationship and their knowledge of their child that the right technology can be introduced at the right time. It is through parents being educated about the technology and apps that are popular that allow them to understand the online world that teenagers are drawn towards. It is though the boundaries that parents set, in "the real world" and in the "online world" that help foster their child's safety and development. And it is through the relationship with their child that parents can create the conditions for open communication should anything happen online that their child would want to talk about.

But what if the parents you work with are coming to this late? What if they're only just coming to realize the negative impact social media is having for their child? What if in their attempts to try and support their child it's resulting in arguments, tears, and emotional turmoil? What if, for their child, the negatives are outweighing the benefits and they don't realize it yet? What if parents feel like they've tried everything and don't know what to do next? If this is the case, then it might be time to advise parents to seek out further support, and the most common starting place is where their child spends half of their childhood, school.

CHAPTER

16

"… But you can't make it drink, or can you?"

https://doi.org/10.1016/B978-0-323-91898-5.00010-2

You can never force someone to change, and if you do then that type of change is never sustainable, and often breeds resentment. But you can help people to identify their values, their goals, their desires and to take responsibility for what their part is in achieving them. Let's be frank for 1 min, manipulation is much easier, it is, it is much easier to manipulate a situation or a young person to try and force the change you think is right for them. But, the impact of that manipulation is often short-lived and in the long term can ruin relationships. Simon Sineak is an author and motivational speaker who once said that "there are only two ways to influence human behavior: you can manipulate it, or you can inspire it." Inspiring a young person to make positive change in their lives is hard—there is no denying that, it will be hard work, but so worthwhile, and can set the scene for personal growth and long-term relationship development. You can open multiple doors for young people, but they must be the ones to step through.

If a young person, or an adult for that matter, does not recognize that there is a need for change then they will not change. So, what is it that schools can offer to support young people struggling with their social media use? And what can other professionals do to help? That is what this chapter will begin to explore, starting with what schools can offer to their communities and ending with what can be done on a 1:1 basis by multiple professional fields.

Schools

Schools are unique organizations for promoting positive change and they are powerful in their ability to reach the hearts and minds of young people. For most developed countries in the world the one commonality across a population is that everyone will have had an experience of "being educated" in one form or another—"what was your school like?" Is one of those questions that you could ask of anyone you meet, and they would have an answer.

So, when it comes to the mammoth task of planning a curriculum to educate the youth of today there's no easy solution, particularly when the world when they "exit" education is likely to be vastly different than when they entered it. When I was at school, I would have never thought it possible that uploading videos on the internet of computer games that you play would be something that could be done to make a living, but here we are in 2021 and it's a lucrative profession for some. When I mention education, I have to be clear that I'm talking about attending and finishing school/college/university. Personally, I feel that learning and education is something that is continual throughout a person's life and never really ends.

Secondary schools have a responsibility to "educate" and this often takes the shape of attending lessons which broadly revolve around: English, Maths, Science, Geography, History, Art, Music, Physical Education, Design and Technology, Modern Foreign Languages, Religious Education, Computing, Citizenship & Personal, Social Health and Economic (PSHE). This is a tough crowd to butt in on, there's not much space to consider building structured sessions on "living with social media." But all is not lost, there are actually plenty of places where the discussions can be fostered, starting within PSHE lessons—where better to tackle to the topic of social media than in lessons designed to explore Personal, Social, Health and Economic influences on our lives. It's time to move beyond safeguarding, it goes without saying that staying "safe online" needs to remain a forefront of discussions for children using the internet, but more is needed. Children need to know about the programming of social media, how behavioral addictions can develop, how their information is used, what cyberbullying can look like and how their self-esteem can be impacted (to name a few). The starting point of promoting change is to bring knowledge into places where it wasn't previously. Teach.

Another option to impart such knowledge would be to host a series of assemblies throughout a school year, tackling one issue at a time for the entire year group. Schools have a captive audience, and while they can't force young people to not use their phones, or not to use certain apps, they can educate young people to be better able to make conscious choices about how they are going to use their time. And to those naysayers who think that "nothing would sink in" and it would be a "waste of time," this is what I say to you:

> Some of the most powerful changes for young people happen when they have been asked the right question, often a question that they do not know the answer to. That question then sits within them until it's ready to be answered.

Those types of questions, or ideas that are shared, plant a seed. Seeds that make take a long time to grow, and some will not, but many will, eventually. And in that space, change is cultivated. Ask yourself, now in knowing what you know about social media, is your phone serving you, or are you serving your phone?

There's a story I often use when training people in using solution focused approaches in schools. It's about an expert therapist working with a client. This client was a 14-year-old who had been struggling with managing their relationships with others amongst other things. In the session with the therapist she only said two words and sometimes just shrugged, those two words?—"Don't know". No matter the questions asked, the most wonderful open-ended crafted questions, by an expert therapist, over a 45-min session, and all they would elicit was a shrug, or a "don't know" from the client. The session finishes and the client returns a week later for the next session... but before the session starts the child's parent asks for a moment with the therapist. The parent says, "I don't know what you did when you last met but my daughter has been completely different at home, it's like having my old girl back again, thank you."

Sometimes the change happens on the inside, we can't forget that in schools. So, you may face an entire classroom of "shrugs" and an entire assembly hall of "whatever" ... but the message will reach a lot of children, eventually. We don't give up on teaching literacy because some children don't enjoy it, we know it's going to be fundamentally useful in adult life to be literate. The same is true of teaching children to swim, to cross the road and to understand the rule of law. Understanding the technology that surrounds us is important knowledge needed for young people to be able to navigate their childhoods safely and their adulthood informed.

While we are talking of "adulthood informed", schools have a place within their community where they can actively be engaging and supporting parents to further their knowledge about social media. Parent workshops and community talks have a great value in supporting parents to be actively informed about the cultural spaces their children occupy. Teach the parents what they need to know in order to make informed decisions about whether or not they will let their children use social media. This can be done by arranging guest speakers to come into the school, I find myself doing more and more of this as time goes by. But given the time to prepare, there is no reason that this cannot be cultivated from within the school staff to deliver in school to the parent community.

There is no consensus approach in how schools and colleges respond to children and their phones. Different schools will have different rules and expectations. I have known schools that will have a "no phones allowed" rule, and if you're caught with your phone it will be confiscated and sent to the office to be collected by the parent at the end of the day. Some schools will allow children to collect their confiscated phones at the end of the day, other schools will have a "drop your phone off at the office if you have to bring it in." Some will have a "once you get to Year 9 you can have a phone in school... but only use them at break time." One thing is consistent across most secondary schools... no matter "the rules", if a child owns a phone, they will probably have it on them in school.

There's more than "the psychological" to consider with phones in school. Most modern-day smartphones are expensive bits of kit, and in secondary school that can result in young people being targeted by thieves for what they own, or even the potential of what they own. There was a time where seeing white earphones meant "iPhone owner" to potential thieves. I'm reminded of a particularly timely theft that happened in one of the schools I was working in.

It was late in autumn and two classes of Year 9's were out for PE, which meant that approximately 60 children were out on the field with their teachers. Nothing out of the ordinary there, it happens day in day out for many schools. What makes this a particularly good time for thieves, is that students have been separated from their property, property that is grouped all together in the changing rooms… an area where security cameras are not allowed to film for obvious reasons (apart from at the entrances). Someone decided to take advantage of this opportunity and made their way into the changing rooms and in less than 60s, managed to go through a third of the blazers hanging up, leaving with 23 smart phones, if he had stayed longer, he would have got more. Take a moment to consider the amount of money that would equate to. Let's say that most smart phones are roughly £500 each, some cost more, some cost less, our thief just walked about of the changing room with £11,500 of property. Once the students returned and noticed their phones were missing it started a CCTV operation that wouldn't have been out of place in a Police Drama… the only difference being that it was headed up by the head of pastoral care for the school and the janitor (who was the best at operating the CCTV camera system). In the end it didn't take long to find the young person responsible for the theft. By working backwards through multiple cameras, they could narrow down who was where during that lesson, and to find the Year 11 young man who went to the toilet during English, via the changing rooms, before returning to his class. The phones were returned, peace was restored, and a classic school punishment ensued. And the motive for such a daring heist? New trainers… He was hoping to sell the phones on, to get some new trainers. Instead he got a fixed term exclusion, some shocked parents and a reputation that is difficult to shake.

Practicalities of having a phone in school aside, research in this area has noted that having a phone out of sight, does not mean it is out of mind. I have been asked in the past whether or not "short technology breaks" would be useful in order to help young people to focus and concentrate in lessons?—to satisfy the urge to check phones so that their minds can once more be back on the subject. My answer to this is that such an approach should only be used for young people who are highly anxious without their phones, rather than for the whole class. Let's not forget that task-switching and multitasking can have a detrimental impact on learning. For secondary aged students I would lean towards the "no phones in lessons at all" stance. For college age students I would suggest that the lecturer sets the rule that if you need to use your phone, leave the room to do so, and then return… but to instill the responsibility that their learning at college level is a choice, you get out what you put in, and to really reflect on if that call/text/social could actually wait until the lecture is over.

There is a clear place where schools and colleges can have a role in responding to young people and their use of social media—through teaching young people and their parents about how this technology works and the impact it can have. But what else can schools and professionals do? What if we have a young person who needs help? In short, that will depend on the young person themselves.

Working 1:1

There are great things about presenting to large groups of parents, or professionals and by working with systemic change points in organizations. You can have an impact at a large level, which in turn can cascade that positive impact and involvement throughout multiple people. However, I still find that some of the most meaningful work takes place at the 1:1 level. Direct work with young people may be time consuming, but it can be time extremely well spent for that individual. I'm reminded of a quotation I've never been able to find the originator of:

> helping one person might not change the world, but it could change the world for one person.

When working directly with young people there are several things that will need to be considered. Firstly, you will need to be following your organizations guidelines on consent, confidentiality and safeguarding. Secondly, the young person is going to have to be willing to be there. This is the fundamental starting point, their willingness to change might not yet have developed, but their willingness to take part in meeting with you *must* be there. If you remember earlier on in this book, I introduced the concept of "the problem owner," this is going to be key here when working directly with young people, particularly regarding social media use. For a reminder of "the problem owner" dilemma, head back to Chapter 6.

When working with a young person to explore their current situation in any given area, it can be useful to consider the Stages of Change Model (sometimes referred to as the Transtheoretical Model).

Stages of change model

Originally developed by Prochaska and DiClemente in the late 1970s, the Stages of Change Model is a six-step process to help people who are reluctant to change, to engage in a process of doing things differently. It helps to provide a framework to change work. The very basic model is outlined below:

1. **Pre-contemplative**—The young person is not yet considering change is good for them. Many young people in this stage are unaware or under-aware of their problems and may not believe that what they are "doing" is causing issues for them.
2. **Contemplative**—The young person is considering the benefits of changing. They are likely weighing up the pros and cons of changing their behavior/situation, but they have not yet made a commitment to change.
3. **Preparation (Decision)**—The young person agrees to work on a plan to change things. They may set targets that they want to achieve. The young person recognizes the benefits of change and will takes steps to change.
4. **Action**—The young person enacts the change as planned (with support). At this stage, the young person wants to keep going with the change and are actively modifying their habits/environment.
5. **Maintenance**—The young person sustains a period of change over time and intends to maintain the positive behavior change going forward.
6. **Relapse**—The young person may make errors and a plan is put place to bring them back on track. At this stage a young person could relapse to any of the previous stages and need support to explore their situation once more, given any new contexts that present themselves.

This model gives a very simple and easy to understand framework to understand where someone might be regarding the change being asked "of them" or coming "from them". Once you have an agreement to work with a young person and have considered the above stages of change model, you will then be in a position to explore in more depth how social media is having an impact on the young person you are working with.

There are multiple ways in which to explore such a phenomenon with a young person. Each individual practitioner may have years of experience and multiple skills sets to draw upon in supporting people to make positive change in their lives. There isn't a "gold standard" approach than can be advocated here. But what I am going to offer is a structured approach to measuring social media impact and a planning framework for what can be done about it. The following resources are meant to add to practitioners "tool kits"—not replace them.

I appreciate that the resources are not easy to "access" in a book format. If you wish to use them in your practice you will find my contact details at the back of this book, get in touch and I will personally send digital copies to you in a printable user-friendly format.

CHAPTER

17

Getting a measure of the situation

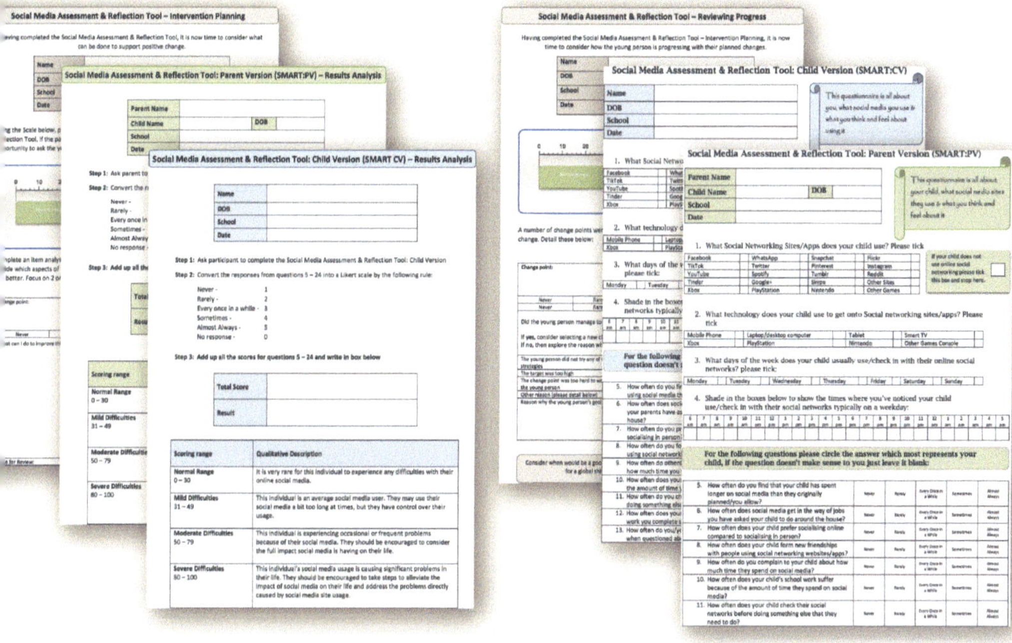

Psychologist's Guide to Adolescents and Social Media
https://doi.org/10.1016/B978-0-323-91898-5.00016-3

There are a number of phases to consider when working for positive change in social media use:

(1) Understanding the individual's social media usage
(2) Planning and implementing an intervention to alleviate any problem points
(3) Reviewing the intervention to see if has worked, and if not, why not?
(4) Planning further interventions if needed
(5) Reviewing the individual's social media usage

The following resources are designed to give a structure to the above process.

Understanding the individual's social media usage

There are two questionnaires I have developed to explore this:

1. The Social Media Assessment and Reflection Tool: Child Version (SMART: CV)
2. The Social Media Assessment and Reflection Tool: Parent Version (SMART: PV)

The SMART: CV allows a child to answer honestly (hopefully) for themselves what social media they choose to use, how they access it, when they access it, the level of impact this is having on their own psychology and whether or not it has impacted their school relationships and attendance.

The SMART: PV allows a parent to report on what they have noticed about their child's social media usage. Covering the same above points, but from a parental perspective.

Having both parent and a child complete the Social Media Assessment and Reflection Tool allows for the opportunity to complete a cross comparison of results—seeing where the similarities lie, differences exist and allowing the opportunity to explore the implications further at a parent–child perception level.

Social Media Assessment & Reflection Tool: Child Version (SMART:CV)

Name	
DOB	
School	
Date	

This questionnaire is all about you, what social media you use & what you think and feel about using it

1. What Social Networking Sites/Apps do you use? Please tick

Facebook		WhatsApp		Snapchat		Flickr	
TikTok		Twitter		Pinterest		Instagram	
YouTube		Spotify		Tumblr		Reddit	
Tinder		Google+		Skype		Other Sites	
Xbox		PlayStation		Nintendo		Other Games	

If you do not use social media in any form, then please tick this box and stop here. ☐

2. What technology do you use to get onto Social networking sites/apps? Please tick

Mobile Phone		Laptop/desktop computer		Tablet		Smart TV	
Xbox		PlayStation		Nintendo		Other Games Console	

3. What days of the week do you usually use/check in with your online social networks? please tick:

Monday		Tuesday		Wednesday		Thursday		Friday		Saturday		Sunday	

4. Shade in the boxes below to show the times where you use/check in with your social networks typically on a weekday:

6 am	7 am	8 am	9 am	10 am	11 am	12 pm	1 pm	2 pm	3 pm	4 pm	5 pm	6 pm	7 pm	8 pm	9 pm	10 pm	11 pm	12 am	1 am	2 am	3 am	4 am	5 am

For the following questions please circle the answer which most represents you, if the question doesn't make sense to you just leave it blank:

5. How often do you find that you've spent longer using social media than you originally planned?	Never	Rarely	Every Once in a While	Sometimes	Almost Always
6. How often does social media get in the way of jobs your parents have asked you to do around the house?	Never	Rarely	Every Once in a While	Sometimes	Almost Always
7. How often do you prefer socialising online to socialising in person?	Never	Rarely	Every Once in a While	Sometimes	Almost Always
8. How often do you form new friendships with people using social networking websites/apps?	Never	Rarely	Every Once in a While	Sometimes	Almost Always
9. How often do others in your life complain about how much time you spend on social media?	Never	Rarely	Every Once in a While	Sometimes	Almost Always
10. How often does your school work suffer because of the amount of time you spend using social media?	Never	Rarely	Every Once in a While	Sometimes	Almost Always
11. How often do you check your social networks before doing something else that you need to do?	Never	Rarely	Every Once in a While	Sometimes	Almost Always
12. How often does your job performance or amount of work you complete suffer because of social media?	Never	Rarely	Every Once in a While	Sometimes	Almost Always
13. How often do you/your friends become secretive when questioned about their social networking use?	Never	Rarely	Every Once in a While	Sometimes	Almost Always

IV. What can be done to help those who need support with their social media use?

14. How often do you cope with difficult parts of your life by thinking about using your social media?	Never	Rarely	Every Once in a While	Sometimes	Almost Always
15. How often do you find yourself thinking about when you will next be able use social media again?	Never	Rarely	Every Once in a While	Sometimes	Almost Always
16. How often do you feel that life without social networking would be boring, empty and joyless?	Never	Rarely	Every Once in a While	Sometimes	Almost Always
17. How often do you snap, yell, or act annoyed if someone bothers you while you are using social media?	Never	Rarely	Every Once in a While	Sometimes	Almost Always
18. How often do you lose sleep because of using social networking sites/apps?	Never	Rarely	Every Once in a While	Sometimes	Almost Always
19. How often do you find yourself thinking about something that's happened online when at school?	Never	Rarely	Every Once in a While	Sometimes	Almost Always
20. How often do you find yourself saying "just a few more minutes" when using social media sites/apps?	Never	Rarely	Every Once in a While	Sometimes	Almost Always
21. How often do you try to cut down the amount of time you spend using social media and fail?	Never	Rarely	Every Once in a While	Sometimes	Almost Always
22. How often do you try to hide how long you've been using your social media?	Never	Rarely	Every Once in a While	Sometimes	Almost Always
23. How often do you choose to spend more time social networking over going out with others?	Never	Rarely	Every Once in a While	Sometimes	Almost Always
24. How often do you feel depressed, moody, or nervous when you are off-line, which goes away once you are back online?	Never	Rarely	Every Once in a While	Sometimes	Almost Always

For the final questions please circle yes or no for your answer:

25. Has anything ever happened on social networking sites that have made you not want to go into school the next day?	Yes	No
26. Have you ever taken time off school because of something that happened on social networking sites?	Yes	No
27. Has anything ever happened on social networking sites that has made you worry in school?	Yes	No
28. Do you access your online social media while in school?	Yes	No
29. Has using online social media made your school friendships stronger?	Yes	No
30. Is there someone in school you would comfortably speak to if you were having difficulties with people on social networking sites?	Yes	No
31. Would you speak to your parents if you were having difficulties with people on social networking sites?	Yes	No
32. Do your parents use social media?	Yes	No

Is there anything else you would like to say?

IV. What can be done to help those who need support with their social media use?

Understanding the individual's social media usage: Results analysis with the child

Once the SMART: CV has been completed it's time to score up the results.

- Questions 1–4 give an overall context to the social media use, exploring what, how and when.
- Questions 5–24 allow for an exploration of the psychology and impact social media has on the psychology of the young person related to risk of behavioral addiction.
- Questions 25–32 allow a brief exploration as to whether the child sees a social media impact in their daily school lives.

The instructions for scoring the SMART: CV are provided overleaf. But the scoring itself should not be the end of the results analysis. In completing the questionnaire young people are embarking on a reflective experience of questioning things they might not have questioned before. Therefore, it is just as important to engage in the reflective questions that follow the completion of the SMART:CV and scoring process. I would recommend scoring the assessment with the young person present so that it can be a collaborative endeavor and exploration.

We are not dealing with finalities and concrete answers here, we are getting alongside a young person with genuine curiosity to help them, and us, explore and try to understand their lived experience.

Social Media Assessment & Reflection Tool: Child Version (SMART CV) – Results Analysis

Name	
DOB	
School	
Date	

Step 1: Ask participant to complete the Social Media Assessment & Reflection Tool: Child Version

Step 2: Convert the responses from questions 5 – 24 into a Likert scale by the following rule:

Never -	1
Rarely -	2
Every once in a while -	3
Sometimes -	4
Almost Always -	5
No response -	0

Step 3: Add up all the scores for questions 5 – 24 and write in box below

Total Score	
Result	

Scoring range	**Qualitative Description**
Normal Range 0 – 30	It is very rare for this individual to experience any difficulties with their online social media.
Mild Difficulties 31 – 49	This individual is an average social media user. They may use their social media a bit too long at times, but they have control over their usage.
Moderate Difficulties 50 – 79	This individual is experiencing occasional or frequent problems because of their social media. They should be encouraged to consider the full impact social media is having on their life.
Severe Difficulties 80 – 100	This individual's social media usage is causing significant problems in their life. They should be encouraged to take steps to alleviate the impact of social media on their life and address the problems directly caused by social media site usage.

Social Media Assessment & Reflection Tool: Child Version (SMART CV) – Results Analysis

Reflection Questions with Child/Young Person:

What went through your mind when completing the questionnaire?

Was there any particular question that really made you think? Which one? Will you tell me about it?

Do you think you have any difficulties with regard to your social media use?

What do you think of the suggested results of the questionnaire?

Social Media Assessment & Reflection Tool: Parent Version (SMART:PV)

Parent Name			
Child Name		**DOB**	
School			
Date			

This questionnaire is all about your child, what social media sites they use & what you think and feel about it

1. What Social Networking Sites/Apps does your child use? Please tick

Facebook		WhatsApp		Snapchat		Flickr	
TikTok		Twitter		Pinterest		Instagram	
YouTube		Spotify		Tumblr		Reddit	
Tinder		Google+		Skype		Other Sites	
Xbox		PlayStation		Nintendo		Other Games	

If your child does not use online social networking please tick this box and stop here. ☐

2. What technology does your child use to get onto Social networking sites/apps? Please tick

Mobile Phone		Laptop/desktop computer		Tablet		Smart TV	
Xbox		PlayStation		Nintendo		Other Games Console	

3. What days of the week does your child usually use/check in with their online social networks? please tick:

Monday		Tuesday		Wednesday		Thursday		Friday		Saturday		Sunday	

4. Shade in the boxes below to show the times where you've noticed your child use/check in with their social networks typically on a weekday:

6 am	7 am	8 am	9 am	10 am	11 am	12 pm	1 pm	2 pm	3 pm	4 pm	5 pm	6 pm	7 pm	8 pm	9 pm	10 pm	11 pm	12 am	1 am	2 am	3 am	4 am	5 am

For the following questions please circle the answer which most represents your child, if the question doesn't make sense to you just leave it blank:

5. How often do you find that your child has spent longer on social media than they originally planned/you allow?	Never	Rarely	Every Once in a While	Sometimes	Almost Always
6. How often does social media get in the way of jobs you have asked your child to do around the house?	Never	Rarely	Every Once in a While	Sometimes	Almost Always
7. How often does your child prefer socialising online compared to socialising in person?	Never	Rarely	Every Once in a While	Sometimes	Almost Always
8. How often does your child form new friendships with people using social networking websites/apps?	Never	Rarely	Every Once in a While	Sometimes	Almost Always
9. How often do you complain to your child about how much time they spend on social media?	Never	Rarely	Every Once in a While	Sometimes	Almost Always
10. How often does your child's school work suffer because of the amount of time they spend on social media?	Never	Rarely	Every Once in a While	Sometimes	Almost Always
11. How often does your child check their social networks before doing something else that they need to do?	Never	Rarely	Every Once in a While	Sometimes	Almost Always

IV. What can be done to help those who need support with their social media use?

12. How often does your child's job performance or amount of work they complete suffer because of social media usage?	Never	Rarely	Every Once in a While	Sometimes	Almost Always
13. How often does your child become secretive when questioned about their social media use?	Never	Rarely	Every Once in a While	Sometimes	Almost Always
14. How often do you think your child copes with difficult parts of their life by thinking about using social media or something that's happened online?	Never	Rarely	Every Once in a While	Sometimes	Almost Always
15. How often does your child talk about when they will be able use social networking sites again?	Never	Rarely	Every Once in a While	Sometimes	Almost Always
16. Do you think your child feels that life without social networking would be boring, empty and joyless?	Never	Rarely	Every Once in a While	Sometimes	Almost Always
17. How often does your child snap, yell, or act annoyed if someone bothers them while they are using social media?	Never	Rarely	Every Once in a While	Sometimes	Almost Always
18. How often does your child lose sleep because of using social media?	Never	Rarely	Every Once in a While	Sometimes	Almost Always
19. How often does your child's conversation get dominated by things that have happened or been said online?	Never	Rarely	Every Once in a While	Sometimes	Almost Always
20. How often does your child struggle to stop using social networking sites when needed?	Never	Rarely	Every Once in a While	Sometimes	Almost Always
21. How often do you try to cut down the amount of time your child spends on social media sites and fail?	Never	Rarely	Every Once in a While	Sometimes	Almost Always
22. How often does your child try to hide how long they've been using their social media?	Never	Rarely	Every Once in a While	Sometimes	Almost Always
23. How often does your child choose to spend more time social networking over going out with others?	Never	Rarely	Every Once in a While	Sometimes	Almost Always
24. How often does your child seem depressed, moody, or nervous when they are off-line, which goes away once they are back online?	Never	Rarely	Every Once in a While	Sometimes	Almost Always

For the final questions please circle yes or no for your answer:

25. Has anything ever happened on social networking sites that has made your child not want to go into school the next day?	Yes	No
26. Has your child ever taken time off school because of something that happened on social networking sites?	Yes	No
27. Has anything ever happened while using social networking sites that has made your child worry in school?	Yes	No
28. Does your child access their social media sites while in school?	Yes	No
29. Has using social media sites made your child's school friendships stronger?	Yes	No
30. Is there someone in school your child would comfortably speak to if they were having difficulties with people on social networking sites?	Yes	No
31. Has your child ever spoken to you about difficulties they are having on social networking sites?	Yes	No
32. Do you use social media?	Yes	No

Is there anything else you would like to say?

IV. What can be done to help those who need support with their social media use?

Understanding the individual's social media usage: Results analysis with the parent

Once the SMART: PV has been completed with the parent, it's time to score up the results. As a reminder:

- Questions 1–4 give an overall context to the social media use, exploring what, how and when.
- Questions 5–24 allow for an exploration of the psychology and impact social media has on the psychology of the young person related to risk of behavioral addiction from a parental perspective
- Questions 25–32 allow a brief exploration as to whether the parent has noticed a social media impact in their child's daily school lives.

The instructions for scoring the SMART: PV are the same as for the child assessment and are provided overleaf. Just like with the SMART: CV the scoring itself should not be the end of the results analysis. I cannot stress enough the value of qualitative data—hearing people's stories and experiences alongside what the numbers may say. In completing the questionnaire parents are also embarking on a reflective experience of questioning things they might not have questioned before. They may have come to realize that they do not know enough about what their child is using as social media, or the times they have access to it. Therefore, it is just as important to engage in the reflective questions with the parents as it is the child. Once more, I would recommend scoring the assessment with the parent present so that it can be a collaborative endeavor and exploration.

There will come a point where professional discretion will need to take place as to decide whether it would be appropriate to have the parent and the child together, to discuss any discrepancies with their reported results and views. The child may wish to keep their responses private from the parent and vice versa. This could be a sensitive topic to approach with the family, which is why remaining respectful to both parties and their views will be important.

Social Media Assessment & Reflection Tool: Parent Version (SMART:PV) – Results Analysis

Parent Name			
Child Name		**DOB**	
School			
Date			

Step 1: Ask parent to complete the Social Media Assessment & Reflection Tool (Parent Version)

Step 2: Convert the responses from questions 5 – 24 into a Likert scale by the following rule:

Never -	1
Rarely -	2
Every once in a while -	3
Sometimes -	4
Almost Always -	5
No response -	0

Step 3: Add up all the scores for questions 5 – 24 and write in 'total score' box below

Total Score	
Result	

Scoring range	**Qualitative Description**
Normal Range 0 – 30	It is very rare for this individual to experience any difficulties with their online social media.
Mild Difficulties 31 – 49	This individual is an average social media user. They may use their social media a bit too long at times, but they have control over their usage.
Moderate Difficulties 50 – 79	This individual is experiencing occasional or frequent problems because of their social media. They should be encouraged to consider the full impact social media is having on their life.
Severe Difficulties 80 – 100	This individual's social media usage is causing significant problems in their life. They should be encouraged to take steps to alleviate the impact of social media on their life and address the problems directly caused by social media site usage.

IV. What can be done to help those who need support with their social media use?

Social Media Assessment & Reflection Tool: Parent Version (SMART:PV) – Results Analysis

Reflection Questions:

What went through your mind when completing the questionnaire?

Was there any particular question that really made you think? Which one? Will you tell me about it?

Do you think your child has any difficulties with regard to their social media use?

What do you think of the suggested results of the questionnaire?

What do you think you could do next in order to support your child?

IV. What can be done to help those who need support with their social media use?

Planning and implementing an intervention

The following resources provide a framework that can be used to plan an intervention. Don't be intimidated by the word "intervention"—it is simply referring to the fact that we are going to "do something" different, and that difference is what is going to "intervene" with the selected problem.

Importantly, intervention planning gives the young person, and the professional working with them, an opportunity to look through the Social Media Assessment and Reflection Tool once more and select some "change points" that the young person would like to work on.

Once the change points have been selected, it's time to explore what their current experience is of that phenomenon, and to find out where they want to get to, what change they want to see. Do they want to move from "almost always" experiencing something to "sometimes"? to "never"? What does the young person believe they can get to?

Once those targets are set it's time to get creative with exploring what can be done to improve things for the young person. There is an emphasis of control being in the young person's hands, exploring what they can do to help themselves. But in addition, there is no doubt that a supportive environment is key to positive change. So, there is space to consider what parents can do to support the young person's efforts.

Planning an intervention is important, there's no point getting results that highlight a difficulty if nothing is going to be done about it. Consider the Stages of Change Model once more and if the young person is ready for change. Remember:

The same + the same = the same. If you don't do anything differently, nothing will change for the better.

Social Media Assessment & Reflection Tool – Intervention Planning

Having completed the Social Media Assessment & Reflection Tool, it is now time to consider what can be done to support positive change.

Name	
DOB	
School	
Date	

Using the Scale below, plot the young person's total score from the Social Media Assessment & Reflection Tool, if the parent has completed the assessment also, plot their score. You can use this opportunity to ask the young person, where they would ideally like to be on this scale.

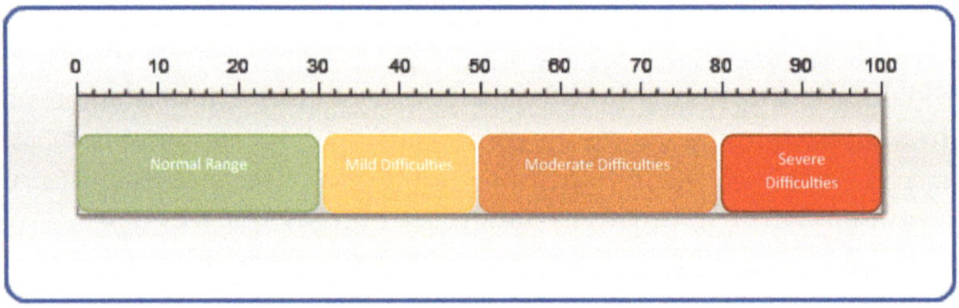

Complete an item analysis of the questionnaire responses (questions 5 – 24) with the young person, decide which aspects of the young person's social media usage that they would like to change for the better. Focus on 2 or 3 to start with.

Change point:				
Never	Rarely	Every once in a while	Sometimes	Almost Always
What can I do to improve this?		What can my parents do to help me improve this?		
Date for Review:				

Social Media Assessment & Reflection Tool – Intervention Planning

Change point:				
Never	Rarely	Every once in a while	Sometimes	Almost Always
What can I do to improve this?		What can my parents do to help me improve this?		
Date for Review:				

Change point:				
Never	Rarely	Every once in a while	Sometimes	Almost Always
What can I do to improve this?		What can my parents do to help me improve this?		
Date for Review:				

IV. What can be done to help those who need support with their social media use?

See below for an example of a completed intervention table: *Example Intervention Table.*

Change point:

How often do you find that you've ... al media than you originally planned?

Ask the young person to also select where they would like to be on this scale = target score

Original Score

Original Score & Target Score

Never	Rarely	Every once in a while	Sometimes	Almost Always

What can I do to improve this situation?	What can my parents do to help me improve this?
Set an alarm reminder for 30 minutes so that I know when I should stop	Buy me an actual alarm clock so I don't need my phone for that
Ask myself 'why' I'm using social media – note down the purpose and maybe what I am trying to escape or avoid doing if I'm procrastinating	Understand that I find it hard to do 2 things at once – I can't use my phone and talk/listen well at the same time
Set a plan for my free time so I know exactly what I want to actually accomplish	To follow the rules that they set – if there is a 'no phones used at the table' rule then they should stick to it as well
At bedtime - leave my phone in another room and use an alarm clock	

Date for Review:

Reviewing progress of the intervention

Once the intervention plan had been created, a date should have been agreed to review the young person's progress with the plan.

The following resources give a framework for exploring how the intervention has been going for the young person. This allows for a quantifiable measure of success or failure with the intervention. This also allows for a qualitative exploration of what may have gone wrong if the young person has not met their planned goals.

If the young person manages to meet their target goals, then it should be celebrated with them. If they have failed to meet their target goals then this should be explored in a guilt-free and blame-free way, try and find out what happened, could it be:

- The young person did not try any of the identified strategies.
- The parent was not able to implement any of the identified strategies
- The target was too high
- Issues outside of the young person's control
- The change point was too hard to work with for the young person
- The young person needs more time
- The social environment acted as a barrier
- Some other reason?

Any perceived failures should be explored in the context of a growth mindset, that failures are the lessons learnt and those lessons should be used to further inform alternative intervention planning. Take forward those lessons and utilize them to refine intervention planning. Do not give up, remind the young person that this simply means that they haven't met their goal "yet", that they are engaging in a process, and processes have movement to them, they have to keep moving for there to be change.

When multiple change points have been worked on, the time will come where a repeat of the SMART: CV should take place. This will then show if over time there has been a shift in a young person's global experience of using social media. A repeat of the SMART: PV can also be done to see if the parent has noticed a difference in their child's presentation. This is a way to test for pre and post intervention effectiveness.

Social Media Assessment & Reflection Tool – Reviewing Progress

Having completed the Social Media Assessment & Reflection Tool – Intervention Planning, it is now time to consider how the young person is progressing with their planned changes.

Name	
DOB	
School	
Date	

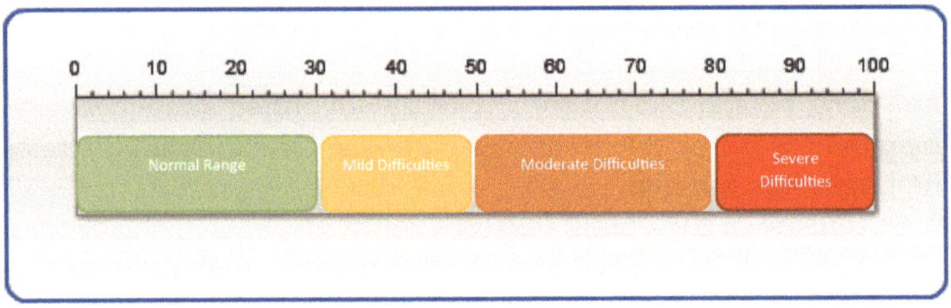

A number of change points were selected in order to narrow down a focus for making positive change. Detail these below:

Change point:				
Never	Rarely	Every once in a while	Sometimes	Almost Always
Never	Rarely	Every once in a while	Sometimes	Almost Always

Did the young person manage to meet their goal? yes / no

If **yes**, consider selecting a new change point to work on & celebrate the success
If **no**, then explore the reason why the intervention didn't work (see below):

The young person did not try any of the identified strategies		The parent was not able to implement any of the identified strategies	
The target was too high		Issues outside of the young person's control	
The change point was too hard to work with for the young person		The young person needs more time	
Other reason (please detail below)		The social environment acted as a barrier	

Reason why the young person's goal was not met:

Return to Intervention Planning

Consider when would be a good time to repeat the Social Media Assessment & Reflection Tool to check for a global shift in the Young Person's experience of using social media

IV. What can be done to help those who need support with their social media use?

Social Media Assessment & Reflection Tool – Reviewing Progress

Change point:				
Never	Rarely	Every once in a while	Sometimes	Almost Always
Never	Rarely	Every once in a while	Sometimes	Almost Always

Did the young person manage to meet their goal? yes / no

If **yes**, consider selecting a new change point to work on
If **no**, then explore the reason why the intervention didn't work (see below):

The young person did not try any of the identified strategies		The parent was not able to implement any of the identified strategies	
The target was too high		Issues outside of the young person's control	
The change point was too hard to work with for the young person		The young person needs more time	
Other reason (please detail below)			

Reason why the young person's goal was not met:

Return to Intervention Planning

Change point:				
Never	Rarely	Every once in a while	Sometimes	Almost Always
Never	Rarely	Every once in a while	Sometimes	Almost Always

Did the young person manage to meet their goal? yes / no

If **yes**, consider selecting a new change point to work on
If **no**, then explore the reason why the intervention didn't work (see below):

The young person did not try any of the identified strategies		The parent was not able to implement any of the identified strategies	
The target was too high		Issues outside of the young person's control	
The change point was too hard to work with for the young person		The young person needs more time	
Other reason (please detail below)			

Reason why the young person's goal was not met:

Return to Intervention Planning

IV. What can be done to help those who need support with their social media use?

See below for an example of a completed review table:

Change point:

How often do you find that you've spent longer using social media than you originally planned?

Original Score & Target Score

Never	Rarely	Every once in a while	Sometimes	Almost Always
Never	Rarely	Every once in a while	Sometimes	Almost Always

Review Score

Did the young person manage to meet their goal? Yes / No

If **yes**, consider selecting a new change point to work on & celebrate the success
If **no**, then explore the reason why the intervention didn't work (see below):

The young person did not try any of the identified strategies		The parent was not able to implement any of the identified strategies	
The target was too high		Issues outside of the young person's control	
The change point was too hard to work with for the young person		The young person needs more time	
Other reason (please detail below)		The social environment acted as a barrier	

Reason why the young person's goal was not met:

Return to Intervention Planning

Remember, if you would like easy to use printable versions of the assessments outlined in the chapter, you will find my contact details in the back of this book, drop me an e-mail and i will send them on to you.

CHAPTER

18

Drawing everything to a close

Psychologist's Guide to Adolescents and Social Media
https://doi.org/10.1016/B978-0-323-91898-5.00021-7

When I first started working as a psychologist and researching social media, I wanted to find a way to share what I had learned with as many people as possible, this book has been my attempt at capturing that information.

My hopes are that having read this book, you will end up with a rounded perspective of the positives that social media can bring to many. And with that, an understanding about the negatives that can be present alongside it.

For those professionals who get to work with parents, I hope you feel more empowered to bring the discussion of social media into a non-judgmental forum with them. To engage parents in reflective conversations that will reverberate within them so that they feel better able to educate their children and empower them to choose their technology wisely. In supporting parents, this topic can become as common a discussion point as the age old "what's happened in school today?". The more parents understand the cultural worlds their children are occupying, the better equipped they are to guide them through into adulthood.

For those professionals who are privileged enough to work with young people, I hope that this book has added to your professional practice, through knowledge gained, perspectives given and in resourcing you to work with those who struggle with their social media use. By the time this book is published there may be multiple others available with different views, arguments, and perspectives. There may be new research papers debunking old ones and innovative steps taken in understanding the phenomena of social media. That is of course the nature and the brilliance of developing psychological understanding. But, no matter the changing face of technology, there is one thing will not fundamentally shift, which is the underlying impact that social media can have on its users… the mixing of technology and people will never be a passive endeavor, but a deeply transformative one. It is essential to approach the intersection of people and technology with a fervent curiosity not a passive indifference. As professionals working with young people, we are in a position to support positive change and growth where it is needed—that will never fundamentally change, we just have to be ready for what the young people will bring through the doors. Understanding the use and experience of social media, I would say, is vitally important to understanding the cultural and social worlds young people are growing up immersed in.

We need to come to a point of informed technology use that serves its users, not hampers their day to day functioning. It starts with awareness, but can't stop there, it takes more than being aware to overcome the status quo. If you want things to be different then you must start doing things differently. For the socially isolated, that might look like turning to social media to connect with others. For those overly connected online and lacking balance in their lives, that may look like adding structure to the time spent online. Whatever the direction one takes with their social media choices, it is important to reflect on the following questions:

IV. What can be done to help those who need support with their social media use?

1. How is your technology use helping you to live life in the way that you want to be living?
2. How is your technology use getting in the way of how you want to be living your life?
3. Do your children (or children you work with) truly have access to broad and balanced life experiences?

The answers to the above questions will indicate if it's time to make a change, and hopefully, what you've discovered in this book will help you on the first step of that journey.

Epilogue

In my normal practice as an Educational Psychologist, I would often be visiting families in their homes, visiting children in their schools, meeting with teachers, meeting with professionals, and conducting consultations from my office. It is not uncommon for Educational Psychologists in the UK to work across an area of 30+ schools. We get around. And then a worldwide pandemic struck, and everything ground to a halt... at least, for a moment. Suddenly denied the ability to work in the "normal way," we kept our distance, in order to keep our communities safe. I've never seen a government organization upgrade their technology so quickly as when Covid-19 showed up. Suddenly, my computer had the capabilities to digitally connect through multiple virtual means... and I had to quickly learn how to use it. Without the technology to do so, my work would have stumbled, hell, it would have fallen flat on its face. I work in a profession that places the utmost value to face-to-face interaction and connection. If the Covid-19 pandemic has taught us anything as professionals it's that our services need to be able to adapt to be delivered in a distanced digital manner should the need arise. I don't believe that "the digital" will ever fully replace the "in person," especially in practitioner psychologist, counseling, social work, mental health, youth work, and teaching professions. But what has happened, and what I believe will grow over time, is that another way of our services being accessed has arrived—the digital way.

This digital way of working allows our services to reach people that may not have had the courage, the means, or the options to meet us in person. It will not be everyone's cup of tea, and if I'm honest, it's not mine, I feel less of a psychologist when working digitally, like those I work with aren't getting the full service and that I'll be missing things that I may have picked up on if I was in the room... subtle changes in body language, the way a tone of voice can shift, the quality rapport that can be generated when two people meet in a space with a common goal. But those thoughts are my load to bear, the clients I work with may be getting exactly what they need from our time together through video conferencing... they may prefer it. The point I'm trying to make is that digital doesn't have to be the enemy, for some people, it will be their preferred way and as professionals we should be able to meet our clients in a way that suits their needs.

There is a growing evidence base to suggest that as communication technology advances, then interventions may be delivered through them for the benefit of their users. Over time I've seen articles noting the use of motivational text messages to support a "stop smoking group," downloadable smartphone games such as "depression quest" exploring choices, consequences, and depressive thoughts, PlayStation games with huge production budgets such as Hellblade: Senua's Sacrifice explore a protagonist with Schizophrenia and even indie games such as Fractured Minds—developed by a 17-year old, exploring anxiety and mental health.

Looking onwards, and with the increase of modern computer gaming and the cross-platform compatibility with social networking, many concepts already researched regarding social media apply to online gaming. However, the differences in use and specifics can elicit different psychological concepts, such as the psychological need to be part of a story. This concept, of being part of a story, is distinct from platforms like Facebook, as the virtual environments in which gaming takes place give rise to "virtual adventures" that individuals can take part in simultaneously with the social benefits.

The medical profession has picked up on these positive effects and become increasingly interested in medical interventions being adapted into games. There is a journal, first published in 2012, called the "Games for Health Journal"—the first peer reviewed journal dedicated to advancing the impact of game research, technologies, and applications on human health and wellbeing. If a journal has been created specifically to contain such research, then it's a sign of changing times. The use of technology and social media games is an extremely valuable and relevant future direction for psychological study, one which I believe will be extremely useful in promoting the psychological health of all users of social media platforms.

Not long ago, I was working in a very cramped Primary School, this is the type of school that was once a church building that got adapted into a school, but never really grew with its student population... every single space within this school is filled. I would often find myself working in a corridor with the young people I needed to see. Space is at a premium here. But what they lack in space, they make up for in ingenuity. I was having a debrief with the deputy head-teacher about my ongoing work and strategies that the school could adopt to support their young people when something caught my attention on the shelf in the office—a virtual reality headset. "what's that?" I asked... I knew what it was, I'm 99% geek when it comes to gaming technology, but where's the fun in that? Sometimes it's better to approach situations from a position of naivety, you learn a lot more. The teacher was excited to show me what they had purchased as a school. "This is the best thing I've bought in a long time," the purpose of which, to provide young people with, what they described as "a mindful moment break." You see, at this school, green space was lacking and the corridors and classrooms were cramped, but what this VR headset did, was allow children who needed a break, who needed space, who needed to calm down, an escape route... one moment they were in a school, the next, on a VR beach, or in a forest, or on the moon. It was a fantastic utilization of technology to overcome the physical limitations of the school to benefit young people in need.

It's not so much of a stretch to envisage putting on a VR headset and finding yourself sitting in front of a client, also in a VR headset, together in a virtual consultation room... and although somewhat apprehensive about the changing nature of technology, I find myself equally quite excited about the possibilities.

Glossary of terms

Blocking You can block someone to unfriend them online and prevent them from starting conversations with you or seeing things you post on your social networking profile. People you block can no longer: See things you post on your profile; Tag you; Invite you to events or groups; Start a conversation with you; Add you as a friend.

Douyin/TikTok Douyin is a Chinese video-sharing social networking service owned by ByteDance. It is used to create short music, lip-sync, dance, comedy and talent videos of 3–15 s, and short looping videos of 3–60 s. TikTok is the international version of the above.

Ecosystemic An ecosystemic perspective of a situation or problem, considers the influencing and interacting factors in a range of environmental systems. These include the influences within a child's school, home, and community. These ideas derive from Bronfenbrenner's (1979) ecological systems theory.

Facebook Facebook is a popular free social networking website that allows registered users to create profiles, upload photos and video, send messages, and keep in touch with friends, family, and colleagues.

FB Messenger Facebook's dedicated messenger application—send text pictures and videos to those whom you are in contact with on Facebook.

Google+ A social network from Google. Some of its tools and features come from existing services and platforms, such as the Picasa photo storing and sharing platform.

Hootsuite A "Social Media Management System" or tool. It helps you keep track and manage your many social network channels.

Instagram Instagram is an online mobile photo-sharing, video-sharing, and social networking service that enables its users to take pictures and videos, and share them either publicly or privately.

Kuaishou Chinese video-sharing mobile app developed by Beijing Kuaishou Technology Co. A mobile app created to make and share GIF pictures.

MSN Messenger It (now discontinued) was an online instant messaging system that allowed you to connect to others online.

Nintendo Wii A games console produced by the company Nintendo that can connect to the internet for social gaming/networking/browsing.

Pinterest Pinterest is a social network that allows users to visually share, and discover new interests by posting (known as "pinning" on Pinterest) images or videos to their own or others' boards.

PlayStation A games console produced by the company Sony that can connect to the internet for social gaming/networking/browsing.

QQ Instant messaging software service and web portal developed by Tencent. QQ offers services that provides online social games, music, shopping, microblogging, movies, and group and voice chat software.

Q Zone Qzone is a social networking website based in China. It allows users to write blogs, keep diaries, send photos, listen to music, and watch videos.

Reddit Reddit is an American-based social news aggregation, web content rating, and discussion website. Registered members submit content to the site such as links, text posts, and images, which are then voted up or down by other members.

Sina Weibo Sina Weibo is a Chinese microblogging website launched by Sina Corporation.

Skype Software which allows you to have a spoken conversation with (someone) over the Internet, frequently also viewing by webcam. Users can also send messages and pictures.

Smart TV A television with the capability to access the internet.
SMART: CV Social Media Assessment and Reflection Tool: Child Version.
SMART: PV Social Media Assessment and Reflection Tool: Parent Version.
Snapchat Snapchat is a mobile messaging application used to share photos, videos, text, and drawings.... which can only be viewed for a small amount of time before they delete themselves.
Spotify Spotify is the world's most popular on-demand music streaming service, allowing browsing and subscription to other people's profiles to discover music tastes and interests.
Tablet A hand held computer with access to the internet.
Tag When you "tag" someone, they'll be notified. Also, if you or a friend tags someone in your post, the post could be visible to the audience you selected plus friends of the tagged person.
Tinder Tinder is a location-based dating and social discovery application that facilitates communication between mutually interested users, allowing matched users to chat.
Tumblr A microblogging platform and social networking website. The service allows users to post multimedia and other content to a short-form blog. Users can follow other users' blogs, as well as make their blogs private.
Twitter An online social networking service that enables users to send and read short 140-character messages called "tweets."
Vine Vine is a short-form video sharing service where users can share six-second-long looping video clips.
Weixin/WeChat WeChat is a Chinese multi-purpose messaging, social media and mobile payment app developed by Tencent. Weixin is the same system but designed for when overseas.
WhatsApp A cross-platform mobile messaging app, which allows you to exchange messages over the internet/mobile data usage, without having to pay.
Xbox A games console produced by the company Microsoft that can connect to the internet for social gaming/networking/browsing.
YouTube A free video sharing website that makes it easy to watch online videos. You can create and upload your own videos to share with others and subscribe to their "channels."

Appendix

The Johari Window

	Known to Self	Not Known to Self
Known to Others	Arena	Blind Spot
Not Known to Others	Facade	? Unknown

Contact details

If you would like to access of the following resources in an easy to print format:

1. Social Media Assessment and Reflection Tool: Child Version (SMART: CV)
2. Social Media Assessment and Reflection Tool: Parent Version (SMART: PV)
3. Social Media Assessment and Reflection Tool: Child Version (SMART: CV)—Scoring Framework and Results Analysis
4. Social Media Assessment and Reflection Tool: Parent Version (SMART: PV)—Scoring Framework and Results Analysis
5. Social Media Assessment and Reflection Tool—Intervention Planning
6. Social Media Assessment and Reflection Tool—Review of Intervention

Then, please do get in touch via the following e-mail address, and I shall personally send them on to you.

I would also love to hear your experiences of using them.

Dr. Pierre Court
drpierrecourt@outlook.com

Sources and References

The following research, articles, books, and websites have informed the content of this book

Adams, D. (2002). *The salmon of doubt: Hitchhiking the galaxy one last time*. UK: William Heinemann Ltd.

Agatston, P. W., Kowalski, R., & Limber, S. (2007). Students' perspectives on cyber bullying. *Journal of Adolescent Health, 41*(6), S59–S60.

Ahn, J. (2011). The effect of social network sites on adolescents' social and academic development: Current theories and controversies. *Journal of the American Society for Information Science and Technology, 62*(8), 1435–1445.

Alloway, T. P. (2007). *Automated working memory assessment (AWMA)*. London: Pearson.

Alloway, T. P., Horton, J., Alloway, R. G., & Dawson, C. (2013). Social networking sites and cognitive abilities: Do they make you smarter? *Computers & Education, 63*, 10–16. https://doi.org/10.1016/j.compedu.2012.10.030.

Alreck, P. L., & Settle, R. B. (1995). *The survey research handbook* (2nd ed.). New York, NY: Irwin/McGraw-Hill.

Alter, A. (2017). *Irresistible: The rise of addictive technology and the business of keeping us hooked*. UK: Penguin Press.

American Psychiatric Association. (1994). *Diagnostic and statistical manual of mental disorders* (4th ed.). Washington, DC: American Psychiatric Association.

Amichai-Hamburger, Y. (2013). Youth internet and wellbeing. *Computers in Human Behavior, 29*(1), 1–2. https://doi.org/10.1016/j.chb.2012.05.023.

Apaolaza, V., He, J., & Hartmann, P. (2014). The effect of gratifications derived from use of the social networking site Qzone on Chinese adolescents' positive mood. *Computers in Human Behavior, 41*, 203–211. https://doi.org/10.1016/j.chb.2014.09.029.

Arteaga Sánchez, R., Cortijo, V., & Javed, U. (2014). Students' perceptions of Facebook for academic purposes. *Computers & Education, 70*, 138–149. https://doi.org/10.1016/j.compedu.2013.08.012.

Asch, S. E. (1951). Effects of group pressure on the modification and distortion of judgments. In H. Guetzkow (Ed.), *Groups, leadership and men* (pp. 177–190). Pittsburgh, PA: Carnegie Press.

Bandura, A. (1997). *Self-efficacy: The exercise of control*. New York: W. H. Freeman & Company.

Benak, J. C. (2001). To quantify experience? Methodological issues in the behavioral/psychological treatment of complex partial seizures. *Seizure, 10*(1), 48–55.

Bevan, J. L., Pfyl, J., & Barclay, B. (2012). Negative emotional and cognitive responses to being unfriended on Facebook: An exploratory study. *Computers in Human Behavior, 28*(4), 1458–1464. https://doi.org/10.1016/j.chb.2012.03.008.

Biesta, G. J. J., & Burbules, N. C. (2003). In M. D. Lanham (Ed.), *Pragmatism and educational research* Rowman and Littlefield.

Bolton, S., Lago, D., & Wright, J. K. (2004). *Writing cures: An introductory handbook of writing in counseling and therapy* (pp. 95–105). New York: Brunner-Routledge.

Boyd, D. M., & Ellison, N. B. (2007). Social network sites: Definition, history, and scholarship. *Journal of Computer-Mediated Communication, 13*, 210–230.

Brenner, W. (1997). Psychology of computer use: XLVII. Parameters of Internet use, abuse and addiction: The first 90 days of the internet usage survey. *Psychological Reports, 80*, 879–882.

Brewster, T. (2020). *Houseparty: Is the hit coronavirus lockdown app safe?*. Retrieved from: https://www.forbes.com/sites/thomasbrewster/2020/03/23/houseparty-is-the-hit-coronavirus-lockdown-app-safe/amp/.

Bright, L. F., Kleiser, S. B., & Grau, S. L. (2015). Too much Facebook? An exploratory examination of social media fatigue. *Computers in Human Behavior, 44*, 148–155. https://doi.org/10.1016/j.chb.2014.11.048.

Buijzen, M., & Valkenburg, P. M. (2005). Parental mediation of undesired advertising effects. *Journal of Broadcasting & Electronic Media, 49*(2), 153–165.

Caldwell, M. A., & Peplau, L. A. (1982). Sex differences in same-sex friendship. *Sex Roles, 8*(7), 721–732.

Caplan, S. E. (2002). Problematic Internet use and psychosocial well-being: Development of a theory-based cognitive-behavioral measurement instrument. *Computers in Human Behavior, 18*, 553–575.

Chang, M. K., & Law, S. P. (2008). Factor structure for Young's Internet Addiction Test: A confirmatory study. *Computers in Human Behavior, 24*(6), 2597–2619.

Chen, R. (2013). Member use of social networking sites—An empirical examination. *Decision Support Systems, 54*(3), 1219–1227. https://doi.org/10.1016/j.dss.2012.10.028.

Chen, S., Weng, L., Su, Y., Wu, H., & Yang, P. (2003). Development of a Chinese Internet addiction scale and its psychometric study. *Chinese Journal of Psychology, 45*(3), 279–294.

Clerkin, E. M., Smith, A. R., & Hames, J. L. (2013). The interpersonal effects of Facebook reassurance seeking. *Journal of Affective Disorders, 151*(2), 525–530. https://doi.org/10.1016/j.jad.2013.06.038.

Cohen, L. (2007). *Research methods in education*. Oxon: Routledge.

Cohen, S., & Wills, T. A. (1985). Stress, social support, and the buffering hypothesis. *Psychological Bulletin, 98*, 310–357.

Colman, A. M. (2006). *Oxford dictionary of psychology* (2nd ed.). New York: Oxford University Press.

Coolican, H. (2004). *Research methods and statistics in psychology* (4th ed.). London, England: Hodder and Stoughton.

Court, P. (2016). *The experience of using online social networking sites for children in UK secondary schools: The impact on cognition, social relationships, sense of self and the role of parents—A mixed method 2 phase analysis*. University of Exeter Doctoral Thesis http://hdl.handle.net/10871/23989.

Cramer, S., Espie, C. A. (2016) Waking up to the health benefits of sleep. Retrieved from: http://www.rsph.org.uk/filemanager/root/site_assets/our_work/areas_of_work/waking_up_to_the_health_benefits_of_sleep/rsph_sleep_report.pdf.

Crawford, S. D., Couper, M. P., & Lamias, M. J. (2001). Web surveys: Perceptions of burden. *Social Science Computer Review, 19*, 146–162.

Creswell, J. W. (2009). *Research design: Qualitative, quantitative and mixed methods approaches*. Thousand Oaks, CA: Sage Publications.

Cronbach, L. (1980). *Toward reform of program evaluation*. San Fransisco: Jossey Bass.

Darley, J. M., & Latané, B. (1968). Bystander intervention in emergencies: Diffusion of responsibility. *Journal of Personality and Social Psychology, 8*, 377–383. https://doi.org/10.1037/h0025589.

Davis, R. A. (2001). A cognitive-behavioral model of pathological Internet use. *Computers in Human Behavior, 17*, 187–195.

De Vaus, D., & A. (2001). *Research design in social research*. London: SAGE Publications Ltd.

Denzin, N., & K., and Lincoln, Y, S. (2000). *The landscape of qualitative research*. London: SAGE Publications Ltd.

Dhir, A., Chen, S., & Nieminen, M. (2015). Predicting adolescent Internet addiction: The roles of demographics, technology accessibility, unwillingness to communicate and sought Internet gratifications. *Computers in Human Behavior, 51*(Part A), 24–33. https://doi.org/10.1016/j.chb.2015.04.056.

Diclemente, C. (2007). The transtheoretical model of intentional behavior change. *Drugs and Alcohol Today, 7*(1), 29–33.

Diddi, A., & LaRose, R. (2006). Getting hooked on news: Uses and gratifications and the formation of news habits among college students in an Internet environment. *Journal of Broadcasting & Electronic Media, 50*(2), 193–210.

Dolev-Cohen, M., & Barak, A. (2013). Adolescents' use of instant messaging as a means of emotional relief. *Computers in Human Behavior, 29*(1), 58–63. https://doi.org/10.1016/j.chb.2012.07.016.

Donath, J., & Boyd, D. (2004). Public displays of connection. *BT Technology Journal, 22*(4), 71–82.

Doty, J., & Dworkin, J. (2014). Parents' of adolescents use of social networking sites. *Computers in Human Behavior, 33*, 349–355. https://doi.org/10.1016/j.chb.2013.07.012.

Dredge, R., Gleeson, J., & de la Piedad Garcia, X. (2014). Cyberbullying in social networking sites: An adolescent victim's perspective. *Computers in Human Behavior, 36*, 13–20. https://doi.org/10.1016/j.chb.2014.03.026.

Drouin, M., Kaiser, D. H., & Miller, D. (2012). *Phantom vibration syndrome. Presented at Midwestern Psychological Association, Chicago, IL.* http://opus.ipfw.edu/psych_facpres/84.

Dyson, A. H., & Genishi, C. (1994). The need for story: Cultural diversity in classroom and community. In *ERIC*. Retrieved from http://files.eric.ed.gov/fulltext/ED365991.pdf.

Elliott, M. S., & Williams, D. I. (2001). Paradoxes of qualitative research. *Counselling and Psychotherapy Research, 1*(3), 181–183.

Eyal, N. (2019). *Indistractable: How to control your attention and choose your life*. UK: Bloomsbury Publishing.

Fenaughty, J., & Harré, N. (2013). Factors associated with young people's successful resolution of distressing electronic harassment. *Computers & Education, 61*, 242–250.

Ferrari, J., Johnson, J., & McCown, W. (1995). *Procrastination and task avoidance: Theory research and treatment*. Springer.

Ferraro, G., Caci, B., D'Amico, A., & Di Blasi, M. (2007). Internet addiction disorder: An Italian study. *CyberPsychology & Behavior, 10*(2), 170–175. https://doi.org/10.1089/cpb.2006.9972.

Festinger, L. (1954). A theory of social comparison processes. *Human Relations, 7*, 117–140.

Field, A. (2013). *Discovering statistics using IBM SPSS statistics* (4th ed.). London: Sage Publications LDT.

Fitzpatrick, R. (1991). Surveys of patient satisfaction: Important general considerations. *Boston Medical Journal, 302*, 887–889.

Floros, G., & Siomos, K. (2013). The relationship between optimal parenting, Internet addiction and motives for social networking in adolescence. *Psychiatry Research, 209*(3), 529–534. https://doi.org/10.1016/j.psychres.2013.01.010.

Forest, A., & Wood, J. (2012). When social networking is not working: Individuals with low self-esteem recognize but do not reap the benefits of self-disclosure on Facebook. *Psychological Science, 23*, 295–302. https://doi.org/10.1177/0956797611429709.

Fowler, F. J. (1993). *Survey research methods*. Newbury Park, CA: Sage Publications.

Frascella, J., Potenza, M. N., Brown, L. L., & Childress, A. R. (2010). Carving addiction at a new joint? Shared brain vulnerabilities open the way for non-substance addictions. *Annals of the New York Academy of Sciences, 1187*, 294–315. https://doi.org/10.1111/j.1749-6632.2009.05420.x.

Freud, A. (1937). *The Ego and the mechanisms of defense*. London: Hogarth Press and Institute of Psycho-Analysis.

Fu, K.-w., Chan, W. S. C., Wong, P. W. C., & Yip, P. S. F. (2010). Internet addiction: Prevalence, discriminant validity and correlates among adolescents in Hong Kong. *The British Journal of Psychiatry, 196*, 486–492. https://doi.org/10.1192/bjp.bp.109.075002.

Gentile, B., Twenge, J. M., Freeman, E. C., & Campbell, W. K. (2012). The effect of social networking websites on positive self-views: An experimental investigation. *Computers in Human Behavior, 28*(5), 1929–1933. https://doi.org/10.1016/j.chb.2012.05.012.

Ghassemzadeh, L., Shahraray, M., & Moradi, A. R. (2008). Prevalence of Internet addiction and comparison of Internet addicts and non-addicts in Iranian high schools. *CyberPsychology & Behavior, 11*, 731–733.

Giménez Gualdo, A. M., Hunter, S. C., Durkin, K., Arnaiz, P., & Maquilón, J. J. (2015). The emotional impact of cyberbullying: Differences in perceptions and experiences as a function of role. *Computers & Education, 82*, 228–235. https://doi.org/10.1016/j.compedu.2014.11.013.

Gould, T. J. (2010). Addiciton and cognition. *Addiction Science and Clinical Practice, 5*(2), 4–14.

Grafanaki, S. (1996). how research can change the researcher: the need for sensitivity, flexibility and ethical boundaries in conducting qualitative researching counselling/psychotherapy. *British Journal of Guidance and Counselling, 24*(3), 329–338.

Greenfield, D. N. (1999). Psychological characteristics of compulsive Internet use: a preliminary analysis. *CyberPsychology & Behavior, 2*, 403–412.

Grieve, R., Indian, M., Witteveen, K., Anne Tolan, G., & Marrington, J. (2013). Face-to-face or Facebook: Can social connectedness be derived online? *Computers in Human Behavior, 29* (3), 604–609. https://doi.org/10.1016/j.chb.2012.11.017.

Griffiths, M. D. (2012). Facebook addiction: Concerns, criticisms and recommendations. *Psychological Reports, 110*(2), 518–520.

Guba, E. G. (1990). The alternative paradigm dialog. In E. G. Guba (Ed.), *The paradigm dialog* (pp. 17–27). Newbury Park, CA: Sage.

Guba, E. G., & Lincoln, Y. S. (1981). *Effective evaluation: Improving the usefulness of evaluation through responsive and naturalistic approaches*. San Fransisco: Jossey-bass.

Guba, E. G., & Lincoln, Y. S. (1994). Competing paradigms in qualitative research. In N. K. Denzin, & Y. S. Lincoln (Eds.), *Handbook of qualitative research* (pp. 105–117). London: SAGE Publications.

Hasson, D., & Arnetz, B. B. (2005). Validation and findings comparing VAS vs Likert scales for psychosocial measurements. *International Electronic Journal of Health Education, 8*, 178–192.

Hitchcock, G., & Hughes, D. (1995). *Research and the teacher. A Qualitative introduction to school-based research* (2nd ed.). London: Routledge.

Howe, K. R. (1988). Against the quantitative-qualitative incompatibility thesis, or, Dogmas die hard. *Educational Researcher, 17*, 10–16.

Howe, N., & Strauss, W. (2000). *Millennials rising: The next great generation*. New York: Vintage Books.

Howitt, D., & Cramer, D. (2005). *Introduction to research methods in psychology*. Pearson Education Ldt.

Indian, M., & Grieve, R. (2014). When Facebook is easier than face-to-face: Social support derived from Facebook in socially anxious individuals. *Personality and Individual Differences, 59*, 102–106. https://doi.org/10.1016/j.paid.2013.11.016.

Jang, K. S., Hwang, S. Y., & Choi, J. Y. (2008). Internet addiction and psychiatric symptoms among Korean adolescents. *The Journal of School Health, 78*(3), 165–171. https://doi.org/10.1111/j.1746-1561.2007.00279.x.

Johansson, A., & Götestam, K. G. (2004). Internet addiction: Characteristics of a questionnaire and prevalence in Norwegian youth (12–18 years). *Scandinavian Journal of Psychology, 45*, 223–229. https://doi.org/10.1111/j.1467-9450.2004.00398.x.

Johnson, R. B., & Onwuegbuzie, A. J. (2004). Mixed methods research: A research paradigm whose time has come. *Educational Researcher*, *33*(7), 14–26.

Judd, T. (2014). Making sense of multitasking: The role of Facebook. *Computers & Education*, *70*, 194–202. https://doi.org/10.1016/j.compedu.2013.08.013.

Katz, J. E., & Rice, R. E. (2002). *Social consequences of Internet use: Access involvement and interaction*. Cambridge: MIT Press.

Khazaal, Y., Billieux, J., Thorens, G., Khan, R., Louati, Y., Scarletti, E., et al. (2008). French validation of the Internet Addiction Test. *CyberPsychology & Behavior*, *11*, 514–525.

Kirschner, P. A., & Karpinski, A. C. (2010). Facebook® and academic performance. *Computers in Human Behavior*, *26*(6), 1237–1245. https://doi.org/10.1016/j.chb.2010.03.024.

Ko, C. H., Yen, J. Y., Yen, C. F., Chen, C. C., Yen, C. N., & Chen, S. H. (2005). Screening for Internet addiction: An empirical study on cut-off points for the Chen Internet Addiction Scale. *Kaohsiung Journal of Medical Sciences*, *21*, 545–551.

Kong, G., Ells, D. M., Camenga, D. R., & Krishnan-Sarin, S. (2014). Text messaging-based smoking cessation intervention: A narrative review. *Addictive Behaviors*. https://doi.org/10.1016/j.addbeh.2013.11.024.

Korkeila, J., Kaarlas, S., Jääskeläinen, M., Vahlberg, T., & Taiminen, T. (2010). Attached to the web: Harmful use of the Internet and its correlates. *European Psychiatry*, *25*, 236–241.

Kubiszewski, V., Fontaine, R., Potard, C., & Auzoult, L. (2015). Does cyberbullying overlap with school bullying when taking modality of involvement into account? *Computers in Human Behavior*, *43*, 49–57. https://doi.org/10.1016/j.chb.2014.10.049.

Kuss, D. J., & Griffiths, M. D. (2011). Online social networking and addiction—A review of the psychological literature. *International Journal of Environmental Research and Public Health*, *8*, 3528–3552.

Kwan, G. C. E., & Skoric, M. M. (2013). Facebook bullying: An extension of battles in school. *Computers in Human Behavior*, *29*(1), 16–25. https://doi.org/10.1016/j.chb.2012.07.014.

Laconi, S., Rodgers, R. F., & Chabrol, H. (2014). The measurement of Internet addiction: A critical review of existing scales and their psychometric properties. *Computers in Human Behavior*, *41*, 190–202.

Langdridge, D. (2007). *Phenomenological psychology: Theory research and method*. Harlow: Pearson Education.

Lee, R. M., & Robbins, S. B. (1995). Measuring belongingness: The social connectedness and the social assurance scales. *Journal Of Counseling Psychology*, *42*(2), 232–241.

Likert, R. (1952). A technique for the development of attitude scales. *Educational and Psychological Measurement*, *12*, 313–315.

Lin, S. S., & Tsai, C.-C. (1999). *Internet addiction among high schoolers in Taiwan*. Retrieved from http://eric.ed.gov/?id=ED437912.

Liu, C., Ang, R. P., & Lwin, M. O. (2013). Cognitive, personality, and social factors associated with adolescents' online personal information disclosure. *Journal of Adolescence*, *36*(4), 629–638. https://doi.org/10.1016/j.adolescence.2013.03.016.

Lu, H. Y. (2008). Sensation-seeking, Internet dependency, and online interpersonal deception. *CyberPsychology & Behavior*, *11*, 227–231.

Luft, J., Ingham, H. (1955). The Johari window, a graphic model of interpersonal awareness. Proceedings of the western training laboratory in group development. Los Angeles: UCLA. Retrieved from http://books.google.co.uk/books?id=r1A3to_7Ih4C&pg=PT130&lpg.

Lyndon, A., Bonds-Raacke, J., & Cratty, A. D. (2011). College students' Facebook stalking of ex-partners. *Cyberpsychology, Behavior, and Social Networking*, *14*(12), 711–716. https://doi.org/10.1089/cyber.2010.0588.

Mariano, C. (1990). Qualitative research: Instructional strategies and curricular considerations. *Nursing and Health Care*, *11*, 354–359.

Marien, H., Custers, R., Hassin, R. R., & Aarts, H. (2012). Unconscious goal activation and the hijacking of the executive function. *Journal of Personality and Social Psychology*, *103*(3), 399–415. https://doi.org/10.1037/a0028955.

Maslow, A. (1954). *Motivation and personality*. New York, NY: Harper.

Mazur, E., & Richards, L. (2011). Adolescents' and emerging adults' social networking online: Homophily or diversity? *Journal of Applied Developmental Psychology, 32*(4), 180–188. https://doi.org/10.1016/j.appdev.2011.03.001.

McCreery, M. P., Kathleen Krach, S., Schrader, P. G., & Boone, R. (2012). Defining the virtual self: Personality, behavior, and the psychology of embodiment. *Computers in Human Behavior, 28*(3), 976–983. https://doi.org/10.1016/j.chb.2011.12.019.

McKenna, K. Y. A., Green, A. S., & Gleason, M. E. J. (2002). Relationship formation on the Internet: What's the big attraction? *Journal of Social Issues, 58*, 9–31.

McLeod, J. (2001). *Qualitative research in counselling and psychotherapy*. London: Sage Publications.

Meerkerk, G. J., Van Den Eijnden, R. J., Vermulst, A. A., & Garretsen, H. F. (2009). The Compulsive Internet Use Scale (CIUS): Some psychometric properties. *Cyberpsychology Behavior, 12*, 1–6.

Miller, R. L., & Brewer, J. D. (Eds.). (2003). *The A-Z of social research*. London: SAGE Publications.

Miyazaki, A., Stanaland, A. J., & Lwin, M. O. (2009). Self-regulatory safeguards and the online privacy of preteen children: Implications for the advertising industry. *Journal of Advertising, 38*(4), 79–91.

Monsen, G., Frederickson, & Cameron. (1998). Problem analysis and professional training in educational psychology: An accountable model of practice. *Educational Psychology in Practice: Theory, Research and Practice in Educational Psychology, 4*(13), 234–249.

Morahan-Martin, J., & Schumacher, P. (2000). Incidence and correlates of pathological Internet use among college students. *Computers in Human Behavior, 16*, 13–29.

Moreno, M. A., Jelenchick, L. A., Egan, K. G., Cox, E., Young, H., Gannon, K. E., et al. (2011). Feeling bad on Facebook: depression disclosures by college students on a social networking site. *Depression and Anxiety, 28*(6), 447–455.

Morrison, C. M., & Gore, H. (2010). The relationship between excessive Internet use and depression: A questionnaire-based study of 1319 young people and adults. *Psychopathology, 43*(2), 121–126.

Moser, C. A., & Kalton, G. (1971). *Survey methods in social investigation* (2nd ed.). London: Heinemann Educational.

Müller, K. W., Dreier, M., Beutel, M. E., Duven, E., Giralt, S., & Wölfling, K. (2016). A hidden type of internet addiction? Intense and addictive use of social networking sites in adolescents. *Computers in Human Behavior, 55*(Part A), 172–177. https://doi.org/10.1016/j.chb.2015.09.007.

Murali, V., & George, S. (2007). Lost online: An overview of internet addiction. *Advances in Psychiatric Treatment, 13*(1), 24–30. https://doi.org/10.1192/apt.bp.106.002907.

Murray, N., & Beglar, D. (2009). *Inside track: Writing dissertations and theses*. Harlow, England: Pearson Longman.

Nagel, T. (1986). *The view from nowhere*. New York: Oxford University Press.

Noyes, D. (2015). *The top 20 valuable Facebook statistics*. Retrieved from: https://zephoria.com/social-media/top-15-valuable-facebook-statistics/.

O'Keeffe, G. S., & Clarke, K. (2011). The impact of social media on children, adolescents, and families. *Pediatrics, 127*, 800–804.

Osbourne, M., & Smith, J. A. (2006). Living with a body separate from the self. The experience of the body in chronic benign low back pain: an interpretative phenomenological analysis. *Scandinavian Journal of Caring Sciences, 20*, 216–222.

Pallanti, S., Bernardi, S., & Quercioli, L. (2006). The Shorter PROMIS Questionnaire and the Internet Addiction Scale in the assessment of multiple addictions in a high-school population: Prevalence and related disability. *CNS Spectrums, 11*(12), 966–974.

Panayides, P., & Walker, M. J. (2012). Evaluation of the Psychometric Properties of the Internet Addiction Test (IAT) in a sample of cypriot high school students: The Rasch

Measurement Perspective. *Europe's Journal of Psychology*, *8*(3), 327–351. https://doi.org/10.5964/ejop.v8i3.474.

Parks, M. R., & Floyd, K. (1996). Making friends in cyberspace. *Journal of Communication*, *46*(1), 80–97.

Paul, J. A., Baker, H. M., & Cochran, J. D. (2012). Effect of online social networking on student academic performance. *Computers in Human Behavior*, *28*(6), 2117–2127. https://doi.org/10.1016/j.chb.2012.06.016.

Perry, B. (2006). *The boy who was raised as a dog: And other stories from a child psychiatrists notebook: What traumatized children can teach us about loss, love and healing*. New York: Basic Books.

Petty, N. J., Thomson, O. P., & Stew, G. (2012). Ready for a paradigm shift? Part 2: Introducing qualitative research methodologies and methods. *Manual Therapy*, *17*(5), 378–384.

Polikinghorne, D. E. (1991). *Qualitative procedures for counselling research*. Cited in Elliott, M. S., Williams, D. I. (2001) Paradoxes of qualitative research, Counselling and Psychotherapy Research, 1 (3), 181–183.

Polit, D. F., & Beck, C. T. (2004). *Nursing research: Principles and methods* (7th ed.). Philadelphia: Lippincott Williams & Wilkins.

Prensky, M. (2001). Digital natives, digital immigrants. On the horizon, 5 MCB. . University Press Retrieved from http://www.marcprensky.com/writing/Prensky%20%20Digital%20Natives,%20Digital%20Immigrants%20-%20Part1.pdf.

Punch, K., & K. (1998). *Introduction to social research*. London: Sage.

Ramsden, G. (2019). *The teenager in the greenhouse: A psychologist's guide to parenting your teenager*. John Catt Educational.

Ramsden, G. (2020). *The Bully in the Greenhouse: exploring why children bully others and what schools can do about it*. UK: John Catt Educational.

Read, J. C., & Markopoulos, P. (2013). Child–computer interaction. *International Journal of Child-Computer Interaction*, *1*(1), 2–6. https://doi.org/10.1016/j.ijcci.2012.09.001.

Reinhold, H. (1993). *The virtual community*. New York: Addison-Wesley.

Ritterfeld, U., Cody, M., & Vorderer, P. (Eds.). (2009). *Serious games: Mechanisms and effects*. New York, NY: Taylor & Francis.

Robson, C. (2002). *Real world research* (2nd ed.). Oxford: Blackwell Publishing.

Robson, C. (2011). *Real world research: A resource for social scientists and practitioner researchers* (3rd ed.). Chichester: Wiley.

Rogers, C. (1961). *On becoming a person: A therapist's view of psychotherapy*. London: Constable.

Rosen, L. D., Mark Carrier, L., & Cheever, N. A. (2013). Facebook and texting made me do it: Media-induced task-switching while studying. *Computers in Human Behavior*, *29*(3), 948–958. https://doi.org/10.1016/j.chb.2012.12.001.

Rosen, L. D., Whaling, K., Rab, S., Carrier, L. M., & Cheever, N. A. (2013). Is Facebook creating "iDisorders"? The link between clinical symptoms of psychiatric disorders and technology use, attitudes and anxiety. *Computers in Human Behavior*, *29*(3), 1243–1254. https://doi.org/10.1016/j.chb.2012.11.012.

Rothberg, M. B., Arora, A., Hermann, J., St. Marie, P., & Visintainer, P. (2010). Phantom vibration syndrome among medical staff: a cross sectional survey. *Boston Medical Journal*, *93*, 69–73.

Rubin, A. M. (1986). Uses, gratifications, and media effects research. In J. Bryant, & D. Zillmann (Eds.), *Perspectives on media effects* (pp. 281–301). Mahwah, NJ: Lawrence Erlbaum Associates.

Sandelowski, M. (1986). The problem of rigor in qualitative research. *Advances in Nursing Science*, *8*(3), 27–37.

Sandler, T. (2005). E-associations: Using technology to connect citizens: The case of meetup.com. In *Conference proceedings from 101st Annual Meeting of the American Political Science Association "Mobilizing Democracy", Washington, DC, USA, 1–4 September 2005.*

Satchell, L., Fido, D., Harper, C., Shaw, H., Davidson, B., Ellis, D., et al. (2020). *Development of an Offline Friend Addiction Questionnaire (O-FAQ): Are people really social addicts?*. Retrieved from: https://psyarixiv.com/7x85m/.

Sechrest, L., & Sidana, S. (1995). Quantitative and qualitative methods: Is there an alternative? *Evaluation and Program Planning, 18*, 77–87.

Seidman, G. (2014). Expressing the "True Self" on Facebook. *Computers in Human Behavior, 31*, 367–372. https://doi.org/10.1016/j.chb.2013.10.052.

Shaw, M., & Black, D. W. (2008). Internet addiction: Definition, assessment, epidemiology and clinical management. *CNS Drugs, 22*(5), 353–365. https://doi.org/10.2165/00023210-200,822,050-00001.

Sheldon, P. (2013). Voices that cannot be heard: Can shyness explain how we communicate on Facebook versus face-to-face? *Computers in Human Behavior, 29*(4), 1402–1407. https://doi.org/10.1016/j.chb.2013.01.016.

Shen, C.-X., Liu, R.-D., & Wang, D. (2013). Why are children attracted to the Internet? The role of need satisfaction perceived online and perceived in daily real life. *Computers in Human Behavior, 29*(1), 185–192. https://doi.org/10.1016/j.chb.2012.08.004.

Sieber, S. D. (1973). The integration of fieldwork and survey methods. *American Journal of Sociology, 73*, 1335–1359.

Slonje, R., Smith, P. K., & Frisén, A. (2013). The nature of cyberbullying, and strategies for prevention. *Computers in Human Behavior, 29*(1), 26–32. https://doi.org/10.1016/j.chb.2012.05.024.

Smahel, D., Helsper, E., Green, L., Kalmus, V., Blinka, L., & Ólafsson, K. (2012). *Excessive internet use among European children*. London School of Economics & Political Science, London, UK: EU Kids Online.

Smith, J. A., Flowers, P., & Larkin, M. (2009). *Interpretative phenomenological analysis: Theory, method and research*. London: Sage.

Smith, P. K., Mahdavi, J., Carvalho, M., Fisher, S., Russell, S., & Tippett, N. (2008). Cyberbullying: its nature and impact in secondary school pupils. *Journal of Child Psychology and Psychiatry, 49*(4), 376–385. https://doi.org/10.1111/j.1469-7610.2007.01846.x.

Smith, J. A., & Osborn, M. (2003). Interpretative phenomenological analysis. In J. A. Smith (Ed.), *Qualitative psychology*. London: Sage.

Sorbring, E., & Lundin, L. (2012). Mothers' and fathers' insights into teenagers' use of the Internet. *New Media & Society, 14*(7), 1181–1197.

SPSS. (2013). *IBM Corp. IBM SPSS Statistics for Windows, Version 22.0.*. Armonk, NY: IBM Corp.

Subrahmanyam, K., Reich, S. M., Waechter, N., & Espinoza, G. (2008). Online and offline social networks: Use of social networking sites by emerging adults. *Journal of Applied Developmental Psychology, 29*(6), 420–433. https://doi.org/10.1016/j.appdev.2008.07.003.

Sutton, J. (2018) Seeing screen time differently. Retrieved from: https://thepsychologist.bps.org.uk/volume-31/march-2018/seeing-screen-time-differently.

Svensson, E. (2001). Construction of a single global scale for multi-item assessments of the same variable. *Statistics and Medicine, 20*(24), 3831–3846.

Tajfel, H. (1979). Individuals and groups in social psychology. *British Journal of Social and Clinical Psychology, 18*(2), 183–190.

Tapscott, D. (1998). *Growing up digital: The rise of the net generation*. New York: McGraw-Hill.

Taylor, J. (2014). Could playing video games help to beat depression? In *BBC news*. Retrieved from http://www.bbc.co.uk/newsbeat/25671185.

Tokunaga, R. (2010). Following you home from school: A critical review and synthesis of research on cyberbullying victimization. *Computers in Human Behavior, 26*, 277–287. https://doi.org/10.1016/j.chb.2009.11.014.

Tosun, L. P. (2012). Motives for Facebook use and expressing "true self" on the Internet. *Computers in Human Behavior, 28*(4), 1510–1517. https://doi.org/10.1016/j.chb.2012.03.018.

van Laerhoven, H., van der Zaag-Loonen, H. J., & Derkx, B. H. (2004). A comparison of Likert scale and visual analogue scales as response options in children's questionnaires. *Acta Paediatrica, 93*(6), 830–835.

Wang, S. S., Moon, S.-I., Kwon, K. H., Evans, C. A., & Stefanone, M. A. (2010). Face off: Implications of visual cues on initiating friendship on Facebook. *Computers in Human Behavior, 26*(2), 226–234. https://doi.org/10.1016/j.chb.2009.10.001.

Watters, C. A., Keefer, C. V., Kloosterman, P. H., Summerfeldt, L. J., & Parker, J. D. A. (2013). Examining the structure of the Internet Addiction Test in adolescents: A bifactor approach. *Computers in Human Behavior, 29*(6), 2294–2302.

Wechsler, D. (2001). *Wechsler individual achievement test-II-abbreviated (WIAT-II-A)*. London: Pearson Assessment.

Weinstein, A., & Lejoyeux, M. (2010). Internet addiction or excessive internet use. *American Journal of Drug and Alcohol Abuse, 36*, 277–283.

Wengraf, T. (2001). *Qualitative research interviewing: Biographic, narrative and semi-structured methods*. SAGE Publications Ldt.

Widyanto, L., & Griffiths, M. (2006). 'Internet addiction': A critical review. *International Journal of Mental Health and Addiction, 4*, 31–51. https://doi.org/10.1007/s11469-006-9009-9.

Wilkinson, S. (1986). *Feminist social psychology*. Milton Keynes: Open University Press.

Williamson, A. (2007). Using self-report measures in neurobehavioral toxicology: Can they be trusted? *NeuroToxicology, 28*, 227–234.

Wilson, R. E., Gosling, S. D., & Graham, L. T. (2012). A Review of Facebook Research in the Social Sciences. *Perspectives on Psychological Science, 7*(3), 203–220. https://doi.org/10.1177/1745691612442904.

Wolcott, H. F. (1990). *Writing up qualitative research*. London: Sage.

Wood, S. K., Eckley, L., Hughes, K., Hardcastle, K. A., Bellis, M. A., Schrooten, J., et al. (2014). Computer-based programmes for the prevention and management of illicit recreational drug use: A systematic review. *Addictive Behaviors, 39*(1), 30–38. https://doi.org/10.1016/j.addbeh.2013.09.010.

Woolfolk, A. E. (1998). *Educational psychology* (7th ed.). Boston: Allyn & Bacon.

Yen, C.-F., Ko, C. H., Yen, J.-Y., Chang, Y.-P., & Cheng, C.-P. (2009). Multi-dimensional discriminative factors for Internet addiction among adolescents regarding gender and age. *Psychiatry and Clinical Neurosciences, 63*, 357–364. https://doi.org/10.1111/j.1440-1819.2009.01969.x.

Young, K. S. (1998). *Caught in the net: How to recognize the signs of Internet addiction and a winning strategy for recovery*. New York: Wiley.

Zhao, E., & Liu, L. (2008). China's generation Y: Understanding the workforce. In *Conference paper on 4th IEEE International conference on Management of Invocation and Technology*.

Index

Note: Page numbers followed by *f* indicate figures, and *t* indicate tables.

A

Addiction, 66. *See also* Internet addiction
Asch Conformity Experiments, 27, 27*f*

B

Behavioral addiction, 76, 80, 166–170
  interpretative phenomenological analysis (IPA), 119–120
  mental experience, 119
Blocking as protection, 167
  defense mechanism, 152–153*t*, 153–154
  online and offline worlds, 154–155
  real-world relationship, 154–155

C

Community guidelines, 175–176
Congruence and true self
  concept, 14
  furries, 17
  harmony, 14
  motives for social media use, 16
  online confidence, 16–17
  people's representation, 15, 15*f*
  Rogers' methods and approach, 14–15
  self-disclosure, 16
  social identity theory, 17–18, 17*f*
  true self-expression, 16
Conscious awareness, 166
Cyberbullying. *See also* Online bullying and in-school
  blocking as protection
    defense mechanism, 152–153*t*, 153–154
    online and offline worlds, 154–155
    real-world relationship, 154–155
  common incident, 49
  definition, 44–45
  group judgment and reaction
    acceptable behavior, 147
    aftermath of negativity, 147
    defensive response, 147–149
    misinterpretation, 149, 149*t*
    repercussions, 146–147, 146*t*
    sense of being, 148–149*t*, 149
    social media as venue, 150
  methods
    cyberstalking, 48–49
    harassment, 45–46
    impersonation, 47–48
    photo and video shaming, 46–47
    subtweeting/vaguebooking, 48
    tools and weapons, 45
    trolling, 49
  negative impact, 146
  person-centered approach, 51–52
  referenced criterion, 51
  school and online bullying, 49–50
  venue and channel for negativity
    misinterpreted messages, 150–151
    risks of social media, 152, 152*t*
    targeted/pulled, 151–152
    twisting, 150
    vulnerability and openness, 152
  victim and perpetrator characteristics, 52
Cybersexual and cyber-relational addiction, 71
Cyberstalking, 48–49

D

Displacement hypothesis, 68
  concept, 32
  media of choice, 31
  technological advances, 32
Distractibility and attention to education, 112

E

Ecological systems theory
  change over time, 7
  chronosystem, 6–7
  connected influences on development and identity, 7
  exosystem, 6
  macrosystem, 6
  mesosystem, 6

Ecological systems theory *(Continued)*
microsystem, 6
multiple relationships, 5, 5*f*
Education about social media
action, 197
contemplative, 197
inspiration, 192
maintenance, 197
manipulation, 192
pre-contemplative, 197
preparation (decision), 197
relapse, 197
schools
adulthood informed, 194
answer to unknown question, 193
knowledge about choices, 193
parent workshops, 194
positive change, 192
practicalities of having phones, 195
psychological with phones, 194–195
rules and expectations, 194
solution focused approach, 193–194
teach safe online, 193
stages of change model, 196–197
working 1:1, 196
Educational impact of social media usage, 169. *See also* Procrastination
cognitive abilities, 84–85
school results, 86
training effect, 85
working memory, 84–85
Emergent themes, 167
Emotional regulation
concept, 36
down-regulation and up-regulation, 36
enjoyable, 37
expressive writing, 36
instant messaging, 36–37
introversion-extroversion, 36–37
levels, 36
private messages, 37
uses and gratifications theory (*see* Uses and gratifications theory)

G
Gambling addiction, 67
Group judgment and reaction, 167
acceptable behavior, 147
aftermath of negativity, 147
defensive response, 147–149
misinterpretation, 149, 149*t*
repercussions, 146–147, 146*t*
sense of being, 148–149*t*, 149
social media as venue, 150

H
Harassment, 45–46
Herd behavior, 101–102
Houseparty
app for quiz lovers, 28
data privacy, 28–29
decision making about engage, 30–31
Douglas Adam rules of technology, 30–31
Epic Games, 29
security, 29–30, 29*f*
statement, 29, 29*f*
trust, 30
Hyperzandualosis, 67

I
Identity and construction of the self, 167
change over time
anticipation, 137
experiences before and after use, 134, 134*t*
familiarity with social media, 136–137
ideal version of one's self, 136
pouting, 136
sense of innocence, 134–135, 135*t*
shift in social media use, 135–136
congruence and true self, 14–18, 15*f*, 17*f*
ecological systems theory, 5–7, 5*f*, 7*f*
identity presentation, 4
Johari Window, 8–9, 8*f*, 10*t*, 10*f*, 11
lesbian, gay, bisexual, transgender, questioning, intersex, asexual, plus (L.G.B.T.Q.I.A.+), 18–19, 19*f*
parent role
boundaries to social media, 141–142
children identity, 141
distraction free task, 142
emotional upset, 143
executive decision for wellbeing, 141, 141*t*
gatekeepers to social media, 142
guardian watch, 142–143
intrusion of privacy, 141
privilege, social media as, 142
procrastination, 142
protective factor for children, 143
part of you
ability to live, 137–138
amount of time spent, 139
continual process, 138

Identity and construction of the self (Continued)
dangers, 139
emotional bereavement, 137–138
feeling of acceptance, 140
life source, 138
self-esteem, 140
sense of being, 137
thought, 138–139*t*, 139
weirdness, 138–139
ship of Theseus, 4–5
social identity theory, 11–14
Impact assessment
intervention planning and implementation
change points, 211
example intervention table, 214–215, 214*f*
supportive environment, 211
positive change of social media, 200
review of the intervention
completed review table, 218, 218*f*
pre and post intervention effectiveness, 215–218, 216*f*
success/failure with intervention, 215
Social Media Assessment and Reflection Tool: Child Version (SMART: CV), 200, 215–218
daily school lives, 203
psychology of young person, 203
reflective experience, 203
Social Media Assessment and Reflection Tool: Parent Version (SMART: PV), 200, 215–218
daily school lives, 208
psychology of young person, 208
reflective experience, 208
social media use, 208
Impersonation, 47–48
Information overload, 71
Informed technology use, 220–221
Instant messaging, 36–37
Internet addiction
behavioral addiction, 76, 80
computer addiction, 71
cybersexual and cyber-relational addiction, 71
definition, 67–68
design of technology and attention
Autoplay, 77–78
ethics of human persuasion, 80
positive intermittent reinforcement, 76–77
slot machines, 76–77
snapchat, 78–79, 78*f*
societal problem, 79–80
diagnostic questionnaire, 72–73, 72*t*
displacement hypothesis, 68
gambling addiction, 67
Hyperzandualosis, 67
information overload, 71
Internet Addiction Test (IAT)
assessment tools, 73–74
behavioral change, 75
internet as conduit to addiction, 75
investigation and discussion, 74
psychological factors, 74
scores, 73, 73*t*
level of impact, 69
measurement, 72–73, 72*t*
net compulsions, 71
offline friend addiction, 80–81
problem owner, 68–70
social networking, 69–70
vs. substance related addiction, 67
terminologies, 66–67
vulnerability
adolescents, 70
categorization, 71–72
newcomers to Internet, 70–71
Interpretative Phenomenological Analysis, 166–167
Interpretative phenomenological analysis (IPA)
assumption, 119–120
benefits and difficulties, 119
stage of process, 120
Isolation reduction, 122

J

Johari Window, 229*f*
as activity with others, 10–11, 10*t*
Arena, 9
Blind Spot, 9
completed example, 9, 10*f*
Façade, 9
multiple interaction influences, 11
representation, 8–9, 8*f*
Unknown, 9

L

Lesbian, gay, bisexual, transgender, questioning, intersex, asexual, plus (L.G.B.T.Q.I.A.+), 18–19, 19*f*
Loss of privacy, 129–130*t*, 130

M
Management of distance, 123, 123t
Monitoring others, 167
audience, 129–130, 129–130t
defense mechanism, 128–129t, 129
loss of privacy, 129–130t, 130
online social gaming, 130
purpose of staying informed, 129–130, 129t
Multiple social networking sites, 168

N
Negative change of social media, 220
Net compulsions, 71
Non-substance related addiction, 67. *See also* Internet addiction

O
Offline friend addiction, 80–81
Online bullying and in-school
direct impact in-school, 158
educational levels/grades, 158
interference of work
attention span, 159
GCSE schoolwork, 158–159
homework, 158
meant to do and actually did, 159–160
task switching, 160
thinking space, 159
threats, intimidation or violence
non-attendance at school, 163
not real life, 162–163
online accusation, 160–161
online altercations, 162
online comment, 161–162
online post, 161–162
schoolwork suffering, 162
Online gameplay, 103
Online gaming, 127–128, 127t, 130, 152

P
Parent-children relationship, 170, 220
Parent responsibility
access to child's device, 188–189
advantage of technology, 187–188
apps on child mobile, 184–185
Burnbook, 186
Calculator%, 186
Chatroulette, 187
Checky, 189
child choice of apps and websites, 184
children access to technology, 179–180
children autonomy during free time, 183
children work out, 180–181
child's development and needs, 178–179
conditions for use, 180
conversations with children, 183
counter-messages, 180–181
education about technology, 182–183, 190
face to face connection, 177–178
Family Sharing, 188–190
Find My Friends, 188
Forest, 189
formal education, 178
HOLLA, 185
IMVU, 185–186
lead by example, 183
Likee, 186, 186f
Qustodio, 189
relational health, 177
RespondASAP, 189
screen rule, 178
screen time, 181
Screentime app, 189
set boundaries, 184
set up rules and practice, 182
3D avatars, 185–186
Wishbone, 187
Yolo, 185
Pathological Gambling, 75
Phantom Vibration Syndrome, 87–88
Photo and video shaming, 46–47
Positive change of social media, 200, 220
Positive intermittent reinforcement, 76–77
Procrastination
academic performance, 88
academic procrastination, 87
bizarre psychological phenomenon, 87–88
concept, 86
fear and anxiety based, 87
harmless and harmful, 86
Phantom Vibration Syndrome, 87–88
pull of technology, 88
social media fatigue, 88
task switching/multitasking, 87
Professional guide, 220
Psychological impacts, 169

R
Reassurance seeking
provocative message, 56t, 57
self-esteem boost, 59
social approval, 58–59, 58f
social responses, 56–57, 56t
social support, 57–58, 57t

Receiving of support, 122
Relational health, 177–178
Relationship maintenance
electronic ranking and positioning, 126
enjoyable times, reminiscing, 127
offline social networks, 127
online gaming, 127–128, 127*t*
reinforce friendship, 127
Research on social media
analysis
days of the week to use/check, 103*f*, 104
Devon School and Midland School participant, 99, 99*t*
gender balance between participants, 99, 99*t*
herd behavior, 101–102
Hootsuite, 101
Houseparty app, 101–102
message alert tone, 105
multiple social media sites/apps, 100–101
online gameplay, 103
participants, year groups and percentage, 98, 98*t*
social networking sites and apps, 99–100*t*, 100
technology to access social networking sites and apps, 102–103, 102*f*
times of the day to use/check, 104–105, 104*f*
visual representation, 100–101, 100*f*
behavioral addiction, 97
interpretative phenomenological analysis (IPA), 120
interview design, 116–117
interview schedule, 117–118
qualitative analysis, 118–120
results, 120
semi-structured interviews, 116
difficulties on social media, 112–113
distractibility and attention to education, 112
internet addiction test
difficulties fit, 109
female experience, 108*t*, 109
gender differences, 109
male experience, 107*t*, 108–109, 108*f*
measurement and theoretical models, 110
multiple assessment, 110–111, 111*f*
overall group experience, 106–108, 106*t*, 106–107*f*
mixed methodology approach, 95–96
parent-child relationship, 113
positives, 112
quantitative and qualitative approach, 95
questionnaires, 96–97
real liking for social media, 97
research questions, 94
results, 98
self-report measures, 97
social networking platforms used, 96–97
Resources, 230
Responsibility
community guidelines, 175–176
parent responsibility (*see* Parent responsibility)
self-governance, 175–177
society responsibility, 174–175

S

School bullying, 49–50
Self-governance
breaking the law/illegal content, 177
community guidelines, 175–176
Community Standards Enforcement Report, 176
cyberpolice, China, 177
General Data Protection Regulation (GDPR), EU, 176
NetzDG law, Germany, 176
policing content, 176–177
Sharing of Abhorrent Violent Material Act, Australia, 176
Self-reflective assessment, 169
Signaling theory
in biology and economics, 54
credibility and trustworthiness, 55
information interpretation, 54, 54*f*
online *vs.* face to face conversation, 56
social media portrayal, 56
social media reputation, 55, 55*f*
words and phrases meaning, 54–55
Social conformity, 27–28, 27*f*, 124–125*t*, 125
Social connectedness
adolescence, 22
Asch Conformity Experiments, 27, 27*f*
counseling, 24–26
description, 22
displacement hypothesis, 31–32
Facebook, 22
within families, 24
global and local social connectedness, 23–24

Social connectedness *(Continued)*
Houseparty app (*see* Houseparty)
MySpace, 23
online and offline social network, 23–24, 33
self-disclosure, 24
sites and apps, 33
social categorization, identification and comparison, 26
social conformity, 27–28, 27*f*
social media, 22, 24–26
social networking, 22, 25–26
YouTube, 23
Social connection, 167
complexities, 125
face to face social connection, 124–125
hold of someone, 122
international social connection, 123, 123*t*
isolation reduction, 122
management of distance, 123, 123*t*
receiving of support, 122
social conformity, 124–125*t*, 125
social inclusion, 124–125
Social identity theory
group memberships, 11
in group-out group bias, 11–12
human connection, 11
social categorization, 12–13
social comparison, 13–14
social identification, 13
stereotyping, 11
Social inclusion, 124–125
Social media choices, 220–221
Society responsibility, 174–175
Stages of change model, 196–197
Subtweeting/vaguebooking, 48
Superordinate themes, 166–167, 169

T
Task switching/multitasking, 87, 158, 160
Theseus ship, 4–5
Trolling, 49

U
Unfulfilled expectations
reassurance seeking
provocative message, 56*t*, 57
self-esteem boost, 59
social approval, 58–59, 58*f*
social responses, 56–57, 56*t*
social support, 57–58, 57*t*
signaling theory, 54–56, 54–55*f*
thought behind an upload
negative and positive emotion, 62
psychological conditions, 61–62
public display of liking, 60
reassurance seeking, 61
self-esteem and self-worth, 59–60
whistle stop tour, 54
Uses and gratifications theory, 143
concept, 37–38
distraction, 39–40
escapism, 39–40
history, 38
identity and connecting to others, 40
positive mood for users, 38–39
principal gratifications, 38
psychological well-being, 40
reasons for choosing social media, 38

V
Venue and channel for negativity, 167
misinterpreted messages, 150–151
risks of social media, 152, 152*t*
targeted/pulled, 151–152
twisting, 150
vulnerability and openness, 152

FSC
www.fsc.org
MIX
Papier | Fördert gute Waldnutzung
FSC® C083411

Kolibri 360 GmbH
Ferdinand-Jühlke-Straße 7
99095 Erfurt, Deutschland
produktsicherheit@kolibri360.de